Coping with Continuous Change in the Business Environment

CHANDOS
KNOWLEDGE MANAGEMENT SERIES

Series Editor: Melinda Taylor
(email: melindataylor@chandospublishing.com)

Chandos' new series of books are aimed at all those individuals interested in knowledge management. They have been specially commissioned to provide the reader with an authoritative view of current thinking. If you would like a full listing of current and forthcoming titles, please visit our web site **www.chandospublishing.com** or contact Hannah Grace-Williams on email info@chandospublishing.com or telephone number +44 (0) 1993 848726.

New authors: we are always pleased to receive ideas for new titles; if you would like to write a book for Chandos, please contact Dr Glyn Jones on email gjones@chandospublishing.com or telephone number +44 (0) 1993 848726.

Bulk orders: some organisations buy a number of copies of our books. If you are interested in doing this, we would be pleased to discuss a discount. Please contact Hannah Grace-Williams on email info@chandospublishing.com or telephone number +44 (0) 1993 848726.

Coping with Continuous Change in the Business Environment

Knowledge management and knowledge management technology

ANTONIE BOTHA
DERRICK KOURIE
AND
RETHA SNYMAN

Chandos Publishing
Oxford · England

Chandos Publishing (Oxford) Limited
TBAC Business Centre
Avenue 4
Station Lane
Witney
Oxford OX28 4BN
UK
Tel: +44 (0) 1993 848726 Fax: +44 (0) 1865 884448
Email: info@chandospublishing.com
www.chandospublishing.com

First published in Great Britain in 2008

ISBN:
978 1 84334 355 4 (paperback)
978 1 84334 356 1 (hardback)
1 84334 355 X (paperback)
1 84334 356 8 (hardback)

Contents

Contents

List of figures and tables

Figures

Tables

About the authors

Antonie C. Botha is an independent IT architect and IT consultant, specialising in enterprise and integration architecting and knowledge management. He has a variety of experience within the information technology industry. Before joining IBM in 1973, he lectured for five years in statistics and computer science at the University of Pretoria. During his 28 years of service in IBM he was involved with government information systems management and systems programming, giving advice and guidance as an IBM systems engineer, IT consultant and IT architect. He holds ten IBM recognition awards for professional excellence. He is the author of a technical IBM publication (*Code Pages and Character Sets Presentation*), a textbook on office systems and a number of journal articles. He has also delivered papers at various symposia and panel forums.

Derrick G. Kourie has been in the Computer Science Department, University of Pretoria since 1978, having previously obtained a PhD in operations research at Lancaster University and worked in industry for a brief spell. He is currently the coordinator of the Fastar and Espresso Research Groups whose joint mission is 'to combine theory and practice to enhance the efficiency and effectiveness of the software process'. His research interests have been wide-ranging, including themes from theoretical computer science, algorithm development, software specification and design, and reflections on the software process. Together with his postgraduate students and co-researchers, numerous peer-reviewed articles on these and related topics have been published. He edits the *South African Computer Journal* and has served on various organising committees, programme committees and review panels of scholarly conferences.

Retha (M.M.M.) Snyman is an associate professor in the Department of Information Science, University of Pretoria. Prior to her current position she was a senior lecturer in the Department of Library and Information

Studies, Technological University of Tshwane. She has gained many years of experience during her engagements with information service organisations. Retha has initiated and offered many courses in knowledge management and supervises several doctoral and masters students. She serves as an external examiner in information and knowledge management for various universities. She has received various research grants and presented papers at local and international conferences. She is also the author or co-author of a number of journal articles on knowledge management.

The authors may be contacted at:
E-mail: *acbotha@iafrica.com*

Preface

Rapid change is a defining characteristic of the modern world. It has a huge impact on society, governments and businesses. Businesses are forced to transform themselves fundamentally to survive in a challenging economy. Transformation implies change in the way business is conducted, in the way people perform their contribution to the organisation, and in the way the organisation perceives and manages its vital assets, which increasingly are built around the key assets of intellectual capital and knowledge.

The latest management tool to respond to the challenges of the economy in the new millennium is the idea of knowledge management. A large body of literature has emerged recently, covering knowledge management and related topics, as well as technologies applicable to knowledge management.[1] However, various academic and practitioner approaches are still necessary to clarify definitions, taxonomies for positioning knowledge management, etc. There is presently some confusion among outsiders to the field as to what the knowledge management phenomenon entails and how to comprehend various claims and issues related to it. Promoters of various technologies are making claims with a view to aligning their products with the current interest in knowledge management. A number of articles covering IT-related subjects are also contributing to this confusion, treating the subject from different perspectives and adopting multifarious 'definitions' of the numerous concepts.

This book aims to clear some of this confusion by proposing a comprehensible set of representative insights and frameworks. It is based on the authors' collective background, which includes not only research into the vast literature on this topic, but also many years of active involvement with, exposure to and experience in the information technology industry. This collective background provides a baseline for synthesising and critiquing many aspects of a fast-evolving knowledge management industry, which is rapidly reaching maturity. The result is a book which not only addresses those themes that are fundamental to knowledge management, but which also identifies recent value-added contributions to the modern knowledge-based business – both of a technological as well as a non-technological nature.

The book is comprised of two parts. The first investigates the concepts, elements, drivers and challenges involved in knowledge management. It describes various perspectives on the many notions in the field. A set of models is proposed for comprehending the positioning, challenges and practical nature of knowledge management.

The second part of the book distils this into an initial technical framework for knowledge management practitioners. By 'technical and technology issues and challenges' we specifically mean to concentrate on the technologies and technical knowledge management approaches a modern organisation can employ to survive and prosper in this rapidly changing business environment.

Note

1. See, for example, the numerous references listed in Liebowitz (1999) and Malhotra (2001). As another example, note that Bontis (2001) cites more than 200 references on the single sub-theme of managing aspects of intellectual capital.

Part 1
A perspective of knowledge and knowledge management concepts

I think therefore I am [*Cogito, ergo sum*]. (René Descartes)

The power of thinking, is knowing what *not* to think about. (Anonymous)

We have modified our environment so radically that we must modify ourselves in order to exist in this new environment. (Norbert Wiener)

The rate and magnitude of change are rapidly outpacing the complex of theories – economic, social, and philosophical – on which public and private decisions are based. To the extent that we continue to view the world from the perspective of an earlier, vanishing age, we will continue to misunderstand the developments surrounding the transition to an information society, be unable to realize the full economic and social potential of this revolutionary technology, and risk making some very serious mistakes as reality and the theories we use to interpret it continue to diverge. (Arthur J. Cordell)

This part of the book provides answers to the 'what' and 'why' questions in regard to knowledge management. It investigates the concepts and elements, drivers and challenges involved in knowledge management. After an introductory chapter (Chapter 1), a chapter on knowledge in general (Chapter 2) lays the foundation for an explanatory chapter (Chapter 3) on knowledge management in particular.

Chapter 4 differentiates the idea of intellectual capital from knowledge management, while Chapter 5 shows how the promotion of organisational learning leads to the knowledge-enabled organisation.

Chapter 6 emphasises that knowledge management mostly takes place relative to communities of practice, while Chapter 7 identifies best practices in the knowledge management context.

Together, the information and perspectives provide the background to the principal conclusions drawn in Chapter 8, some of which are expanded upon in the second part of the book.

Introduction

For the things we have to learn before we can do them, we learn by doing them. (Aristotle)

What we learn and what we remember determine largely who we are. Memory, not merely facial and physical appearance, defines an individual. (Joe Z. Tsien)

For the first time in the history of mankind, we are close to having the biological understanding, the economic ability and the cultural willpower to change the intelligence of future generations. *But we do not yet understand what intelligence is.* (Amir Aczel)

When the pace of change outside an organization becomes greater than the pace of change inside the organization, the end is near. (J. R. Walter, President of AT&T)

This chapter introduces the idea of knowledge management, by pointing to the context in which it has emerged, namely a rapidly changing global business environment. Attention is drawn to the fact that although the idea of knowledge management is well established, there is nevertheless a large degree of confusion about the scope and meaning of the term. This leads to a statement of the goals of the book, as well as an outline of the book's structure.

Rapid and constant change: the new business environment

We live in an era of rapid change. Don Tapscott articulates this well in his much referenced book *The Digital Economy*:

Today we are witnessing the early, turbulent days of a revolution as significant as any other in human history. A new medium of human communications is emerging, one that may prove to surpass all previous revolutions – the printing press, the telephone, the television – in its impact on our economic and social life. The computer is expanding from a tool for information management to a tool for communication ... enabling a new economy based on the networking of human intelligence ... The Age of Networked Intelligence is an age of promise. It is not simply about the networking of technology but about the networking of humans through technology ... But the Age of Networked Intelligence is also an age of potential peril. For individuals, organizations, and societies that fall behind, punishment is swift ... This is an age of networking not only of technology but of humans, organizations, and societies. (Tapscott, 1996)

Davis and Meyer (1998) provide thorough coverage of this rapid change and its resulting implications and effects, in the appropriately named book *Blur: The Speed of Change in the Connected Economy*.

In his book, *The Third Wave*, Alvin Toffler (1981) describes the creation of wealth in terms of three broad waves:

- *first wave – the agricultural era*: wealth creation was and still is tightly attached to land;
- *second wave – the industrial era*: wealth creation happens through industrial production, including mass production, mass consumption, mass education, mass media all linked together and served by specialised institutions;
- *third wave – the information era*: wealth creation is tightly linked to information and knowledge handling.

Some 14 years later, Alvin and Heidi Toffler expanded on *The Third Wave* in another influential book, *Creating a New Civilization: The Politics of the Third Wave*. They state:

That term 'civilization' ... includes such varied matters as technology, family life, religion, culture, politics, business, hierarchy, leadership, values, sexual morality and epistemology. Swift and radical changes are occurring in every one of these dimensions of society. Change so many social, technology and cultural elements at once and you create not just a transition but a transformation, not just society but the beginnings, at least, of a totally new civilization. (Toffler and Toffler, 1995)

In the foreword to Toffler and Toffler's book, Newt Gingrich incisively comments:

> The Tofflers correctly understand that development and distribution of information has now become the central productivity and power activity of the human race ... on virtually every front we see the information revolution changing the fabric, pace and substance of our lives. (Gingrich, 1995)

Rather than discuss the very interesting implications for whole societies and governments, the present book will restrict itself to the prominent implications this new era holds on the existence and survival of modern-day companies and institutions.[1]

In an interview conducted by *Business Management Asia* about his article 'Is knowledge the ultimate competitive advantage?', Dr Yogesh Malhotra was asked why he had argued that sometimes, merely possessing knowledge is not enough, but that application was everything. Malhotra replied:

> The key ideas that influence the current global business scenario can be summed up simply in one phrase: *radical discontinuous change*. Ideas such as change management, learning and unlearning, adaptation, agility and flexibility have been popular over the past few years. However, in the post-1990s era, the rapidity and radical nature of change has assumed unprecedented proportions that defy the past logic based on pre-determination and pre-definition. This has put a premium on thinking beyond benchmarking and best practices, and developing innovative business models that self-obsolete marginal value propositions and processes before competition does so.
>
> From a business strategic perspective, knowledge management is about obsolescing what you know before others do, and profiting by creating the challenges and opportunities others haven't even thought about. In the bigger picture, the focus of knowledge management is on the ever-changing environment in which societies, organisations and individuals live, work, learn, adapt and survive. (Malhotra, 2003)

Malhotra (1993) previously argued that the survival and growth of organisations in an increasingly turbulent environment would depend upon effective utilisation of information technology for aligning the organisational structure with environmental preferences and creating symbiotic interorganisational structures.

This trend of constant change requires businesses to transform themselves fundamentally in order to survive and prosper in a challenging new economy. Transformation implies change in the way business is conducted, in the way people perform their contribution to the organisation, and in the way the organisation perceives and manages its vital assets, which are increasingly built around the key assets of intellectual capital and knowledge.

Over a number of decades, organisations have employed various techniques and management tools to manage and adapt to the required change. In the 1980s, the main management tool for changing organisations was to focus on quality. 'Total quality' and 'continuous improvement' were management tools seen as vital to respond to the required change. Also seen during the 1980s – in our view – was an overemphasis on a complete and a far too mechanistic modelling of the way business is conducted.

During the 1990s, 'business process re-engineering' (BPR) became the key management tool for change. BPR implementation aims to re-engineer old business processes, organisational structures and practices that have become inappropriate for modern, rapidly changing business challenges. Lately, however, BPR is no longer seen as a panacea, as many reporters maintain that only a third of BPR projects can be considered to be successful.[2] Although the theory on which BPR is based is sound, the key failures are cultural, mainly because of people's resistance to change (such as a lack of executive support) as well as unrealistic expectations. Furthermore, the main goal for BPR was streamlining the business by reducing costs, with the greatest focus on reducing head count. Employees therefore became sceptical towards programmes introduced in the name of BPR. Re-engineering is a necessary but insufficient condition for competitiveness. The goal should be more than just cost control; it should be a drastic transformation of customer service, innovation and responsiveness to the challenges of modern times.[3] Today it is recognised that *success* in the new economy will require companies to follow two interrelated strategies:

- to invent new business processes, new businesses, new marketplaces and new customers – not just to re-engineer old processes; and

- (vitally for companies, and probably most importantly) to grow and exploit the intellectual assets of the organisation.

For a long time it has been recognised that technology – and specifically information technology (IT) – serves as a key enabler of business change and innovation. This insight has recently been expanded, in the sense that we now realise that technology can be strategically employed to become a key driver of change and innovation. Thus, it is not simply the case that necessary change can be facilitated (enabled) by technology; rather, the very presence of technology stimulates (drives) a need for change. We can refer to many sources for this realisation, such as the numerous publications of respected industry observers and consulting groups such as Gartner Group and META Group, as well as the well-articulated perspectives of the need to align business and IT as far as strategy and execution is concerned;[4] the latter is however beyond the scope of the present book. Figure 1.1 illustrates the relationship between IT and business; the bottom right block depicting IT's enabling role, and the top right block, its driver role.

Figure 1.1 Business and IT relationship

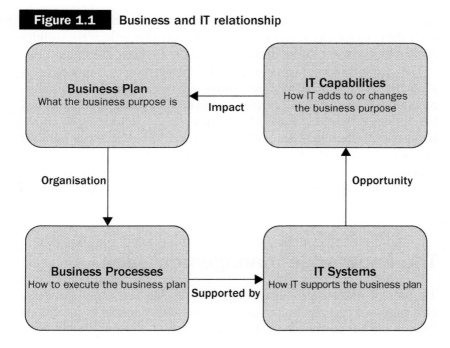

We will restrict ourselves here to mentioning briefly just one notable report from the Gartner Group – *The Technology-Enabled Enterprise*. The report highlights, inter alia, the important role of knowledge and knowledge management in the early twenty-first century. The authors predict that the information technology professional will be faced with the challenges and opportunities caused by the heightened competition of a global economy. They write: 'No longer viewed solely as a tool of process efficiency and effectiveness in many industries IT will be a determinant of survival and prosperity' (Schlier, Hunter, Harris and Berg, 1998).

IT will become the competitive resource to differentiate and provide competitive advantage. The factors driving demand for IT in the new economy – with knowledge management as a prominent factor – are summarised by the Gartner report as follows:

- the emerging global economy – globalisation;
- dramatic changes in terms of competition;
- competition-driven changes in enterprise strategy and structure;
- enterprise critical success factors;
- continuous enterprise transformation; and
- knowledge management.

These drivers of demand will create new IT critical success factors and drive the need for a new vision of IT architecture that reflects the realities of the successful enterprise of the early twenty-first century.

The use of technology – especially information technology – is changing strategic business expectations in terms of speed of execution, time limitations, reduction or even elimination of distance barriers, and perceptions of services delivered. The modern user, customer, or citizen has become increasingly demanding and expects to transact with business in a way that can mostly or even only be achieved via technology-based support systems. These systems are primarily integrated with processes and technology that is based on information, knowledge, and the knowledgeable people involved – the so-called knowledge workers.[5]

The knowledge management idea

The idea of 'knowledge management' is a contemporary response to the challenges of the economy in the new millennium. Even though humankind has perennially relied on knowledge for solutions, the recent emergence of, and emphasis on knowledge management as a critical topic, is rooted in technological developments. More specifically, it is related to the ease of access and affordability created by new technologies, primarily internet-based technologies. Knowledge management is not an end in itself but rather a means to an end. Knowledge management is considered a key part of the strategy to use expertise to create a sustainable competitive advantage in the present business environment. The contemporary enterprise faces a number of business drivers that seriously challenge the organisation's ability to survive and prosper. These business drivers and modern trends include:

- an overload of information and opportunities;
- a shortage of some resources and an abundance of others;
- increasing investment in people and information; and
- the resultant uncertainty in handling these issues when dealing with shrinking response times.[6]

Central to an approach to counter these challenges, is the realisation of the importance of knowledge, both about the external business environment and about the available internal expertise. The strategic choice is a knowledge-focused evolving into a knowledge-enabled strategy: the more an enterprise's market value is determined by intellectual capital, the more knowledge-focused its strategic response should be to knowledge management business drivers. A key idea in this regard is the following:

> The major competitive advantage of an organisation is its knowledge expertise – it is the primary differentiator in a hugely competitive business environment.

It can thus be concluded that knowledge management and related concepts and notions need to be understood firmly as well as effectively positioned and employed to support the modern business organisation in its quest to survive, grow and prosper.

Notes

1. A vast literature has evolved to cover this very interesting subject. See, for example, Toffler (1981, 1990); Sunter (1992, 1996); Davis and Botkin (1995); and Grulke and Silber (2000).

2. See for example Tapscott (1996).
3. More detail beyond the scope of this book is covered in Tapscott (1996). See also Table 1.1 of Tapscott (1996: 30–1), which compares various attributes of total quality, re-engineering, and business transformation approaches.
4. For the classic article on business and IT alignment, see Henderson and Venkatraman (1993).
5. We discuss these aspects in detail later in this book.
6. See for example a good coverage in Toffler (1991) as well as the well-respected publications of Sunter (1992, 1996); Grulke and Silber (2000); Visser and Sunter (2002); Malhotra (2003).

2

Knowledge perspectives and concepts

It is ironic that the science of the 20th century is based on Relativity, Quantum Effects and the Theory of Chaos; and that we were guilty of not managing knowledge. (Anonymous)

Background

The study of learning and of its key component, knowledge, dates back at least to the days of the philosophers Plato and Aristotle. Aristotle is purported to have said: 'For the things we have to learn before we can do them, we learn by doing them'.[1] Modern day thinkers, artificial intelligence scientists, and business management experts such as Peter Drucker, Alvin Toffler and Ikujiro Nonaka have spent much time and energy in grasping the importance of knowledge, in creating an awareness of its value and of the vital need for its 'management' in modern organisations.[2]

Prusak (2001) looks at the history of the knowledge management subject area and offers insights into what knowledge management means today and where it may be heading in the future. He maintains that knowledge management is a practitioner-based response to real social and economic trends, which include the following three major trends:

- globalisation;
- ubiquitous computing; and
- the knowledge-centric view of the organisation.

Globalisation has introduced unprecedented complexity, large volumes of global transactions, as well as an ever-increasing change in the business environment. It has added an increasing number of new participants and products, as well as channels for access and distribution. Only information technology infrastructures, support tools and systems can handle these effectively. Taking Prusak's (2001) words, organisations must ask themselves, 'what do we know, who knows it, and what do we know that we should know?'

The trend towards ubiquitous computing increases the unintended value of specific knowledge that cannot be digitised, such as judgment, design, leadership, better decisions, innovation and humour. The low cost of communication today has given virtually unlimited access to digitised information, raising the value of those skills that cannot be digitised. The contemporary view of an organisation is that although it embodies a collection of capabilities, it is constrained in its effectiveness by its current cumulative skills and know-how – its *knowledge assets*. These capabilities are mostly built from the tacit and explicit knowledge that exist in the organisation and turn out to be a major competitive differentiator in the new society.

Most of the content, emphasis on, and energy for knowledge management has originated from the three preceding eras, namely:

- the information management era;
- the quality movement; and
- the human capital era.

Information management is the approach and practice that focuses on how information is managed – independently of the information technologies. The information considered here consists of documents (in various formats and media), data and structured messages. Similar to information management, knowledge management shares a user perspective – i.e. it focuses on value as a function of user satisfaction rather than on the efficiency of the technology that handles the information. It also focuses on the quality of the content.

The quality approaches of the 1980s and 1990s focused on internal customers, improving processes, and shared goals. Quality management was most effective for manufacturing processes. Knowledge management has a broader scope in that it includes processes that do not seem to lend themselves to measurement or even to clear definition.

The human capital approach has a sound theoretical base. In practice though, understanding of the value of human capital is not yet well established. The focus is mostly on the financial advantage of investing in individuals through education and training. Many organisations, however, still view their employees and their education as expenses rather than investments. By definition, human capital focuses on the individual, whereas knowledge management work is concerned with groups, communities and networks (Prusak, 2001).

Varieties of knowledge

Nonaka describes knowledge as coming in two basic varieties: tacit and explicit;[3] or to put it differently, as uncodified knowledge and codified knowledge (Nonaka, 1991; Nonaka and Takeuchi, 1995).[4] We realise that a number of authors have criticised Nonaka on philosophical grounds in this respect, pointing out that knowledge in essence cannot purely be represented explicitly. These views consider the duality of knowledge as an interlinked mixture of implicit (tacit) and explicit knowledge. In fact, the duality of knowledge implies that tacit and explicit knowledge are co-dependent and any view of knowledge involves both tacit and explicit knowledge.[5] A practical view of knowledge is that tacit and explicit knowledge are not absolute opposites, but that they form a spectrum. Understanding them is best achieved at the extremes of the spectrum. We agree in principle that knowledge is essentially a pure human faculty, which is still far from being completely understood. However, we also recognise the importance of Nonaka's contribution to this study area, shifting the focus away from a philosophical-only view towards a much more practical business view. Our approach in this book is to employ the view of Nonaka cautiously and avoid falling into the same trap as many academics and practitioners by confusing the notions of 'information' versus 'knowledge' as well as 'information management' versus 'knowledge management'.

According to Nonaka (1991), explicit knowledge comes in the form of artefacts such as books, documents, white papers, databases and policy manuals. Tacit knowledge, in contrast, can be found in the heads of employees, the experience of customers, and the memories of stakeholders. Tacit knowledge is hard to catalogue, usually built on experience, difficult to document in any detail, and may be short-lived. Both types of knowledge are important and according to Nonaka (1991) it is the interaction between tacit knowledge and explicit knowledge that creates learning in the organisation. The organisational learning process involves capturing, exchanging and creating the knowledge in a continuous interaction of these two knowledge varieties – a never-ending, closed-loop knowledge transformation process.[6] This concept is illustrated in Figure 2.1.

Business knowledge may also be divided into individual, organisational and structural knowledge. Individual knowledge resides only in the minds of the employees. Organisational knowledge results from the learning that occurs on a group or division level. Structural knowledge is embedded in the culture and make-up of the organisation through processes, manuals, business rules and codes of conduct and ethics. Figure 2.2 illustrates this notion.

It should be noted that all of these types of business knowledge can also be classified as either tacit and/or explicit (Tapscott, 1996; Stewart, 2001).

Knowledge is also broader than the notion of intellectual capital. Intellectual capital refers to the commercial value of trademarks, licences, brand names, formulations, methodologies, intellectual content and patents. Knowledge is broader in that it is also dynamic as a result of action and interaction between people in an organisation

Figure 2.1 Organisational learning process

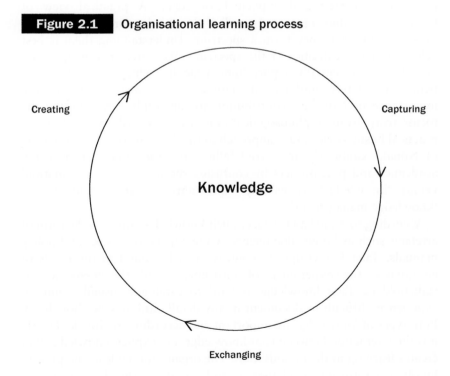

Figure 2.2 Business knowledge

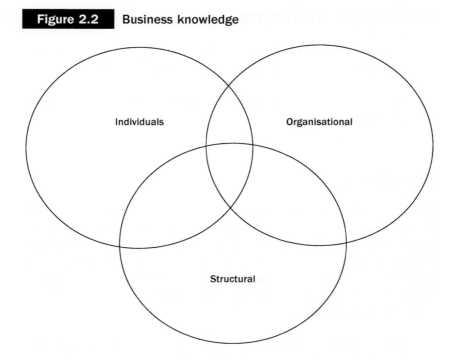

using information, knowledge and learning while interacting with each other.[7]

Knowledge is much more than just information, although it is only a special form of information (Firestone, 2003). Only when people are using information can it be transformed into or regarded as knowledge. With the modern overload of information one can have too much information; however, it is hard to conceive that one can have too much knowledge.

Hence, as an initial practical approach to comprehend the notions of data, information and knowledge – summarising many references in the literature – the following view is proposed:[8]

- knowledge is actionable information;
- information is organised/analysed data; while
- data consists of facts and figures, having no meaning out of context and interpretation.

Following this introductory view of the notion of knowledge, the next section explores knowledge concepts in more depth.

Knowledge concepts

> Knowledge is of two kinds: We know a subject ourselves, or we know we can find information upon it. (Samuel Johnson)

> Wisdom consists of knowing what to do with what you know. (Anonymous)

Introduction

In this section the basic concepts and nature of knowledge are described. We start this review and seek the opinions of various authors in various disciplines of study; later on, we attempt to clearly define the notion of 'knowledge' in its current context as well as identify different types of knowledge handling. We contribute by interpreting with our own insights and ideas about the notion of knowledge.

Thomas Stewart writes:

> It is a defining fact about organizations in the Information Age: Knowledge and information take on their own reality, which can be detached from the physical movement of goods and services. From this divergence comes at least two important implications. First, knowledge and the assets that create and distribute it, can be managed, just as physical and financial assets can be. Indeed, intellectual and physical-financial assets can be managed separately from one another; they can be managed together; they can be managed in relation to one another. Second: If knowledge is the greatest source of wealth, then individuals, companies, and nations should invest in the assets that produce and process knowledge. (Stewart, 1997)

While practising in industry, however, the authors were often exposed to the many viewpoints of people with vested interests in viewing the concept of knowledge from their respective expertise domains. This can be summarised as follows:

- *for human resource management*: 'knowledge can only be in the minds of people';
- *for document management and librarians*: 'knowledge is in documents';

- *for information system management*: 'knowledge management is information management with the word *information* changed to *knowledge*'; and

- *for knowledge engineering*: 'knowledge is something which can be captured in computer applications'.

It therefore seems worthwhile to examine the concept of knowledge more clearly.

Some ideas about the term 'knowledge'

According to Snowden (1998), 'It is not necessary, realistic or sensible to devote time to defining knowledge. What is important is to achieve an understanding of what is meant to use knowledge in contrast to information.' Notwithstanding this view, this book proceeds from the view that we should at least grasp the complexity of the term 'knowledge' and relate it to the term 'information'. Because the notion of knowledge is complex, various attempts have been published to better grasp it. Snowden uses the metaphor of a map and a guide to distinguish between knowledge and information:

> A map is a set of data organised into a coherent and reusable form – it is information. The guide, on the other hand, is knowledgeable. She does not need to consult a map, takes into account recent experience and has the ability to relate my ability to her knowledge of the terrain. The guide is the fastest way to achieve my objective, provided that I trust her. If I do not have that trust, and am not prepared to take a risk of experimentation, then I will fall back on information – the map. (Snowden, 1998)

Authors in artificial intelligence and especially expert systems – also known as 'knowledge engineering' – came to an association between knowledge and expertise (Luger and Stubblefield, 1989; Rich and Knight, 1991). Waterman articulates this as follows:

> The goal of AI scientists had always been to develop computer programs that could in some sense think, that is, solve problems in a way that would be considered intelligent if done by a human ... Various attempts over a number of decades were made to achieve this goal. In the late 1970s AI scientists began to realize *something quite important*:

> To make a program intelligent, provide it with lots of high-quality specific knowledge about some problem area.
>
> This realization led to the development of special-purpose computer programs, systems that were expert in some narrow problem area. (Waterman, 1993)

These programs are known as *expert systems*. The process of building these is referred to as *knowledge engineering*. The expert in this case is a human:

> An expert is a person who, because of training and experience, is able to do things the rest of us cannot; experts are not only proficient but also smooth and efficient in the actions they take. Experts know a great many things and have tricks and caveats for applying what they know to problems and tasks; they are good at ploughing through irrelevant information in order to get at basic issues, and they are good at recognizing problems they face as instances of types with which they are familiar. Underlying the behaviour of experts is the body of operative knowledge we have termed expertise. (Waterman, 1993)

Expert systems rely on a corpus of knowledge. The knowledge is derived or captured from the expertise of human experts – sometimes without the capturers realising/grasping the embedded semantics and implications of the knowledge items. The knowledge is explicit to the expert system and organised to simplify decision making. The knowledge is explicit and therefore also accessible (unlike most conventional programmes).

Thus, a first conclusion we can derive for this study from artificial intelligence and expert systems is that human knowledge is closely linked to the notion of expertise. It is highly personal and difficult to transfer or document as the expert often finds it difficult to express the reasoning behind his/her expertise. This thinking of the 1980s and 1990s was based on the premise that knowledge is 'nothing but' a set of rules, and that knowledge engineering was about getting these rules from the heads of experts into expert system shells. Some authors have optimistically maintained that all human knowledge could eventually be encapsulated in vast 'knowledge bases'. This is a very mechanistic view of the concept of knowledge. Today we realise that this view is far from the abilities of human beings, humbling us in grasping the limitations of our current technologies compared with human cognitive capabilities.

The study of expert systems has taught a number of valuable lessons that are applicable to this study. In some cases, artificial expertise located within an organisation is preferred to human expertise; in other cases the reverse is true. One advantage of artificial expertise is its permanence. Human expertise can quickly fade, and must constantly be practised and rehearsed to maintain proficiency in some problem area. Artificial expertise is usually more applicable to and useful in narrow domains of knowledge. To replicate in an expert system the human ability of a broad focus and deployment of commonsense knowledge is still just a distant dream for the expert systems builders of today. Other characteristics sometimes considered to differentiate artificial from human expertise are listed in Tables 2.1 and 2.2.[9]

Human expertise relies on human intelligence and the knowledge that a human applies to become and remain an expert. There exists a fascinating

Table 2.1   Artificial expertise preferred to human expertise

Human expertise	Artificial expertise
Perishable	Permanent
Difficult to transfer	Easy to transfer
Difficult to document	Easy to document
Unpredictable	Consistent
Expensive	Affordable

Table 2.2   Human expertise preferred to artificial expertise

Human expertise	Artificial expertise
Creative	Uninspired
Adaptive	Needs to be told
Sensory experience	Symbolic input
Broad focus	Narrow focus
Commonsense knowledge	Technical knowledge

interplay between intelligence, knowledge, learning, language, memory, and the unique abilities of human behaviour such as understanding, recognition of patterns, and ability to abstract and generalise. A number of these topics are areas of study in artificial intelligence, psychology, education, etc. However, we are touching on them here because they overlap with the focus of knowledge management.

We will concentrate here first on the more abstract notion of knowledge versus information. At a very basic level, we may distinguish between knowledge, information and pure data by referring to their abstraction levels. Although Snowden (1998) does not promote or support this approach, such a distinction nevertheless gives us some insight into the notions of data, information and (explicit) knowledge – as in the accompanying representation. We differentiate here between three types of knowledge, namely explicit knowledge, tacit knowledge and embedded knowledge as illustrated in Figure 2.3.

This representation as different abstract levels by no means indicates a dependence of knowledge on (pure) information. There is a co-dependence between knowledge and information although the human expert often

Figure 2.3 Data, information and knowledge

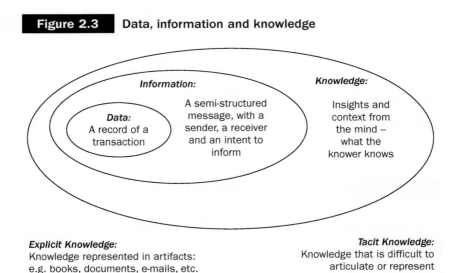

Information:
A semi-structured message, with a sender, a receiver and an intent to inform

Data:
A record of a transaction

Knowledge:
Insights and context from the mind – what the knower knows

Explicit Knowledge:
Knowledge represented in artifacts:
e.g. books, documents, e-mails, etc.

Tacit Knowledge:
Knowledge that is difficult to articulate or represent

Imbedded Knowledge:
Knowledge contained in processes, products, rules and procedures

Source: Idea and content adapted from a variety of sources including various IBM presentations on e-business.

cannot express the specific information on which some knowledge may depend, and also often has no clear wording or formulation of the reason for a particular decision or action – which was taken because of certain expertise, knowledge or intuition.

Turban and Frenzel's (1992) definitions of data, information and knowledge in artificial intelligence are:

- *Data*, i.e. numeric (or alphanumeric) strings that by themselves do not have a meaning. They can be facts or figures to be processed.

- *Information*, i.e. data organised so that it is meaningful to the receiver of the information.

- *Knowledge* has several definitions.
  - a clear and certain perception of something;
  - understanding;
  - learning;
  - all that has been perceived or grasped by the mind;
  - practical experience and skill;
  - acquaintance or familiarity;
  - cognisance, recognition; and
  - organised information applicable to problem solving.

Table 2.3 illustrates the differences in characteristics between the notions of information and knowledge.

Sowa (1984, cited in Luger and Stubblefield, 1993) describes that 'Knowledge encompasses the implicit and explicit restrictions placed upon objects (entities), operations, and relationships along with general and specific heuristics and inference procedures involved in the situation being modelled'. The ability to form higher-level abstractions from the particulars of experience is one of the most powerful and fundamental abilities of the human mind. Abstractions allow us to understand the full range of instances in a domain. In the words of Luger and Stubblefield (1989, 1993), 'A picture may be worth a thousand words, but an abstraction can define the important features of an entire class of pictures … Ultimately, *most of our ideas are about other ideas*.'

Knowledge as used by a computer consists of facts, concepts, theories, heuristic methods, procedures and relationships. Knowledge in this context is also information that has been organised and analysed to make it understandable and applicable to problem-solving or decision making. This angle on the notion of knowledge is inherently

Table 2.3 Information versus knowledge

Information	Knowledge
Information is linked to data	Knowledge relates to data and information but may not be linked to it
Quantity: lots of information	Much less knowledge
Information is sometimes context-based	Knowledge is always context-based
Information can be created by people and computers	Knowledge can only be created by people
Information is easier to understand and transfer	Knowledge is sticky and is very context-based
Information is often static	Knowledge is often dynamic
Information is single loop learning	Knowledge is double loop learning
Information can be easily linked	Knowledge requires a framework to make sense
Information is costly to create and maintain	Knowledge is more costly to create and maintain
Information can be used by anyone anytime	Knowledge often has time and target value

covering a representable type of knowledge – so-called explicit knowledge.

In businesses and organisations in general we mainly encounter knowledge in three forms:

- *explicit knowledge*, as represented in databases, memos, notes, documents, etc.;
- *embedded knowledge*, which is encountered in business rules, processes, manuals, in the organisation's culture, codes of conduct and ethics, etc.; and
- *tacit knowledge*, which is present in the minds of human stakeholders.

Figure 2.4 presents the hierarchy of these three types of knowledge within organisations, and how they relate to the values, norms and culture of the organisation.[10,11]

The process of using data and information as well as of acting upon it, creates knowledge. Knowledge is an individual's or organisation's understanding of reality – of what works and what does not work. Knowledge can be seen as a spectrum ranging from pure tacit know-how,

Figure 2.4 Three varieties of knowledge

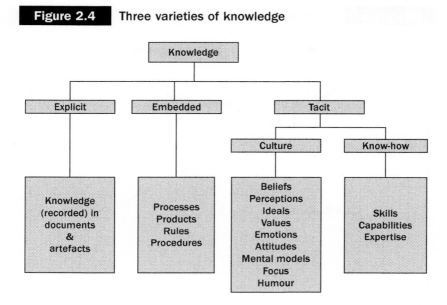

competence, expertise, values and norms to mostly explicit interpreted knowledge. The notion of knowledge is best understood at the extremes of this spectrum. In most cases where we deal with knowledge we have to consider the duality of knowledge – a combination of tacit and explicit. This is illustrated in Figure 2.5. Therefore, knowledge can be purely tacit knowledge or a combination of tacit and explicit knowledge. This differentiates knowledge from (pure) information.

We close this section by positioning the different types of knowledge that occur within an organisation.

Different types of knowledge

For our practical and technological approach to the subject, we recognise and differentiate between five different types of knowledge,[12] namely:

- *Know-what*: refers to knowledge about facts or some truth; also known as *declarative knowledge*. An example of declarative knowledge is knowing certain facts, such as who is the president of the World Bank or that the world is a globe and not flat. Declarative knowledge also represents knowing what the knowledge means and implies.

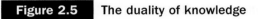

Figure 2.5 The duality of knowledge

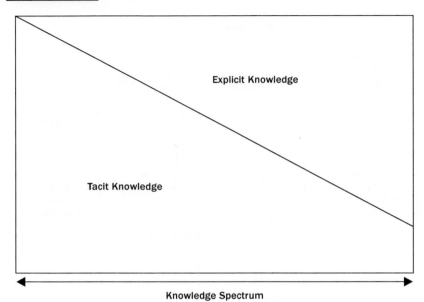

Knowledge Spectrum

- *Know-why*: refers to knowledge about principles and laws in nature, the human mind and society. It involves deep knowledge of cause-and-effect relationships.

- *Know-how*: refers to skills, i.e. the ability to do something; that is to apply 'know-what' knowledge to complex real-world problems. This is also known as *procedural knowledge*. In procedural knowledge, there is an end goal which requires a series of steps to be accomplished, with the execution of those steps driven by internal procedural rules. Procedural knowledge can vary in complexity from simple, such as selecting personal computing functions when utilising a keyboard, to very complex, such as riding a bike. Most procedural knowledge is tacit – it cannot be articulated.

- *Know-who*: involves information about who knows what and who knows what to do. It is typically a kind of knowledge developed and kept within the boundaries of a group such as an organisation or community of practice. As the complexity of the knowledge increases, cooperation between groups tends to develop and people build respect and understanding of who knows what and who to approach for specific knowledge.

■ *Know-when*: refers to knowledge involving timing. One of the most valuable types of knowledge in a business context is predictive knowledge – the ability to look ahead to a certain condition and adjust before that condition occurs. Also valuable is adaptive knowledge – the knowledge that guides an organisation to change itself when the business environment demands it.

These types are illustrated in Figure 2.6.

The knowledge worker and innovator are continually involved in learning and experimentation with the goal to move from superficial knowledge to deep understanding. The distinction is between knowing how things are done and knowing why they occur. As Garvin states:

> Knowing how is partial knowledge; it is rooted in norms of behavior, standards of practice, and settings of equipment. Knowing why is more fundamental: it captures underlying cause-and-effect relationships and accommodates exceptions, adaptations, and unforeseen events. The ability to control temperatures and pressures to align grains of silicon and form silicon steel is an example of

Figure 2.6 **Five types of knowledge**

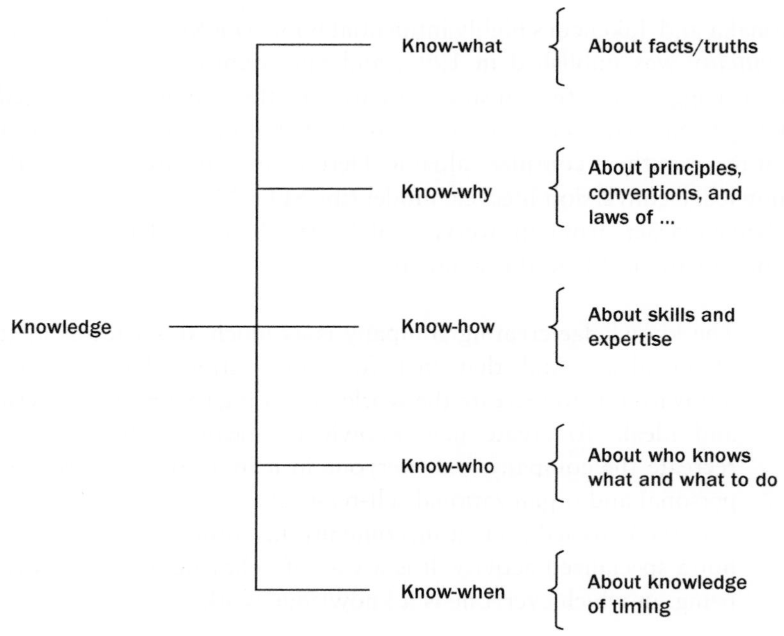

knowing how; understanding the chemical and physical process that produces the alignment is knowing why. (Garvin, 1993)

This view of knowledge should be seen as the baseline of how knowledge will be regarded in the rest of this book, namely as a duality of tacit and explicit knowledge, which is best comprehended at the extremes and where our particular emphasis is more on the explicit side.

There is a reason to believe that the greatest advantage from the use of knowledge will come from topics where the knowledge is generally not explicitly available. In many cases this knowledge is only in the heads of individuals and has not been captured for use by others. To take advantage of this tacit knowledge, enterprises try to capture and convert it into explicit knowledge for others access and use.

A much referenced approach to how this can be done in practice can be articulated in terms of the knowledge conversion lifecycle, which is the topic of the next section.

The knowledge conversion lifecycle (SECI Model)

Nonaka and Takeuchi's highly influential book *The Knowledge-Creating Company* was published in 1995, and may rightly be considered the main trigger for the business focus on the value of knowledge management. They made a number of contributions to this subject area that many authors consider valuable. Here we are only interested in their knowledge conversion lifecycle model (the SECI Model).

Some extracts from an overview of Nonaka's article that predates the book are applicable in this context:

> The knowledge-creating company is as much about ideals as it is about ideas. And that fact fuels innovation. The essence of innovation is to recreate the world according to a particular vision and ideal. To create new knowledge means quite literally to recreate the company and everyone in it in a non-stop process of personal and organizational self-renewal.
>
> In the knowledge-creating company, inventing new knowledge is not a specialized activity. It is a way of behaving, indeed a way of being, in which everyone is a knowledge worker...

New knowledge always begins with the individual ... [In each case] an individual's personal knowledge is transformed into organizational knowledge valuable to the company as a whole. Making personal knowledge available to others is the central activity of the knowledge-creating company. It takes place continuously and at all levels of the organization. (Nonaka, 1991)

As mentioned previously, Nonaka and Takeuchi (1995) suggest that two types of knowledge exist, namely tacit and explicit. Table 2.4 lists more detail.

The two types of knowledge – tacit and explicit – can be presented in a 2 × 2 tabular form to derive Nonaka and Takeuchi's knowledge conversion lifecycle (SECI Model).

These four patterns of knowledge creation in an organisation are closely linked in a knowledge creation cycle of learning. This knowledge creation and learning cycle, termed 'knowledge conversion', is presented in Table 2.5.

It can be regarded as a never-ending cycle: identifying tacit knowledge; making as much of it as possible explicit so it can be formalised, captured and leveraged; encouraging the new knowledge to be absorbed and become tacit (Stewart, 1997). In the knowledge-creating company,

Table 2.4 Tacit and explicit knowledge

Tacit knowledge	Explicit knowledge
Knowledge of experience (body skills)	Knowledge of rationality (mind)
Simultaneous knowledge (here and now)	Sequential knowledge (there and then)
Analogue knowledge (practice)	Digital knowledge (theory)

Table 2.5 Knowledge conversion

Knowledge conversion	Tacit knowledge	Explicit knowledge
Tacit knowledge	Socialisation (Sympathised knowledge)	Externalisation (Conceptual knowledge)
Explicit knowledge	Internalisation (Operational knowledge)	Combination (Systemic knowledge)

all four of these patterns exist in a dynamic interaction – a kind of 'spiral of knowledge' (Nonaka, 1991).

Figure 2.7 illustrates this with a simplistic representation; many other views are also possible.

These four different patterns are summarised as follows:[13]

- From *tacit to tacit* – socialisation/sharing – this pattern enables the learning of skills through observation, imitation and practice, making the skills part of one's own tacit knowledge 'base', thus learning through a 'socialisation' process. Knowledge is the by-product of experience and interaction. We learn by assimilating meaning from and remembering our dynamic interactions and experiences. This is still a limited form of knowledge creation because the knowledge seldom becomes explicit and can therefore not easily be leveraged by the organisation as a whole.

- From *tacit to explicit* – externalisation through capture/articulation – this exchange converts tacit into explicit knowledge, allowing it to be shared and exploited by others in the company.

Figure 2.7　Knowledge conversion lifecycle (simplistic view)

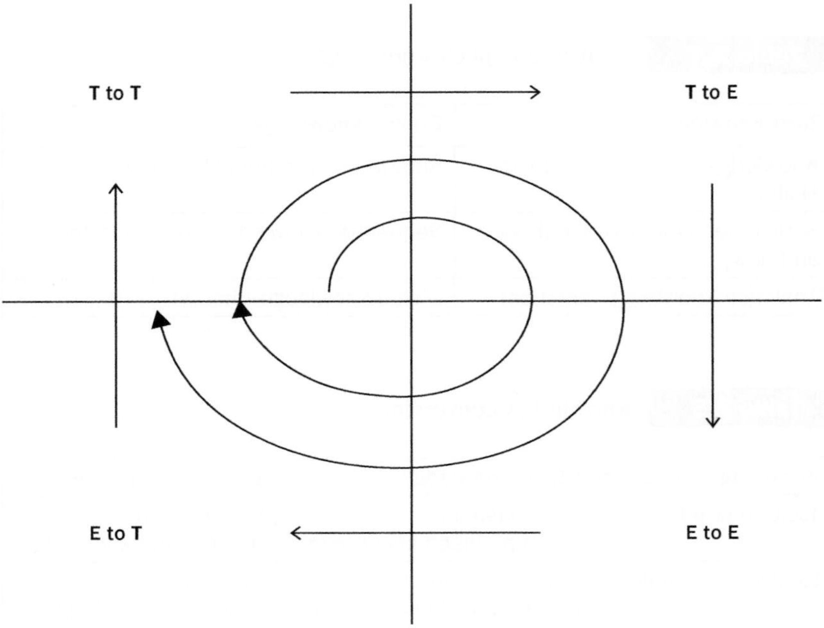

- From *explicit to tacit* – internalisation/learning – as new explicit knowledge is shared and made available throughout the company, other employees begin to 'internalise' it. In other words, they are broadening, extending and reframing their own tacit knowledge. In this way the organisation is continuously updating its knowledge base and the knowledge workers use it as part of the background of tools and resources needed to perform their jobs.

- From *explicit to explicit* – combination through copying and distributing – this is combining discrete pieces of explicit knowledge from different sources to form new knowledge, which is the main task of the knowledge worker.

In 1998 Nonaka expanded the SECI model by introducing the concept of *Ba* (or place) (Depres and Chauvel, 2000). A *Ba* in knowledge management is a space for dynamic knowledge conversion. Four *Bas* are defined by Nonaka (Figure 2.8):

Figure 2.8   *Ba* and the SECI Model (adapted by Depres and Chauvel, 2000 from Nonaka, 1991)

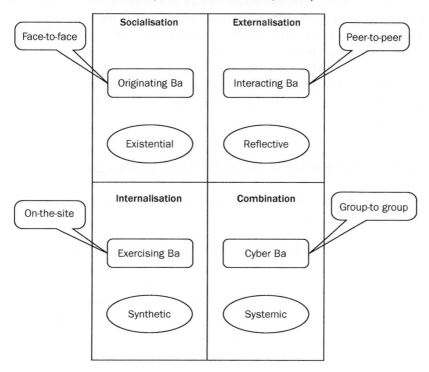

- *Originating Ba*: a space where individuals share emotions, feelings, experiences, etc.
- *Interacting Ba*: a space where tacit knowledge is made explicit.
- *Cyber Ba*: a space of interaction in a virtual world. It implicates the combination of new and existing explicit knowledge to generate new explicit knowledge throughout the organisation.
- *Exercising Ba*: a space that facilitates the conversion of explicit knowledge into tacit knowledge.

From this description of *Ba* it is clear that knowledge is context-dependent. It cannot be separated from its 'place' in any meaningful way. Each knowledge-creating process requires a *Ba* (a space), which should be recognised by the organisation (Depres and Chauvel, 2000).

The knowledge conversion lifecycle is a powerful model for knowledge management. It clearly indicates that knowledge management should at least be concerned about managing the opportunities for enabling the sharing, capturing, learning and distribution of knowledge. As this book is focusing on the technical aspects of knowledge management, we need to consider technical infrastructure as well as representation and support technologies to enhance these abilities. The last part of the book will focus in detail on these support technologies and utilise the knowledge lifecycle model extensively. In Table 2.6 we summarise and combine these aspects and hint at some of the relevant technologies.

At this point however we elaborate on a theme just mentioned in the previous paragraph: the need for managing knowledge. This is the topic of the next section.

Why knowledge has to be managed

In a global economy, knowledge may be a company's greatest competitive advantage.

If you're renting knowledge, make sure you take steps to retain it too.

What sounds like workplace gossip is often a knowledge network updating itself. (Thomas H. Davenport and Laurence Prusak)

The best brains on a particular subject frequently are spread around the world. The system that best unlocks its collection of

Table 2.6	Knowledge conversion lifecycle

Knowledge conversion	Tacit	Explicit
Tacit	Socialisation Sharing Meetings and discussions Chat rooms/synchronous collaboration Informal e-mail Conferencing tools E-meetings Synchronous collaboration (chat)	Externalisation Articulation, capturing Write a report Authoring tools Collaborative filtering Capture information in course of work Answering questions Annotation
Explicit	Internalisation Learning Learn from a report Summarisation, navigation Detect and visualise relationships Personalise task and context Visualisation Browsable video/audio presentations	Combination Copying, distributing E-mail a report Current awareness – subscription Content maps for knowledge browsing Organise or classify content or people Advanced text search Document categorisation

minds will be the one that wins in the marketplace. (Robert Buckman, Buckman Laboratories)

Knowledge Management alone is not the value. The value is winning in the marketplace. (Todd Garrett, Senior Vice President, Chief Information Officer, Procter and Gamble Company)

Knowledge plays a vital role for the existence and survival of organisations in the modern knowledge-based economy. As this study area is all but simple, we need to take cognisance of various aspects that affect the acceptance, necessity and eventual adoption of knowledge management in the modern business. These aspects include the following:

- there is a strong drive within modern organisations to become so-called learning organisations;

- there is a need to manage the knowledge assets and intellectual capital of the organisation;
- various practical matters have to be considered, such as:
  - how to 'manage' knowledge; or – at a minimum – how to raise awareness of its value and its unique nature;
  - how to obtain, discover and apply knowledge and where its best practices fit;
  - how to encourage and drive the sharing of knowledge within the enterprise;
- there is a need to devise a set of frameworks and models for knowledge management; and
- it is of interest to critically assess predictions about knowledge management and to therefore obtain a glimpse of the future of the field.

People know more than they realise. Over the years, they develop large internal 'repositories' of skills, information and ways of approaching challenges, and how to get things to 'work' or 'work out'. Organisations too are stacked with explicit knowledge: various rules of thumb, values, intuitions, various rules of behaviour, etc. As was seen with the history of total quality management, tacit knowledge is unexpressed, it is often unexamined; it can go wrong without one being aware of the fact. Stewart articulates it well:

> The outstanding virtue of tacit knowledge is that it is automatic, requiring little or no time or thought. But every virtue has a set of reciprocal vices, and tacit knowledge has three: *It can be wrong; it's hard to change; and it's difficult to communicate.* Tacit knowledge tends to be local as well as stubborn, because it is not found in manuals, books, databases, or files. It is oral. (Stewart, 1997)

Knowledge is regarded as a vital asset of the modern organisation. In most cases knowledge manifests itself as the only real differentiator between organisations; in terms of the organisation's capabilities, responsiveness or agility, adaptability to change when needed, adding value to customers and all stakeholders, etc. Because knowledge is so vital as an asset of the organisation it has become mandatory to manage knowledge properly. This is not generally recognised, however, as many organisations do not embark on programmes and strategies to manage their knowledge assets. The reason for this phenomenon is the lack of realisation of the importance of knowledge, mixed and confused with the subtle differences between information management and knowledge management as disciplines and strategies.

Only in recent years is knowledge management becoming regarded as a critical success factor for the modern organisation's survival, following many attempts at tackling similar and related issues on a strategic and operational level. One of the main contributors to this has been a growing realisation of how businesses themselves may be negatively affected by staff lay-offs and knowledge worker resignations.

Many strategists are careful in supporting yet another 'management fad', as so many recent strategic promising management tools have turned out to be just that. During the 1980s and 1990s many highly praised management tools such as 'total quality management', 'business process re-engineering', 'scenario planning', etc. were tried with varying degrees of success (see Ilbury and Sunter, 2003).

Since about 1996, strategists have focused on the discipline of knowledge management.[14] Knowledge management not only has the primary task of making the right knowledge easy to find, but to locate, validate and share any knowledge contained in the organisation.

Knowledge management is therefore a deliberate strategy to get the right knowledge to the right people at the right time to assist the employees and other stakeholders to share and put information and knowledge into action so as to improve organisational performance.

Knowledge management is not a radical paradigm shift as such. It is rather a framework and a change of focus to build on past experiences and to create new ways of exchanging knowledge. The past focus and experiences were mostly based on managing explicit knowledge kept in artefacts as well as tacit knowledge present in clever people. The new ways of exchanging knowledge are happening in communities of practice, knowledge-rich intranet sites, and rich collaboration between stakeholders.

Knowledge management is primarily a multi-disciplined area of study and practice. It is mostly a concern of management science and business management. In the modern world, however, these disciplines are intimately involved, and closely linked and supported by technology – especially information technology. Knowledge management is about managing knowledge as one of the most vital assets of the organisation, and creating a learning organisation that can adapt in an agile manner. Knowledge management is mostly about leveraging knowledge in order to adapt to change, in order to survive and grow the organisation. Information technology is perceived to be the prime enabler of organisational change and innovation – especially in offering support with vital infrastructure and tools to ease and speed up the ability to manage the knowledge assets while coping with rapid change.

For most organisations, the adoption of a knowledge-focused strategy represents a transformation and requires a shift in the culture (i.e. values and focus) of the organisation. It requires a shift in focus from:[15]

- individual to team;
- activity to results;
- completion to evolution;
- escalation to collaboration;
- content to context;
- knowing to learning.

The organisation must shift to a perspective that sees knowledge as an asset owned and maintained by the team, not by an individual. The focus of the team is to capture and improve the collective knowledge, not just to solve individual customer problems, but to improve organisational learning.

These insights have led businesses to seriously consider 'managing' their knowledge assets and answer questions such as the following:

- *How is knowledge shared?* This is particularly pertinent because of the trend of knowledge workers becoming more mobile.
- *How is knowledge retained?* Businesses have to consider trends such as downsizing and retrenchments.
- *How is knowledge obtained?* This is important because of the rapid business change currently occurring in the new economy.

Miscellaneous insights about knowledge

We don't know what we know until someone asks us. (David Snowden)

Companies don't own the knowledge … at best, they lease it from the employees. (Hubert Saint-Onge)

In the introductory part of the book we described the richness of the notion of knowledge from various perspectives and conclude here with a few summary statements about the uniqueness and counterintuitive nature of the term 'knowledge'.

As Coleman (1997) describes, knowledge is unique and different from capital, labour and land – the key ingredients of the 'old' economy – in important ways, such as:

- ability to multiply;
- if knowledge is shared it belongs to all who share – 'sell it or give it away and you still have it!' (Coleman, 1997);
- knowledge costs little to reproduce but costs a lot to create;
- sending a message on the internet is virtually free;
- knowledge is difficult to measure, weigh or count;
- measurement is only done in very indirect ways – such as the number of patents issued;
- knowledge has a 'time value' which is a key characteristic;
- knowledge and insight hold value only for a short time – they must be replenished;
- knowledge comes in tacit and explicit varieties, with the following characteristics:
    - tacit
        - owned by individuals and very personal;
        - a set of skills, understanding, experience and insights;
        - also embedded in products or in the company's processes;
    - explicit
        - can be owned by organisations, individuals or groups;
        - can be recorded or described;
        - documentation is often in electronic form in corporate documents, PCs or on the internet.

A few things we have learned about knowledge that may seem counterintuitive can be summarised as follows:[16]

- Knowledge is not pristine – it is messy and chaotic.
- How well organised is our own knowledge?
- It is not static, it is dynamic.
- Do any of us feel we are done with learning? Do we have complete knowledge about anything?

- It is as much about context as content.

- Information out of context is useless. We have a lot to learn about context.

- It is not about technology – even though we argue in this study in favour of the important role played by knowledge management technology. It is about people, values, connections and creating knowledge flows as supported by technology.

- Knowledge is the by-product of experience and interaction with others.

- Customers know more than vendors give them credit for – we have created an arbitrary boundary between us and our customers which is not helpful.

- The most valuable things we know become clear as a result of demand.

- Knowledge is personal. How important is what we know to who we are? Knowledge is a significant element in our identity.

Summary

As mentioned in Chapter 1, we are experiencing a rapidly changing business environment. This forces organisations to reinvent themselves in many ways, and especially to grow and to exploit the intellectual assets of the organisation. Knowledge is becoming the real differentiator for an organisation to survive and be successful in the highly competitive modern economy. It is therefore vital for organisations to exploit their knowledge assets, create new ones, as well as grow an environment of knowledge awareness, continuous learning and sharing of knowledge.

In this chapter we explored the varieties and different concepts of the term 'knowledge'. There is a natural conversion cycle of knowledge and it needs to be 'managed'. The many notions related to knowledge management are the topics set for the next chapter.

Notes

1. See www.quotations.about.com.
2. See articles and books such as Toffler (1970, 1981); Drucker (1993); Nonaka and Takeuchi (1995); Tapscott (1996); Stewart (1997, 2001); Malhotra (2001a, 2001b, 2003); Prusak (2001); Sveiby (2001a, 2001b).

3. The word 'tacit' comes from the Latin, meaning 'to be silent or secret'. 'Explicit', also from Latin, means 'to unfold' – to be open, to arrange, to explain. It also means 'to document' (Stewart, 2001).
4. The classic (philosophical) works on tacit knowledge are Polanyi (1964, 1967).
5. See for example Hildreth and Kimble (2002) and Liebenberg (2003).
6. This is discussed in more detail later in this book.
7. The notion of intellectual capital is described in more depth later in this book.
8. We will analyse, use and debate this general notion of knowledge later.
9. Adapted from the classic work of Waterman (1993).
10. See also Figure 2.3.
11. In the rest of this book we will use only the two forms – tacit and explicit – and draw no distinction between explicit and embedded knowledge.
12. We utilise here sources such as tutorials adapted from eKnowledgeCenter.com as well as Spek and Spijkervet (1996, cited in Baek, Liebowitz, Prasad and Granger, 1999) and Quinn, Anderson and Finkelstein (1996).
13. From various sources such as Nonaka (1991), Depres and Chauvel (2000), etc.
14. It is however still very early to judge success or failure.
15. Consortium for Service Innovation (Canada) (year unknown).
16. Ibid.

3

Knowledge management perspectives and concepts

The fundamental building material of a modern corporation is knowledge. Using knowledge to make money is the real challenge. (Valery Kanevsky, Hewlett-Packard Company)

Knowledge management is really about recognizing that regardless of what business you are in, you are competing based on the knowledge of your employees. (Cindy Johnson, Director of Collaboration and Knowledge Sharing at Texas Instruments)

If TI only knew what TI knows. (Jerry Junkins, ex-CEO of Texas Instruments)

Introduction

Modern knowledge management is an emerging discipline – barely 10 years old and still in an immature state – with many concepts and ideas still evolving. In many ways its elusive nature and lack of clear definition can be quite confusing for observers, practitioners and academics. In order to better comprehend the notion of knowledge management one may approach it from different perspectives. We follow here the list of perspectives suggested by Beckman (1999) and contribute by synthesising the ideas of a number of authors as well as adding and interpreting our own insights.

Beckman (1999) distinguishes between six perspectives in a thorough survey of the literature about knowledge management, namely:

- conceptual;
- process;

- technology;
- implementation;
- organisational; and
- management.

This chapter focuses briefly on the conceptual, process and technology perspectives, and some practical issues that are mostly implementation-related. The technology perspective is expanded later on in much more detail, and forms the main topic of the second part of this book.

The following topics are addressed as part of the *conceptual perspective*:

- definitions of knowledge management;
- principles of knowledge management; and
- a proposed conceptual knowledge management framework.

In the *process perspective* we propose a process for managing knowledge.

In the *technology perspective* we take a brief look at:

- the IT infrastructure required for knowledge management;
- knowledge representation;
- knowledge acquisition;
- knowledge repository and 'knowledge bases'; and
- knowledge transformation.

In the knowledge management *implementation perspective* we concentrate on:

- certain success factors;
- challenges; and
- knowledge management strategies.

We close this chapter by positioning knowledge management in relation to the two related notions of 'information management' and 'business intelligence'.

The conceptual perspective

The conceptual perspective is concerned with the definition of knowledge management, and describes a framework of knowledge management which is useful for comprehending and positioning knowledge management.

Definitions of knowledge management

Because knowledge management is still a new area of study, different authors define knowledge management in different ways. We suggest the following two definitions as our general and working definition of knowledge management. Both were used in practical consultation and derived from various sources, mostly from practical consulting material used in consulting engagements:

- *High-level definition of knowledge management*: Knowledge management is the discipline of managing the processes of knowledge creation, organising and sharing in an organisation.

- *Working definition of knowledge management*: Knowledge management is a discipline whose objective is to systematically leverage expertise and information to improve organisational:

  - efficiency (by reusing captured intellectual assets);
  - responsiveness (by organising resources to respond to threats and opportunities);
  - competency (by managing knowledge transfer to improve employee skills); and
  - innovation (by bringing people together across time and geography to share ideas).

These two definitions have proven useful for different occasions and formulate the essence of knowledge management in a practical way. The working definition is particularly useful in the focus of this book as it spells out the practical and technical value of knowledge management.

Knowledge management principles

Principles are basic statements of intent with an important role in strategic activities. A number of authors have proposed principles to follow while managing knowledge. After an organisation has agreed upon a set of knowledge management principles, it can create detailed approaches and action plans based upon these principles. We regard the views of Davenport (1998) as well-experienced and well-accepted in the knowledge management community. His ten general principles of knowledge management – regarded as a classic in the knowledge management field – can be summarised as:

- Knowledge management is expensive ('but so is stupidity!') – secure sufficient funds.

- Effective management of knowledge requires hybrid solutions involving both people and technology – technology on its own will not be sufficient.

- Knowledge management is highly political – take care of the organisational politics or the system will never get going.

- Knowledge management requires knowledge managers – appoint appropriate staff.

- Knowledge management benefits more from maps than models, more from markets than hierarchies – stop talking and do something to show results.

- Sharing and using knowledge are often unnatural acts – such behaviour therefore needs to be encouraged.

- Knowledge management means improving knowledge work processes.

- Providing access to knowledge is only the beginning of knowledge management.

- Knowledge management never ends.

- Knowledge management requires a knowledge contract.

In addition, knowledge management principles of O'Dell and Grayson (1998) and Tobin (2003) are summarised in Table 3.1.

From these principles it is clear that organisations need to be serious about their knowledge management activities or they will be wasting their money.

A conceptual framework for knowledge management

> The fundamental building material of a modern corporation is knowledge. Using knowledge to make money is the real challenge. (Valery Kanevsky, Hewlett-Packard Company)

In this section we consider how to represent the aspects of knowledge management, utilising an existing practical framework to clarify many of the confusing viewpoints and perspectives of this field, with a specific focus on knowledge management.

Over a number of years, various authors have contributed to the challenge of clearly presenting the different aspects of knowledge management and their mutual relationships. One of the most useful

Table 3.1	Summary of the knowledge management principles of O'Dell and Grayson with Essiades (1998) and Tobin (2003)

O'Dell and Grayson with Essiades (1998)	Tobin (2003)
Business values drive transfer benefits	Knowledge management is a discipline
Transfer of best practices is the most common and most effective knowledge management strategy	One champion is not enough
Knowledge management must be woven into the corporate infrastructure	Cultural change isn't automatic
Funding ear-marked for knowledge management is rare	Create a change management plan
Having the 'right' cultural is critical	Stay strategic
Successful knowledge management efforts employ a 'push-me-pull-you' approach	Pick a topic, go in-depth, keep it current
If it works, it really works	Don't get hung up on the limitations
Top-level support is a must	Set expectations or risk extinction
Technology is a catalyst but no panacea	Integrate knowledge management into existing systems
Mature knowledge management efforts lead to transition from nurturing to measuring	Educate your self-service users

frameworks published – which the authors have employed in a number of practical consulting situations on collaboration – resulted from research done by Waite and Company (1997) sponsored by Lotus Consulting. This paved the way to clearly position knowledge management in relation to its related concepts. We briefly describe this framework in the following paragraphs.

As can be seen in Figures 3.1 to 3.4, the framework divides the work complexity dimension into three categories, namely 'information flows', 'knowledge flows' and 'work flows'. The second dimension is the organisational complexity. This dimension is also divided into three categories, namely 'automated work group', 'integrated enterprise' and 'extended enterprise'.

As indicated in Figure 3.1, the enterprise knowledge management solutions category is positioned to serve the integrated enterprise (on the vertical axis) in terms of knowledge flows (shown on the horizontal axis).

The enterprise knowledge management category is thus distinguished from the enterprise-wide communications category, which supports the information flows. It is also distinguished from the enterprise process innovation category, which relates to work flows. Moreover, Figure 3.1 differentiates enterprise knowledge management from smaller-scale workgroup collaboration and from extended enterprise electronic community development. The corresponding block in Figure 3.2 shows that the resulting collaboration (knowledge flows) across departmental boundaries allows organisations to better leverage intellectual capital and to benefit from best practices.

Knowledge management captures information that otherwise resides in the experiences of individuals or in functional silos. Knowledge management puts it into context so that employees may use it to improve the quality of their decisions, and to systematically incorporate new learning. A 'community of practice' – which we describe in detail later – is one type of knowledge management solution (Figure 3.3).

The illustrations in Figure 3.3 and Figure 3.4 clearly position where workgroup technologies fit as business solutions and they also indicate the positioning of the technologies for messaging and collaboration.

Figure 3.1   Lotus Solutions Framework – part 1

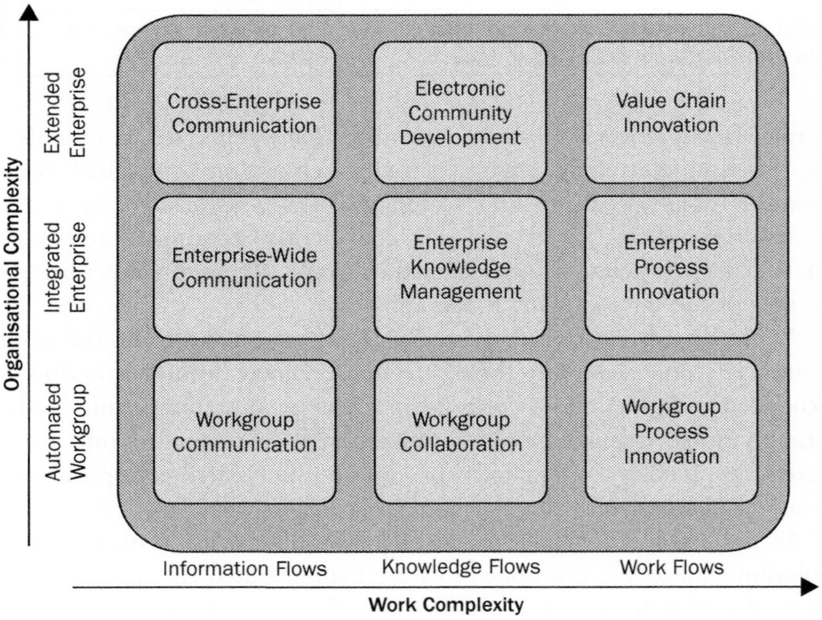

Figure 3.2 Lotus Solutions Framework – part 2

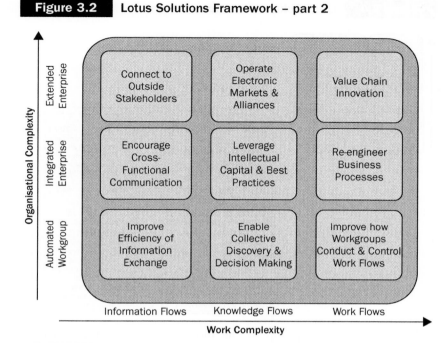

Figure 3.3 Lotus Solutions Framework – part 3

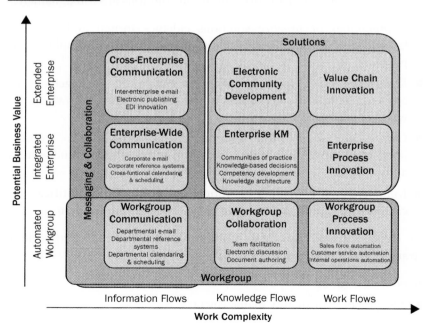

Figure 3.4　**Lotus Solutions Framework – part 4**

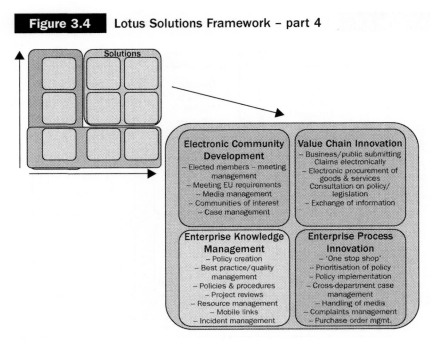

The third category group in the model groups the four business solutions of the framework. In terms of the enterprise knowledge management solutions category, important solutions are listed, namely:

- *Communities of practice* solutions enhance formal and informal knowledge sharing of best practices among people with similar work practices.

- *Knowledge-based decisions* solutions enable the management of ongoing identification, extraction and distribution of knowledge to workers making decisions.

- *Competency development* solutions enable companies to leverage intellectual capital and deliver core business knowledge to individuals and groups.

- *Knowledge architecture* solutions enable the identification, categorisation, and maintenance of key business information.

As Figure 3.4 indicates, these solutions can be expanded into various strategic and practical activities and initiatives such as:

- policy creation;
- best practices or quality management;

- policies and procedures;
- project reviews;
- resource management;
- mobile links; and
- incident management.

Where applicable, we will return to some of these collaboration solutions in the second part of this book.

The process perspective

> Knowledge by itself is not powerful. *Applied knowledge* is powerful![1] (Anonymous)

Different knowledge management processes

Before knowledge, experience and expertise can be effectively leveraged and transformed into valuable organisational assets they must be formalised, distributed, shared and applied. This implies that knowledge is managed through a process. A number of authors[2] have proposed models for this knowledge management process. In all of them it is assumed that steps and activities are often concurrent, sometimes repeated, and not always in linear sequence. In the following we propose our view of the business processes in which knowledge fulfils an important role.

Knowledge processes

A number of 'knowledge processes' can be found in business; for example, research and development (R&D), planning, market research, customer service, consulting, and decision making. These are typical knowledge-work processes performed by knowledge workers. A number of processes are obvious components of knowledge management such as knowledge creation, documentation, validation and distribution.[3] Each process has a knowledge component. Some, such as R&D, concentrate on creating knowledge, while some, such as market research, are mostly concerned with discovering knowledge. Some processes focus on organising or packaging knowledge. These processes can be categorised into three processes as we discuss next.

Knowledge management, therefore, deals with knowledge processes that affect a knowledge-focused organisation. There are three primary interrelated knowledge processes, each with several sub-processes:

- knowledge creation and sensing;
- knowledge sharing and dissemination;
- knowledge organising.

Knowledge usage is the result of these knowledge processes.

Knowledge creation and sensing

Knowledge production or discovery is a process that creates new knowledge through the regrouping and combination of older concepts as well as the sensing and invention of new ones. All knowledge creation – individual, team, community and organisation – occurs through learning and is constructed from other knowledge ideas, information, data and new insights.

When a question is asked or a hypothesis is developed, one step in knowledge production is to search for and retrieve older knowledge statements to try to prove the new hypothesis. New knowledge is created when new concepts are reformulated from older concepts. The formulation may produce a lot of knowledge or may simply bring about small improvements to current concepts that increase their explanatory and predictive power. The creation of a knowledge idea stems from a supply chain of knowledge, information and data. For example, knowledge can be constructed through knowledge gathering from classes and formal training, experts, seminars, previous knowledge, assumptions, social networking, literature, or a combination of these.

Knowledge sharing and dissemination (or transfer)

Even if vast pools of high-quality knowledge exist, the knowledge may be worthless without effective dissemination (also known as 'diffusion'). Knowledge dissemination is the process by which new knowledge is communicated through certain channels over time among the members of a team or organisation. This can occur in many different ways:[4]

- *Education*: Education from an expert to a novice is an ancient method of knowledge dissemination. Effective transfer of knowledge is dependent on factors such as the teacher's and the student's abilities as well as the relationship between them.

- *Sharing*: People share ideas and knowledge with other people formally or informally on a regular basis. Successful businesses focus on promoting knowledge sharing and reward those that do.

- *Storytelling*: This ancient technique of transmitting multiple dimensions of knowledge has recently been 'rediscovered' to be very beneficial for knowledge dissemination.

- *Writing and publishing*: The skill of writing in a way that encourages the reader while maximising understanding is a key success factor for knowledge dissemination.

- *Exposing*: Designing and constructing the environment to expose knowledge workers to high-quality sources of knowledge, making it easy to find high-quality knowledge sources and expertise when needed, should be key focus areas for knowledge dissemination.

Knowledge organisation

Knowledge organisation presupposes that knowledge already exists and that it is beneficial to capture that knowledge. The company might, for example, want to capture the knowledge of another firm by acquiring the firm, hiring employees from that firm or by bringing in external consultants, reverse-engineering some of their products, or researching the knowledge by examining published papers and articles.

This knowledge acquisition and organisation process will be examined in detail in the second part of the book.

Knowledge management process model

We propose the following knowledge management process model as illustrated in Figure 3.5.

The knowledge management process model is comprised of the three knowledge processes that give rise to knowledge usage, namely:

- knowledge creation and sensing,

- knowledge sharing and dissemination; and

- knowledge organisation.

Eight key activities may be identified which take place as part of the knowledge management processes. These activities are:

- *Create and sense*: two activities that result in new knowledge or new assemblies of existing knowledge.

Figure 3.5 Knowledge management process model

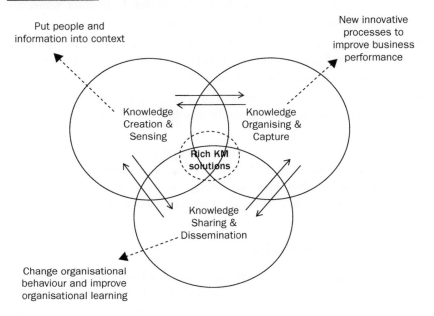

- *Capture*: activities that record and convert tacit knowledge to explicit knowledge, i.e. that move knowledge from the individual to the team, community and the enterprise.

- *Organise*: activities that classify, map, index and categorise knowledge for navigation, storage and retrieval.

- *Personalise*: activities that internalise and make knowledge specific to individuals or communities.

- *Share and collaborate*: two activities that apply knowledge to business decisions or opportunities. The 'collaborate' activity is recursive; it continually generates feedback that affects and is integrated into other processes.

- *Access*: activities that disseminate knowledge to users, display knowledge (translate, format and publish), and access knowledge (browse, search and examine).

These processes and activities are related in Figure 3.6. The figure additionally displays which activities are more human-focused and which are more technology-focused.

| Figure 3.6 | Knowledge management process model – activities |

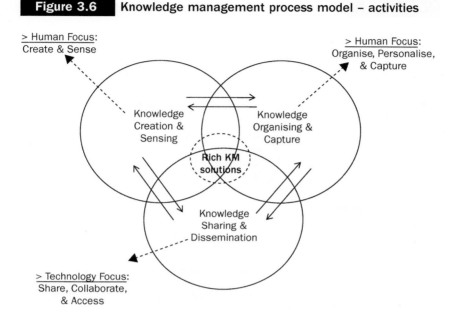

> Human Focus:
Create & Sense

> Human Focus:
Organise, Personalise,
& Capture

Knowledge
Creation &
Sensing

Knowledge
Organising &
Capture

Rich KM
solutions

Knowledge
Sharing &
Dissemination

> Technology Focus:
Share, Collaborate,
& Access

Levels and evolution of knowledge management

Figure 3.7 presents our view of three different knowledge management levels that can be observed as knowledge management activities increase in an organisation.

By just sharing knowledge the business value is relatively lower than when sharing is augmented by applying knowledge specifically through collaboration between knowledge workers. The highest business value is obtained when knowledge is constantly created, shared and applied. We then expect to see a high level of innovation in the organisation.

Figure 3.7 shows how moving from sharing to collaborating and to innovating relates to a number of key knowledge-related areas of business. These include work complexity, organisational learning, the required technical sophistication to implement and maintain these knowledge areas, and the symbiosis between technology and people. Shortly after the year 2000 it seems that knowledge management was not high on the key strategy list of organisations for a brief period. However, this has clearly changed recently as most organisations nowadays are giving attention to knowledge management.[5] We argue here that knowledge management is regarded today as a key strategy, especially for knowledge-based organisations. We also propose that

Figure 3.7 Three levels of knowledge management

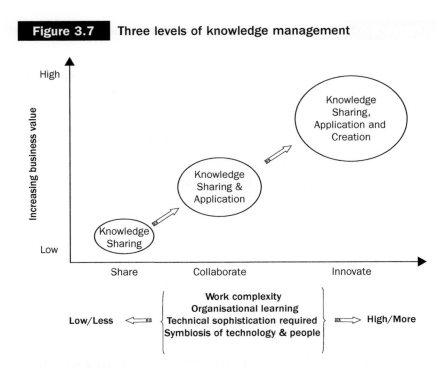

knowledge management should be regarded as a natural evolution for modern businesses in managing the challenges of the business environment. Knowledge management is 'built' on 'layers' of previous approaches to tackle these challenges. This evolution towards knowledge management, both in business and technology, is illustrated in Figure 3.8.

The notion of knowledge management described so far may be referred to by the term 'first generation knowledge management' (KM1). In KM1 we recognise a first generation of knowledge management. Some authors prefer to differentiate between two generations of knowledge management. This view is particularly promoted by Firestone and McElroy (2003) who refer to the latest emphasis on knowledge management as 'The new knowledge management'. The main differences between these 'generations' of knowledge management are summarised below:

- First generation knowledge management (KM1):
  - it is assumed that knowledge already exists;
  - there is primarily a technology focus.

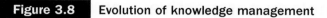

Figure 3.8 Evolution of knowledge management

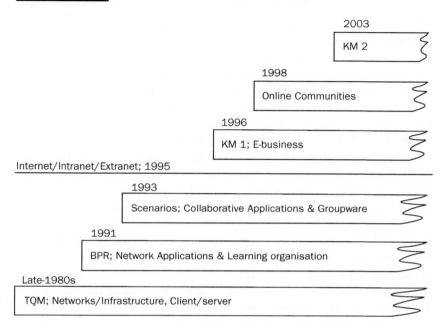

- as far as knowledge is concerned the focus is on knowledge integration;
- KM1 is not strongly concerned with knowledge production.

- Second generation knowledge management (KM2):
  - it is assumed that knowledge does not necessarily exist beforehand;
  - the focus is on knowledge production and integration;
  - knowledge is more a human social system behaviour, driven by individual and shared processes.

Firestone and McElroy (2003) also published an extended knowledge management lifecycle and described its components in depth. This view is aligned with our own views about the subject, although we argue that businesses should not underestimate the importance of many aspects of KM1, which laid the foundation for KM2. While progress is made with further research and development on knowledge management, the present book contributes to this field by proposing models and a technology framework that are applicable to both generations of knowledge management.

The technology perspective – an overview

This section gives an overview of the technology perspective. A detailed description is covered in the second part of this book, where we propose a new view of the technology perspective. This view is related to the knowledge management process model proposed in the previous section.

Many experts differ in their opinions regarding the value of IT to enable knowledge management.[6] This is specifically the opinion with regard to the value of expert systems. Davenport and Prusak (1998) asserted throughout their book that knowledge management is much more than technology, but 'techknowledgy' (their term) 'is clearly a part of knowledge management'. They also state: 'Knowledge derives from minds at work ... Successful knowledge transfer involves neither computers nor documents but rather interactions between people.'

Nevertheless, the availability of certain technologies such as Lotus Notes and Lotus Domino, as well as the ubiquitous World Wide Web has been a major catalyst for the awareness and acceptance of the knowledge management paradigm. Beckman (1999) has contributed a lot of work in support of the value of IT, formulating and integrating the concepts of knowledge representation, knowledge repositories and automated knowledge transformation. Other approaches found in the many sources on knowledge management have focused on developing software products that implement many of these concepts.[7] For example, Jackson (2001) identifies six areas of technology for the knowledge management enterprise, namely:

- document management;
- information management;
- searching and indexing;
- communications and collaboration;
- expert systems; and
- enterprise software (including vertical portals).

In the second part of the book, we propose our own categories of knowledge management technology as part of our knowledge management technology framework. This includes a category of knowledge management technology infrastructure.

Here we summarise the topic of IT infrastructure required for knowledge management as background for the section on the implementation perspective.

IT infrastructure required for knowledge management

Having an IT infrastructure in place to facilitate sharing of knowledge is a huge advantage in an organisation. Knowledge and expertise can only be effectively applied if they are easily accessible, understandable and retrievable.

An IT knowledge network will preferably include the following components:

- a knowledge base or repository – most likely a database that houses unstructured information;
- a directory of knowledge source and locality of expertise;
- a directory of learning resources; and
- groupware for collaboration between the knowledge workers.

The IT component may include the following elements:

- IT architecture interfaces and standards;
- IT platform – hardware and software for program execution as well as storage subsystems;
- communication – networking and security for structured data and multimedia data such as image, voice and video;
- information content – structured and unstructured information;
- software applications may include:
  - office automation and groupware;
  - decision support systems and executive information systems;
  - advanced information retrieval systems/engines;
  - intelligent systems such as expert systems, machine learning and knowledge discovery;
  - process modelling and simulation;
  - transaction systems such as functional information systems, including finance, marketing, human resources, information systems, etc.;
- user support, including help desks and electronic learning.

All of these technologies can be applied for knowledge management with strong agreement among experts about the value of internet-based networking and groupware technologies for knowledge sharing.

The implementation perspective

The implementation perspective on knowledge management concerns factors that facilitate the success of knowledge management projects, along with those challenges that may be foreseen and avoided. Here we summarise, for completeness, different aspects of the following:

- IT infrastructure implementation;
- critical success factors;
- prerequisites and challenges;
- types of knowledge projects.

We close with some ideas about knowledge management implementation steps.

IT infrastructure implementation

The need for an IT infrastructure to support knowledge management has been emphasised previously. Four phases may need to be addressed in the deployment of such an IT infrastructure.[8] The order of these phases may change depending on particular business needs:

- *Phase 1*: Establish an information systems and IT infrastructure.
- *Phase 2*: Create knowledge repositories.
- *Phase 3*: Develop expert system applications.
- *Phase 4*: Develop knowledge discovery capabilities.

Critical success factors for knowledge management

A number of authors have written about critical success factors for knowledge management, notably the well-respected Davenport and Prusak (1998). They defined nine factors leading to knowledge project success:

- A *knowledge-oriented culture*: Building a positive knowledge-friendly culture is the most important factor. There are three aspects to this:
  - employees must have a positive orientation to knowledge;

- there should be no factors inhibiting the sharing of knowledge;
- the type of knowledge management project must fit the culture.

■ *Technical and organisational infrastructure*: Employ a uniform set of technologies that are compatible with the knowledge project. Establish appropriate organisational structures, roles and skills to support the knowledge project.

■ *Senior management support*: Executive-level support is important in implementing the changes associated with the knowledge management project.

■ *A link to economics or industrial value*: Knowledge management can be expensive and therefore must be justified through economic benefit or industry success.

■ *A modicum of process orientation*: Knowledge processes should be implemented to govern the knowledge management activities.

■ *Clarity of vision and language*: The terms and concepts used in the knowledge management programme should be well defined, as terms like 'information', 'knowledge' and 'learning' can be widely interpreted.

■ *Non-trivial motivational aids*: Employees need to be motivated to share and use their knowledge. However, the tactics and incentives used should have a long-term impact.

■ *Some level of knowledge structure*: The structure of the organisational knowledge base should be redefined to reflect new learning and growth. This will make it easy for users to find the information they are seeking.

■ *Multiple channels for knowledge transfer*: The knowledge manager must realise that knowledge is transferred through multiple channels – online discussions, face-to-face contact, reports and journals, etc. – and should seek to incorporate these into the knowledge system.

Prerequisites and challenges

Beckman (1999) lists several challenges in implementing knowledge management in the typical organisation. We quote Beckman on four of these:

■ 'First, knowledge is often hoarded, rather than shared.

■ Second, valuable knowledge developed by others is often ignored, rather than applied in daily work situations.

- Third, knowledge and expertise are often not valued by the corporate culture, by failing to measure intellectual assets.

- Fourth, employees who share knowledge and expertise are considered naive, rather than rewarded for their valuable organizational behaviour.'

Types of knowledge projects

Davenport and Prusak (1998) found that knowledge management projects fall into three broad categories based on the objectives of the project. These are described as follows:

- *Knowledge repositories*: The aim of these projects is to capture the knowledge embedded in various resources (e.g. documents, reports, journals, memos, presentations etc.) and to structure and store it in a repository for easy access and retrieval. They found three types of repositories:
  - *External knowledge*: for example, repository of competitive intelligence gathered from trade journals, market research, analyst reports etc.
  - *Structured internal knowledge*: for example, repository of research reports, product-oriented marketing material and methods. This centres more on gathering information that most users interpret as knowledge.
  - *Informal internal knowledge*: for example, discussion database full of know-how. This gets people to articulate their tacit knowledge but not in a structured format.
- *Knowledge access and transfer*: The aim of these projects is to facilitate access to and transfer of knowledge among a community of users. These projects focus on finding the knowledge and transferring it to the people that need it. It is about connecting the possessors of knowledge to the prospective users – which can be a complex activity.
- *Knowledge environment*: The aim of these projects is to establish an environment conducive to knowledge management. This is done through various methods: change organisational culture, behaviour and attitudes to knowledge, improve the knowledge management processes, measure and improve the value of knowledge capital.

Davenport and Prusak (1998) note that in 'real' life, almost all projects are a combination of these three different types, although the focus may be on one aspect only, or the priorities between the three aspects may change.

Ideas about implementation steps

KPMG recently published an insightful brochure that sketches five implementation steps of a successful knowledge management implementation, as shown in Figure 3.9. Successful implementation is done in a systematic way, building on successive 'layers' of increasing knowledge-rich organisational capability – away from a 'knowledge-chaotic' business situation towards an ideal of a 'knowledge-centric' situation. Along the way, the organisation becomes knowledge-aware, then knowledge-enabled and knowledge-managed. Their methodology to perform this implementation is their intellectual capital and therefore not published. Their approach involves an assessment of the particular engagement's layer of knowledge capability followed by a deliberate series of consulting guidance and advice to guide the organisation towards the ideal 'knowledge-centric' capability.

We close this chapter with a brief comparison of knowledge management and the notion of information management. We also position business intelligence in relation to knowledge management.

Figure 3.9   **KPMG's five-step implementation stack**

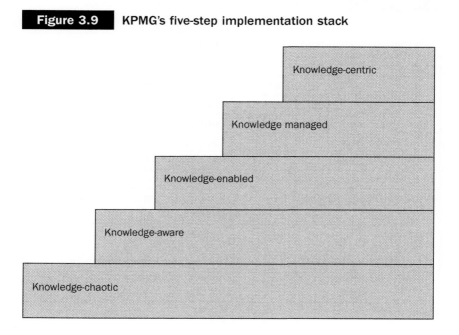

Positioning knowledge management, information management and business intelligence

Information management versus knowledge management

It is beneficial to compare main differences between information management and knowledge management in table form. Table 3.2 illustrates these differences.

Denham Grey articulates these differences well when he states:

> Much of what purports to be knowledge management is in reality information management. The distinction I like to make is this: working with objects (data or information) is Information Management and working with people is Knowledge Management. Information Management is about documents, CAD drawings, spreadsheets, program code. IM means ensuring access, security, delivery, and storage. It deals exclusively with explicit

Table 3.2   Information management versus knowledge management

Information management	Knowledge management
High volume of transactions	Low volume of transactions
Low cost (value) per transaction	High value (cost) per transaction
Well-structured procedures	Ill-structured procedures
Output measures defined	Output measures less defined
Focus on process	Focus on problems and goals
Focus on efficiency	Focus on effectiveness
Handling of 'data' ('pure' information)	Handling of concepts (notions)
Predominantly clerical workers	Knowledge workers – managers and professionals
Examples: • 'Back office' • Mortgage servicing • Payroll processing • Cheque processing	Examples: • Loan department • Asset/liability management • Planning department • Corporate banking

Source: Adapted from McNurlin and Sprague (2002).

representations. Creation, use, learning, meaning, understanding, and negotiation are *not* core issues but efficiency, timeliness, accuracy, veracity, speed, cost, storage space and retrieval *are* central concerns in Information Management. (Grey, 1998)

Business intelligence versus knowledge management

Business intelligence is often seen as being synonymous or at least similar to knowledge management. In this book we regard business intelligence as an application and technology area of knowledge management, depending on how it is employed and used. Table 3.3 (summarised from a number of sources) illustrates some of the vast differences between these two notions.

Cody, Kreulen, Krishna and Spangler (2002) argue that business intelligence and knowledge management may eventually be merged into a new discipline that handles data, unstructured information and knowledge. They call this discipline 'BIKM'.

Summary

It is clear that knowledge management as a discipline can be viewed from different perspectives and is inherently very rich in nature and concept. This results in differentiation between different organisations depending

Table 3.3 Business intelligence versus knowledge management

Business intelligence	Knowledge management
Performed by knowledge workers	Widespread sharing by all
Memory of customers	Corporate memory
Prospects/forecasts	Competition/engineering
ROI business critical	ROI emerging
Financial change	Cultural change
Analytics and mining	Push/pull/filter agents
Clustering	Categorisation
Multidimensional data and views	Knowledge maps

on how effectively knowledge is adopted strategically and exploited tactically. In this chapter we synthesised the different perspectives from many sources, thus contributing to the comprehension of this widely studied but sometimes confusing area. We specifically contributed by proposing our own knowledge management process model and by putting forward our view of three different 'levels' of knowledge management sophistication.

In the next chapter we briefly describe some applicable aspects of the notion of intellectual capital.

Notes

1. In other words, it is not so important what you know, but what you do with what you know.
2. See, for example, Demarest (1997), Cohen (1998), Depres and Chauvel (1999), Collison and Parcell (2001), Von Krogh, Nonaka and Aben (2001), Birkinshaw and Sheenan (2002).
3. See Stewart (2001) for more detail.
4. Adapted from eKnowledgeCenter online course. The best knowledge dissemination takes place in communities of practice as we will strongly argue in Chapter 6.
5. See many sources such as the respected discussion forum www.brint.com as well as industry observers such as the Gartner Group.
6. See, for example, (Sveiby, 2001a) and (Malhotra, 2001a) as well as a number of discussion forums such as those covered in www.brint.com (regarded as a primary knowledge management website).
7. One should note that a variety of (old) technologies applicable to the knowledge management ideals have been available for quite a number of decades; for example, the telephone as communication medium.
8. Adapted from Beckman (1999).

4

Intellectual capital

Intellectual Capital is packaged useful knowledge. (Thomas A. Stewart)

Without a strategy for taking knowledge to market, knowledge management is meaningless. Selling knowledge products is one of the major business opportunities of our time. (Thomas A. Stewart)

Intellectual capital has grown so important that it, rather than ownership of physical assets, explains why companies come into being and why their boundaries fall where they do. Knowledge creation gets to the very core of what makes a firm ... I invent, therefore I am. (Thomas A. Stewart)

In this chapter we summarise and synthesise various perspectives and considerations about the term 'intellectual capital' (also known as 'intellectual assets') as far as knowledge management is concerned. An extensive literature covers the subject of intellectual capital; the most prominent are the two books of Thomas Stewart (1997, 2001). The term is often confused and misused in various contexts. One specific area of confusion is the difference between intellectual capital and intellectual property, which we describe next.

Intellectual capital is not intellectual property

We start by differentiating the two notions of intellectual property and intellectual capital. Intellectual property is the set of assets that includes copyrights, patents, semiconductor circuit layouts rights, and various design rights. The set also includes trademarks and service marks. Auditing intellectual property is a well-known practice but is generally not particularly useful. For example, it is rather useless to know that one owns a patent but not have the information about its commercial potential or its return on investment. Intellectual property assets are usually considered from a legal perspective. Intellectual property and intellectual capital are therefore considered mutually exclusive. Intellectual property may be seen as an output of intellectual capital (Bontis, 2001).

Intellectual assets are increasingly important to enterprise competitiveness and market value. Protection was traditionally afforded only to patents and copyrights; now, mission-critical business and technical processes are also regarded as intellectual property. Key employee competencies, business data and market data are considered mission-critical intellectual capital. Competitive advantage is gained when these 'knowledge assets' are enriched with employee insight and applied within the context of enterprise business principles, past experience and strategic direction.

Managing the different forms of intellectual capital

According to Stewart (2001) intellectual capital (knowledge assets) takes just two forms. First, we get the semi-permanent body of knowledge, the expertise and know-how that develops in a person, or is related to a task or an organisation. This body of knowledge may include communications or leadership skills, understanding a particular field or industry, or being familiar with the organisation's processes, values and culture (often articulated as: 'this is how we are doing it here').

The second kind of intellectual capital (knowledge assets) is the tools that augment the body of knowledge; either by making available the related facts, data or information, or by delivering expertise and contacts to other expertise when needed, in other words by leveraging available expertise. Stewart's example is: 'Phone numbers are not intellectual capital; phone books are.'

In the second part of this book, we argue that this second form of intellectual capital is best supported by knowledge management technology that is specifically designed to manage intellectual capital.

Drucker (1993) describes the arrival of a new economy that he refers to as the 'knowledge society'. He claims that in this society, knowledge as intellectual capital is not just another resource alongside the traditional factors of production, namely labour, capital and land – but the only meaningful resource today.

'Because knowledge has become the single most important factor of production, managing intellectual assets has become the single most important task of business', states Stewart (1997) in his much referenced book *Intellectual Capital – The New Wealth of Organizations*. Although conventional assets of organisations will persist, knowledge as an asset is gaining in importance as a product of knowledge workers and in processes that add value to work. As we progress more and more into the knowledge-based era, knowledge will inevitably become a more important asset of modern organisations – eventually becoming the most important asset.

Intellectual assets are powerful – they appreciate rather than depreciate with use. Use of intellectual assets is a necessary condition of innovation, inspiration, problem resolution and value creation. Intellectual capital is the most important source of future value for all organisations, yet it is the least understood, always being used but rarely managed.

Definition of intellectual capital

To answer the question: 'What is intellectual capital?' we should note that organisational knowledge assets consist of talent, skills, know-how, know-what and relationships (with their related infrastructure of devices and communication networks) that can be used to create wealth and survive. Within the context of this book, an asset is something that transforms raw material into something more valuable (Stewart, 2001).

Many companies today, however, have almost no physical assets at all. Examples include advertising agencies as well as consulting and computer services companies, which make use of a lot of information technology and own relatively few physical assets such as desks, chairs, computer equipment, and some (perhaps shared) conference and training facilities. Other examples are the professional services industry and new knowledge-based companies such as Google. Stewart states:

Intelligence becomes an asset when some useful order is created out of free-floating brainpower – that is, when it is given coherent form (a mailing list, a database, an agenda for a meeting, a description of a process); when it is captured in a way that allows it to be described, shared, and exploited; and when it can be deployed to do something that could not be done if it remained scattered around like so many coins in a gutter ... Like beauty, knowledge exists in the eye of the beholder ... There's a vital lesson here: Knowledge assets, like money or equipment, exist and are worth cultivating only in the context of strategy. You cannot define and manage intellectual assets unless you know what you are trying to do with them. (Stewart, 1997)

As a guideline for defining intellectual capital, one can start off with the notion that intellectual capital is the sum of an organisation's patents, processes, employees' skills, technologies, information about customers and suppliers, and (age-old) experience.[1] These exist in the form of procedures and networking – internally and externally – with business colleagues and business partners. Stewart (2001) quotes the definition of Klein and Prusak (1994) as follows: 'Intellectual material that has been formalized, captured, and leveraged to produce a higher-valued asset'.

Stewart (2001) adds to this a working definition of intellectual capital, namely that 'Intellectual capital is packaged useful knowledge'.

Large global companies such as IBM[2] are inclined to define their own view of intellectual capital to reflect the unique assets of the particular organisation.

We use the following definition as adapted from Stewart (2001): 'Intellectual capital is the knowledge about how to transform raw material and make it more valuable'.

Some of this material may be physical. For example, the knowledge of the formula for Coca-Cola is an intellectual asset about how to transform a (secret) mixture of sugar, water, carbon dioxide and certain flavourings into the most well-known soft drink. The raw material may also be intangible, such as knowledge. For example, a lawyer takes the facts of a law case – the raw material – interprets, combines and enhances them by using his/her knowledge of law, supported by searching capabilities into similar cases – the intellectual asset – to produce an opinion or a legal brief. This output has a higher value when compared with the original facts alone (Stewart, 2001).

Intellectual capital domains

It has become the norm to consider the organisation's intellectual capital as consisting of three domains, namely: human capital (such as its talent, skills and expertise), structural capital (such as its intellectual property, patents, methodologies, software assets, documents and procedures), and relational capital (its relationships with clients, market participants and suppliers).[3] Every company possesses a unique mixture of all three of these, but depending on the industry or type of company, emphasis is placed on one of them more than the others. Intellectual capital can be viewed as the sum of these sub-domains. The catering industry illustrates the point rather well (Stewart, 2001). The leading restaurant succeeds mainly because of the human capital of its chef; the franchiser relies on the structural capital of its special recipes and effective processes; while a speciality restaurant excels because of its customer capital because the waiting staff provide a personalised treatment of the customers and know their exact preferences.

In the real world, when companies are compared – say in a similar industry and with very similar access to knowledge and information – the reason why one company outperforms the other is twofold:

- it is embedded in its human, structural and relational capital, not in its tangible assets;[4]
- it depends largely on how this company exploits or manages these intangible assets.

The intellectual capital model in Figure 4.1 is built upon the notion that intellectual capital resides in three strategic places in the organisation, namely its people, its structures and its external relationships (with customers and business partners) (Stewart, 1997). Thus, intellectual capital can be divided into the three domains of human capital, structural capital and relational capital. Each of these three domains is intangible and reflects the knowledge assets of the company – but can still be measured and managed. If divided as such it becomes possible to identify tacit as well as explicit knowledge in each of them. Tacit knowledge is mostly found in human and customer capital, in people and relationships. Most of the stock and flow of intellectual capital is tacit. Most work involves explicit and tacit knowledge in combination. 'Most knowledge management, however, limits itself to explicit knowledge; if it doesn't ignore tacit knowledge, it does a lousy job of getting at it' (Stewart, 2001).

Figure 4.1   The intellectual capital model

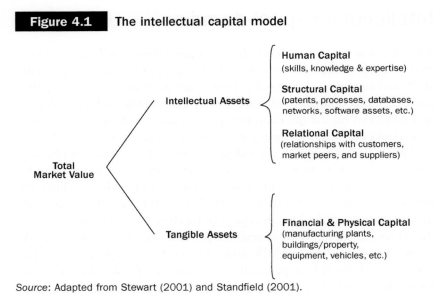

Source: Adapted from Stewart (2001) and Standfield (2001).

It is important to note that intellectual capital is not created from discrete parts of human, structural and relational capital but from the interplay among them.

In the following we briefly describe each of these intellectual capital domains.

Human capital

Human capital is made up of the capabilities of the individuals in the organisation that can aid in providing solutions to customers. It is the source of innovation and renewal, resulting from the competence of the individuals. For our purpose it suffices to state that competence is know-how plus the ability of reflection. It is the expertise of mastering the rules of the profession so well that they are obeyed as a matter of second nature.

Structural capital

A collection of human capital (of smart people) on its own may not produce the flow and sharing of knowledge in the organisation.

Knowledge needs to be leveraged by sharing and transporting or diffusing it. This requires structural intellectual assets, such as information systems, knowledge processes, competitive and market intelligence, knowledge of market channels, and management focus. Stewart (1997) articulates this need for management focus: 'Like human capital, structural capital exists only in the context of a point of view, a strategy, a destination, a purpose'.

Structural capital packages human capital and permits it to be used again and again to create reusable value. Stewart adds to this:

> What leaders need to do ... is contain and retain knowledge, so that it becomes company property. That's structural capital ... The structural capital is more important ... Even the smartest people in the world need a mechanism to assemble, package, promote, and distribute the fruits of their thinking. (Stewart, 1997)

Drucker (as quoted in Stewart, 1997 and 2001) says that 'Only the organization can provide the basic continuity that knowledge workers need in order to be effective'.

Structural capital belongs to the organisation as a whole. It can be reproduced and shared. As Stewart (1997) argues, 'Rapid knowledge sharing, collective knowledge growth, shortened lead times, more productive people – these are the reasons for managing structural capital'.

Relational capital

Relational capital is the value of the organisation's relationships with the people with whom it does business. These relationships include customers, citizens and market business partners, including the relationships with suppliers. In the words of Stewart (1997), 'It's the depth (penetration), width (coverage) and attachment (loyalty) of our franchise ... It's the likelihood that our customers will keep doing business with us'. Relational capital is recognised in many forms, such as compliant letters, renewal rates and referrals. Relational capital is based in learning, in access, and in trust.

We illustrate the positioning of the three domains of intellectual capital in Figure 4.2 and show the relative difficulty in developing and managing these three domains.[5]

Figure 4.2 Positioning the three domains of intellectual capital

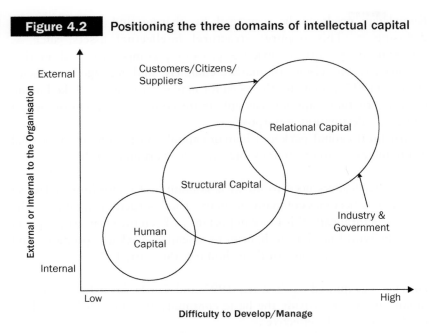

Closure and summary

Corporations are projecting their knowledge products and themselves in a paradigm that focuses on knowledge and knowledge management. Examples are:[6]

- ABB, the Swedish manufacturer of electrical machinery, says of itself, 'We build knowledge'.
- *Fortune* magazine claims it 'replaces what the martinis destroyed'.
- Ford says 'Ride New Ideas'.
- Eli Lilly reminds 'Knowledge is powerful medicine'.
- IBM's famous slogan is 'THINK', and they name their laptop a ThinkPad.

The IT industry is increasingly moving into selling knowledge. This includes products and services such as configuration, systems integration and consolidation, consulting, network design, etc. A sizable portion of IBM's revenue stems from licensing and rights to its huge base of patents and other intellectual capital.

We summarise this chapter by combining the different intellectual capital domains into Table 4.1 in terms of their essence, scope, parameter and codification difficulty.

Table 4.1 Comparison of the three domains of intellectual capital

Domain	Human	Structural	Relational
Essence	Intellect	Routines	Relationships
Scope	Internal within employee	Internal organisational links	External organisational
Parameters	Volume	Efficiency	Longevity, durability
Codification difficulty	High	Medium	Highest

Source: Adapted from Bontis (2001).

In the next chapter we take a closer view at organisational learning and the notion of the learning organisation.

Notes

1. Adapted from Stewart (2001).
2. IBM Asset Web's definition is similar to the following: 'Intellectual capital consists of information, code, software programs, knowledge, objects, experience, wisdom and/or ideas that are structured to enable reuse to deliver value to customers and shareholders'.
3. Standfield (2001) extends Stewart's model to include/rephrase 'customer capital' to 'relational capital' and 'social capital'. Intellectual capital is described in depth in Stewart (1997).
4. This is confirmed by a number of case studies such as described in Stewart (2001).
5. Adapted from Bontis (2001).
6. Adapted from Stewart (2001).

Organisational learning and the learning organisation

Stick close to your desks and never go to sea
And you all may be rulers of the Queen's Navee! (W. S. Gilbert[1])

Introduction

We begin by quoting from the executive summary of the well-known business management consultant Peter Drucker:

> Twenty years from now, the typical business will have half the levels of management and one-third the managers of its counterpart today. Work will be done by specialists brought together in tasks forces that cut across traditional departments. Coordination and control will depend largely on employees' willingness to discipline themselves.
>
> Behind these changes lies information technology. Computers communicate faster and better than layers of middle management. They also demand *knowledgeable users* who can transform their data into information.
>
> Information-based organizations pose their own *special management problems* as well: motivating and rewarding specialists; creating a vision that can unify an organization of specialists; devising a management structure that works with task forces; and ensuring the supply, preparation, and testing of top management people. Solving these problems is the management challenge for the rest of the century. (Drucker, 1988; emphasis added)

These words were prophetic; the 1990s saw dramatic trends in flatter organisations[2] and increased use of outside (knowledgeable) consultants.

Some of Drucker's insights can be emphasised by quoting from one of his earlier articles:

> The typical business will be knowledge-based, an organization composed largely of specialists who direct and discipline their own performance through organized feedback from colleagues, customers, and headquarters. For this reason, it will be what I call an information-based organization.
>
> But as soon as a company takes the first tentative steps from data to information, its decision processes, management structure, and even the way its work gets done, begin to be transformed … Information is data endowed with relevance and purpose. Converting data into information thus requires knowledge. And knowledge, by definition, is specialized. (In fact, truly knowledgeable people tend toward over-specialization, whatever their field, precisely because there is always so much more to know.)
>
> The information-based organization requires far more specialists overall than the command-and-control companies we are accustomed to … In its central management, the information-based organization needs few, if any, specialists … So the organization that will be developed will go beyond the matrix and may indeed be quite different from it. One thing is clear, though: it will require greater self-discipline and even greater emphasis on individual responsibility for relationships and for communications … The other requirement of an information-based organization is that everyone takes information responsibility. (Drucker, 1988)

Drucker (1988) describes three major revolutions in the concept and structure of organisations. The first took place between 1895 and 1905. It distinguished management from ownership. It established management as a work and a task in its own right.

The second revolution took place in the early 1920s. This was the development of the modern organisation, introducing the command-and-control model, with an emphasis on decentralisation – departments and divisions, central service staff, personnel management, the whole system of budgets and controls, and the important distinction between policy and operations.

The third revolution is taking place now: the shift from the command-and-control organisation to the information-based organisation, the organisation of knowledge specialists. The existence of this third revolution and how it relates to knowledge management is supported by authors such as Toffler and Toffler (1995), Tapscott (1996), Grulke and Silber (2000), Malhotra (2001a, 2004), Stewart (2001), Ponzi and Koenig (2002) and Koenig (2004, 2005).

Stakeholders not just shareholders

One of the major implications of the modern business environment is the recent demand on modern businesses to expand their focus and not only concentrate on adding value for their shareholders. It has become critical for organisations to focus beyond the shareholders, and on to the broader group of their stakeholders.[3] This is explained well by Visser and Sunter (2002) in their book *Beyond Reasonable Greed: Why Sustainable Business is a Much Better Idea*. Organisations are expected to satisfy the needs of their shareholders, employees and business partners while fulfilling modern obligations such as their legal, social and environmental responsibilities. Modern demands place more emphasis on how organisations perceive their societal roles and how the expertise within the organisation is forced to diversify and expand continuously according to stakeholder demands. The typical organisation needs to become ever more agile to respond to the rapid changing environment and should develop and retain vastly increasing knowledge-based capabilities in order to survive.

The result of these observations about the demands on the modern organisation is that organisations should adapt over time by concentrating on continuous learning of their people – knowledge workers as well as other employees. This should happen with a much more concentrated focus on on-the-job learning, in addition to formal class-based and instructed education and training. In order to grow, everyone within the organisation, as well as those closely involved as external business partners, is obliged to continuously learn in a focused way.

The link between learning, working and innovation

Brown and Duguid have contributed to the idea of a close link between learning, working and innovation. We quote them on some of the relevant ideas:

> Working, learning, and innovating are closely related forms of human activity that are conventionally thought to conflict with

each other ... Much conventional learning theory, including that implicit in most training courses, tends to endorse the valuation of abstract knowledge over actual practice and, as a result, to separate learning from working and, more significantly, learners from workers ... [W]e view learning as the bridge between working and innovating ... [E]volving communities-of-practice are significant sites of innovating...

To foster working, learning, and innovating, an organization must close that gap. To do so, it needs to reconceive of itself as a community-of-communities, acknowledging in the process the many non-canonical communities in its midst ... [T]o understand the way information is constructed and travels within an organization, it is first necessary to understand the different communities that are formed within it and the distribution of power among them. Conceptual reorganization to accommodate learning-in-working and innovation, then, must stretch from the level of individual communities-of-practice and the technology and practices used there to the level of the overarching organizational architecture, the community-of-communities...

Our argument is simply that for working, learning, and innovating to thrive collectively depends on linking these three, in theory and in practice, more closely, more realistically, and more reflectively than is generally the case at present. (Brown and Duguid, 1991)

We illustrate this idea in Figure 5.1.

Transforming the way to learn

According to Davis and Botkin (1995), the existence of the knowledge business is transforming the way we learn. The knowledge business is mastering the opportunity presented by the knowledge revolution in significant ways, some of which we list as follows:

- Business is coming to bear the major responsibility for the kind of education that is necessary for any country to remain competitive in the new economy.

- The marketplace for learning is being redefined dramatically to lifelong learning, whose major segments are customers, employees and students.

Figure 5.1   Learning, working, and innovation interrelationships

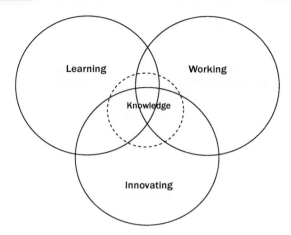

- Any business can become a knowledge business by putting data and information to productive use, creating knowledge-based products and services that make its customers smarter.

- A new generation of smart and humanised technologies may revolutionise learning by employees and customers in business before it affects students and teachers in schools.

- Business-driven learning will be organised according to the values of today's information age: service, productivity, customisation, networking, and the need to be fast, flexible and global.

These points of view are important because businesses should not focus only on knowledge per se or even on knowledge management. In the new millennium a prime focus area for success is about individual learning and specifically about organisational learning.

In order to address the challenge of organisational learning, we next describe our own view of the nature of the modern knowledge-based organisation and focus thereafter on organisational learning.

The knowledge-based organisation

Seen in a mechanistic way an organisation is an example of an open system that processes business input and produces business output. But,

Figure 5.2   An organisation's three domains

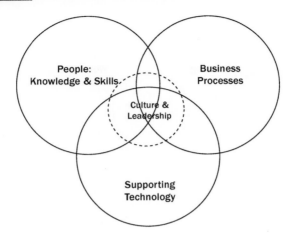

from a more knowledge-focused view, an organisation consists of three domains: people with their knowledge and skills, business processes, and supporting technology, as illustrated in Figure 5.2.

The organisation has a life of its own because it consists of individual human beings, their structures and cooperation, how they behave, their culture, their external image, their morale and leadership, as well as how they organise themselves through processes, and how they are supported by technology. An organisation is thus far more than a mechanistic robot-like information-processing engine. Knowledge of knowledge workers and their dynamics, along with the way in which ever-evolving technology is exploited and employed for business support, make businesses much more like living organisms that learn and grow in order to survive and prosper. It is in essence a complex and adaptive (learning) system that needs to react to external opportunities and threats in order to grow and survive.

In the following sections we develop and describe models and aspects that are typical of those organisations that are exploiting knowledge and in doing so become knowledge-based. We consider aspects of the knowledge worker, a model for the knowledge-based organisation, as well as those characteristics that are applicable to the topic of this book.

The age of the knowledge worker

In this section we take a look at the knowledge worker, who plays an important role in knowledge management.

A traditional company is largely a collection of physical assets, with owners who are responsible for maintaining them, and who appoint people to operate them. In contrast, a knowledge company differs from this model in many ways, because not only are the key assets intangible, but also it is neither clear who owns them, nor who is responsible for maintaining them. As described in Chapter 4 where we cover intellectual capital, the typical knowledge-based organisation may own only a few traditional assets. As Stewart (1997, 2001) points out, 'The knowledge company doesn't care about owning capital. In fact, the fewer assets the better; so long as it has intellectual capital.' Stewart also quotes Paul A. Strassman,[4] author of the book *The Business Value of Computers*, who calculated the annual cost of equity capital for 3,000 US companies compared with their information expenses. More than 90 per cent of the companies spent more on information. The median company paid nearly five times more.

More and more people spend their working life involved with information, ideas and knowledge. Table 5.1 illustrates the major transformation in organisational make-up as the information era is progressing.

One can conclude that an ever-growing proportion of all workers today are 'knowledge workers'. Stewart (1997) maintains that knowledge-intensive companies – those that have 40 per cent or more knowledge workers – accounted for 28 per cent of total US employment in the late 1990s, but produced 43 per cent of new employment growth. It should also be noted that on top of an increase in people doing knowledge work, the knowledge content of all work is also increasing – including within agricultural, blue-collar, clerical and professional work.

The increasing percentage of knowledge workers has fundamentally changed the nature of work, including that of managers. Managerial work used to be described by the acronym POEM (plan, organise,

Table 5.1   Transformation in organisations

Year	Production workers (%)	Personal service (%)	Managerial and administrative (%)	Technical and professional (%)
1900	73.40	9.00	13.30	4.30
1940	57.20	11.70	23.60	7.50
1980	34.20	13.30	36.10	16.10

Source: From Stewart (1997); data taken from the US National Bureau of Standards.

execute and measure), a characteristic of industrial Taylorism.[5] Knowledge work, however, is vastly different from industrial era work. It is mostly professional in nature. Professionals are measured not by the tasks they perform but by the results they deliver. Unlike the industrial worker, the professional interacts more with peer experts than with the managerial hierarchy to complete tasks and projects. When work is about knowledge, the professional work model is followed rather than the bureaucratic model. This results in 'flatter' organisations and new managerial methods. Mass production industrial work required command-and-control management with the 'boss' knowing more than the employee. Knowledge workers are most likely employed because they know things their 'bosses' don't. Knowledge workers, working alone or in teams, plan, organise and execute many aspects of their own work, with some worker measurement done by computer. This has resulted in a reduced need for middle management and therefore generally 'flatter' organisation structures. The requirement for management in the information era is firmly on 'leadership' as opposed to management. The most valuable parts of knowledge-based work involve pure human capabilities such as sensing, judging, creating, collaboration and relationship building.

Additionally, the typical knowledge worker experiences a largely undefined working environment with a multitude of ill-defined outcomes. On top of this, the knowledge worker experiences a number of role changes during a typical working day. For example, he/she can act as a project manager in one meeting, then be a subject matter expert in the next meeting, changing roles again later by responding to a request for input to a remote group or team. This same knowledge worker may be involved in a separate community of practice in his/her semi-private time after working hours.

An enterprise model

A number of authors have described models of the organisation. For example, we have already noted the model described by Sveiby (2001b), who specifically approached this topic from a managerial and knowledge-based perspective. We propose here, however, our own enterprise model of the modern knowledge-based organisation. This consists of various strategic, tactical and operational business models employed within and by the organisation. Our enterprise model is illustrated in Figure 5.3. This model describes the complexity of the

Figure 5.3 Enterprise model

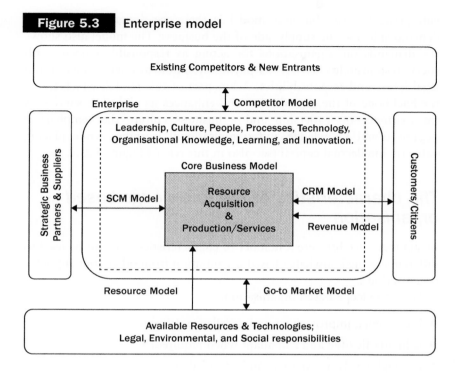

modern business environment and how organisations organise themselves to operate and grow in such an environment.

The main purpose of the modern business is to produce products or deliver services required from its customers in cooperation with its strategic business partners through its different relationship models. We emphasise two specific relationship models, namely the customer relationship model and the supply chain model. These models are built based on the organisational knowledge about the particulars and specific needs of the customers. The models also add value by exploring relationships and cooperation with strategic business partners and suppliers.

The modern organisation utilises its go-to-market business model to use the business environment to serve its customers while defending itself against its competitors or new entrants into its market via its competitor model. The typical e-business model of operation relies on cooperation with its strategic business partners and suppliers while adding value for its customers, in many instances acting more and more as a virtual enterprise. Its core business model is therefore designed to link the demand side and the supply side of the business. The model also shows the demands on organisations for acting as responsible citizens with social responsibility as well as paying attention to environmental and legal issues and responsibilities. A key part of this model, which forms the backbone of the organisation and enhances its ability to survive, is the existence of leadership and a business culture that emphasises organisational knowledge and organisational learning, while placing value on intellectual capital (see also in this regard Figure 5.2).

The characteristics of the knowledge-based organisation

In summary, we list here a number of characteristics that can be used to differentiate the knowledge-based organisation from other contemporary organisations.

The knowledge-based organisation:

- is customer, improvement and excellence-driven;
- is highly flexible and can adapt when required;
- has high levels of expertise and knowledge;
- has high rates of organisational learning and innovation;
- is innovative and IT-enabled;
- is self-directed and managed – employing leaders rather than managers;
- has a culture of being proactive and futuristic;
- values expertise and sharing of knowledge.

The knowledge-based organisation is continuously learning in order to survive and grow. We address the matter of successful learning by an organisation in the next section.

Successful enterprise learning

The successful enterprise uses its knowledge assets to learn from that which has been sensed in its business environment, and by innovating new products, services, channels and processes. It then transforms itself rapidly by its innovations and excels in exploiting opportunities and overcoming challenges. This enterprise is enabled by information, knowledge and technology. It wins because of its knowledge of

Figure 5.4 Successful enterprise learning

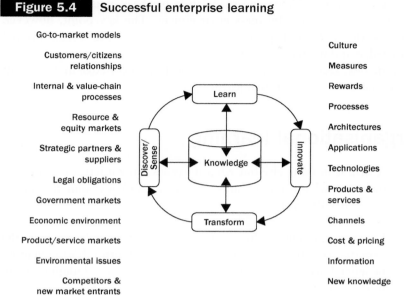

Go-to-market models

Customers/citizens
relationships

Internal & value-chain
processes

Resource &
equity markets

Strategic partners &
suppliers

Legal obligations

Government markets

Economic environment

Product/service markets

Environmental issues

Competitors &
new market entrants

Discover/Sense

Learn

Knowledge

Innovate

Transform

Culture

Measures

Rewards

Processes

Architectures

Applications

Technologies

Products &
services

Channels

Cost & pricing

Information

New knowledge

customers, products, internal and cross-organisation processes, and the business environment. This is illustrated in Figure 5.4.

This diagram draws attention to the complexity of the business environment and indicates how the successful organisation responds to the many and diverse parameters. External parameters in the left-hand side of the diagram include many related financial events and trends, legal obligations, the dynamics of internal and value-chain processes, as well as different environmental and other business issues. On discovering or sensing these parameters the organisation responds by accumulating or updating this new or changed knowledge and in doing so continues to learn as an organisation. This learning – as we will discuss in detail in the following sections – includes acting on the new knowledge and reflecting on the implications imposed on the organisation and its business. The cycle indicated in Figure 5.3 leads to processes of innovation to counter the effects of, or take advantage of the new knowledge acquired. The result of this innovation affects the internal parameters listed on the right-hand side of the diagram and usually leads to a transformation in the way the organisation does business.

The diagram combines a number of ideas about the successful enterprise by emphasising the role played by organisational knowledge and organisational learning. We also illustrate the continuous cycle that the modern knowledge-based organisation has to exercise in the current dynamic and complex business environment. The key point, however, remains the core and prime position taken by the organisational knowledge and its management.

In the next section we explore this important knowledge management aspect, namely organisational learning.

Organisational learning

> A firm is nothing else but what it knows, how it harnesses and co-ordinates what it knows, and how fast it can know something new. (Laurence Prusak)

> Learning can only be done in two ways: Either one learns from the expertise of others who know or by trial-and- error. It's much more beneficial to learn from others as children do. (adapted from traditional wisdom)

> Why is there always time to do it over, but never time to do it right first? (Anonymous)

> An organization's ability to learn, and translate that learning into action rapidly, is the ultimate competitive business advantage. (Jack Welch, chairman of General Electric)

In this section we explore the important knowledge management aspect of organisational learning. Knowledge management and its learning aspect, as discussed so far, logically imply that an organisation has to employ and grow its intellectual capital and knowledge assets. In doing so the organisation needs to embark on an organisational learning programme. In the following section we briefly discuss organisational knowledge and the definition of a learning organisation, concluding with some applicable remarks about the knowledge-enabled organisation.

Organisational knowledge

We pointed out previously that organisational knowledge consists of five different types of knowledge: know-what, know-why, know-how, know-who and know-when. Our view is that organisational knowledge is constituted by the collected knowledge of individual knowledge workers who share their knowledge while interacting with other employees. We can derive two key characteristics of organisational knowledge from this. Firstly, organisational knowledge is knowledge that is shared among organisational members. We particularly note a number of views of authors indicating that although organisational knowledge is created via individual knowledge, one may regard organisational learning – which is closely related to organisational knowledge – as another case of 'the whole being greater than the sum of its parts'. Secondly, organisational knowledge is distributed – being created and managed by individuals who act autonomously within a decision domain.

These two characteristics are conflicting, which increases the difficulty of managing organisational knowledge. Therefore, it is necessary to construct a powerful, intelligent information infrastructure to support knowledge management. We have already described one such construct when we described the knowledge creation lifecycle of Nonaka and Takeuchi (1995) in Table 2.6. In the second part of this book we will expand this concept, introduce other alternatives, and describe the detail of this infrastructure.

The concept of collective learning is investigated in various fields of study but is still not well understood. In the following we will touch on some of the issues that these studies have addressed where applicable to our particular focus. In this section we therefore summarise and synthesise various perspectives and considerations related to organisational learning. In the next section, we take a closer look at the concept of a learning organisation.

What is a learning organisation?

Senge (1990) has helped popularise the concept of the learning organisation. He briefly defines a learning organisation as 'an organisation that is continually expanding its capacity to create its future'. According to Garvin (1993), 'A learning organisation is an organisation skilled at creating, acquiring, and transferring knowledge, and at modifying its behaviour to reflect new knowledge and insights'. Gilley and Maycunich (2000) describe a learning organisation as an organisation that learns powerfully and collectively, continually transforming itself to more effectively manage knowledge and empower its people to learn as they work, utilising technology to maximise learning and production. These organisations must continually refresh and update their intellectual capital. This is the process of organisational learning.

In *The Fifth Discipline*, Senge (1990) distinguishes between two different types of learning in organisations. 'Adaptive learning', is essentially 'survival learning', whereas 'generative learning' is learning that enhances an organisation's capacity to create. Senge stresses that the two types of learning must be joined. Argyris (1991) and Hitt (1995) refer to these two types of learning as single-loop learning and double-loop learning. In single-loop learning the members of an organisation respond to changes in the internal and external environment by detecting errors, which they then correct. An individual working at a single loop level just conforms to the set standards and norms and will focus on solving the problem.

Double-loop learning occurs when flaws are detected and corrected in a manner that results in the modification of an organisation's underlying norms, policies, strategies, objectives and assumptions associated with the norms. People operating at a double-loop level will not just conform to the standards and norms that have been set, but will also question whether the standards and norms are the proper ones, and will ask what could be done to redesign the system so that problems cannot occur again.

Considering the above description of the two types of learning it is clear that the traditional organisation is more aligned to single-loop learning, and the learning organisation with double-loop learning. However, an organisation needs both types of learning, although according to Hitt (1995) we should recognise that double-loop/generative learning is on a higher level and that it provides guidance for single-loop/adaptive learning.

All knowledge creation occurs through learning. Learning or knowledge creation takes place at three levels: the individual, the team and the organisation. When an individual learns,[6] he/she creates personal knowledge even though that knowledge might not be new to other individuals. Collective knowledge creation is when a set of rules believed to be true – called a knowledge claim – is either submitted to the group by an individual or the group co-creates the knowledge claim through collaboration. In this sense, a group learns. The group's knowledge claim may or may not be new to other groups within an organisation. If it is new, and a substantial number of peer groups believe the knowledge claim to be true, then the knowledge claim becomes organisational knowledge, and thus the organisation learns.

Therefore, the creation of new knowledge is the point at which individual and organisational learning come together. Essentially then, in the modern organisation the act of working and that of learning are the same.[7]

The way that learning is connected to working takes place in the conceive, act and reflect learning spiral, as illustrated in Figure 5.5.

These activities – as we will argue in the second part of this study – can be supported by technology such as groupware and so-called knowledge portals.

We should point out here that the organisation cannot create knowledge without individuals. It is, therefore, important for the organisation to provide the context and to support and stimulate the activities for creating knowledge. Organisations therefore have to change their thinking about learning. This is illustrated in Figure 5.6.

Figure 5.5 Learning spiral

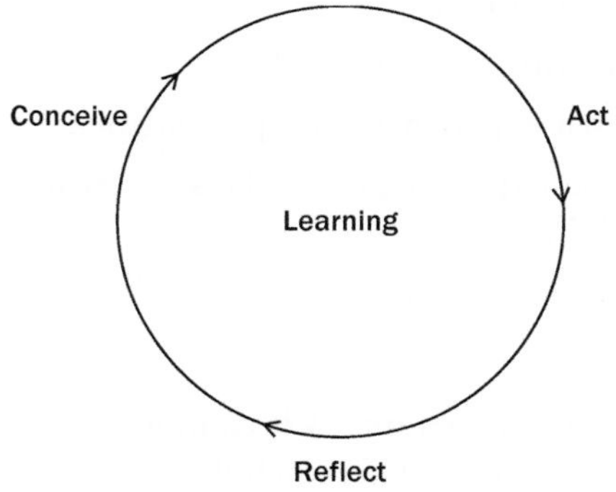

```
        Conceive              Act

                Learning

              Reflect
```

Figure 5.6 Individuals learn in the context of the organisation

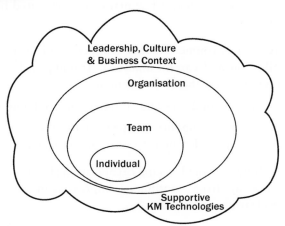

Three critical issues must be addressed before a company can truly become a learning organisation, writes Harvard Business School professor David Garvin (1993):

- first, is the question of meaning: a well-grounded, easy-to-apply definition of a learning organisation;
- second, comes management: clearer operational guidelines for practice; and
- finally, better tools for measurement can assess an organisation's rate and level of learning.

Garvin states that learning organisations are skilled at five main activities:

- systematic problem solving.
- experimentation with new approaches.
- learning from own experiences and past history.
- learning from the experiences of others (even doing SIS – 'stealing ideas shamelessly').
- transferring knowledge quickly and efficiently throughout the organisation.

As one cannot manage something if it cannot be measured, a complete learning audit is a must. This includes measuring cognitive and behavioural changes as well as tangible improvements in results. Garvin finally warns that learning organisations are not built overnight, but are the result of carefully cultivated attitudes, commitments and management processes. He lists a few major steps required to become a learning organisation:

- Firstly, foster an environment that is conducive to learning (including time for reflection and careful analysis). Training in brainstorming, problem solving, etc. is therefore essential.
- Secondly, open up boundaries and stimulate the exchange of ideas.
- Thirdly, once a more supportive open environment is established, management can create learning forums; invite strategic reviews; etc.

He argues forcefully that the learning organisation should make a subtle shift in focus, away from continuous improvement and towards a commitment to learning.

Marquardt (2000) believes that learning organisations learn more effectively from their mistakes, make more organisational use of their employees at all levels of the organisation, shorten the time required to implement strategic changes and stimulate improvement in all areas of the organisation.

From organisational learning to the knowledge-enabled organisation

> When I started my job at [the newspaper] Svenska Dagbladet I was taught that it was a Publishing Company. A few years and a dozen management books later I was working in an Information Company. Now I am employed by a Know-How Company. A career without even having to change employer! I sometimes wonder whether the development only has happened in the heads of some authors. (Journalist in 1989, quoted by K.-E. Sveiby)

Because of its relevance to this book, we will give a brief summary of a well-researched subject: the knowledge-enabled organisation.[8]

Organisational learning, as discussed previously, can only take place through the collective learning of individuals who then share their insights and experiences across the organisation to enable it to change and enhance its response to environmental stimuli. Kim (1993) develops this in his model of organisational learning. In this model, individuals improve their mental models, which are their internal images, values, norms and principles of how the business world works, through an experiential learning cycle that Kim has termed 'observe-access-design-implement'. These mental models are shared and made explicit to become shared mental models. Through sharing, actively interacting and experimenting, the mental models are further refined and improved. Over time, the shared mental models are incorporated into the organisation. This change in behaviour related to the new shared mental model is what we associate with organisational learning.

The knowledge-enabled organisation is therefore the result of a progression through an organisational learning process. As illustrated in Figure 5.7, a process has to be completed whereby mental models are developed for the creation and sharing of individual and organisational tacit knowledge to create tacit and explicit knowledge within teams, communities and the whole organisation.

Figure 5.7	From organisational learning to a knowledge-enabled organisation

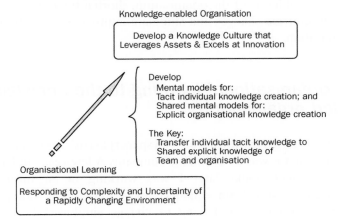

The key ingredient of organisational learning is the ability to transfer individual tacit knowledge to shared explicit knowledge and spread it across the organisation. As Tobin states:

> When a company learns to utilise and foster the growth of the knowledge and skills of all employees across all functions and levels, integrate learning activities into every employee's work, encourage and reinforce all modes of learning, and align all of this learning with the company's strategic business directions, it becomes a knowledge-enabled organisation. (Tobin, 1997)

Tobin (1997) states that a knowledge-enabled organisation is one in which:

- the company recognises that the collective knowledge and skills of its employees provide the company's only source of competitive advantage;
- the company uses the knowledge and skills of all employees, regardless of level, function or location, to help meet individual, functional, department and overall company goals;
- every employee has the means to locate the knowledge and skills of other employees to improve individual and company performance;
- the company provides sufficient just-in-time learning opportunities to all employees to enable them to gain the knowledge and skills needed to do their jobs;

- the company builds a culture that nurtures a positive learning environment.

Tobin argues that individuals and organisations learn through experience and discovery, which is supported by sharing knowledge and providing access to knowledge at the point where it is needed. He is convinced that the knowledge-enabled organisation provides a more effective context and environment for continuous learning than large investments in training.

We want to add to this argument by re-emphasising the model in Figure 5.2, in which we maintain that successful organisational learning and the knowledge-enabled organisation is the result of a symbiosis of people (with their knowledge), businesses processes and supporting technology. This is achieved through the successful learning cycle, as illustrated in Figure 5.4.

Summary

In this chapter we described our view of the modern organisation, its required focus on its stakeholders rather than only its shareholders – the so-called stakeholder capitalism versus shareholder capitalism, as well as the importance of learning and what the learning organisation entails. We presented and proposed different models for ease of comprehension. They include the three domains of an organisation (see Figure 5.2), the enterprise model (see Figure 5.3), and a model for the successful enterprise learning cycle (see Figure 5.4). We also emphasised the reality that individual learning takes place in the context of the organisation (see Figure 5.6).

It should be clear from the descriptions that knowledge management plays an important role in positioning the modern learning and knowledge-enabled organisation to grow and survive in a highly competitive business environment.

In the next chapter we discuss a key phenomenon important for knowledge management, namely communities of practice.

Notes

1. The power of knowledge!
2. See Rajan and Wulf (2003).

3. Stakeholders include shareholders, employees, customers/citizens, business partners, suppliers, as well as social, environmental and government responsibilities.
4. See website: www.strassman.com.
5. After Frederick Winslow Taylor, the industrial engineer who founded Scientific Management at the turn of the twentieth century. His contribution was the value of managerial brainpower or 'father knows best' management (Stewart, 1997).
6. Actually, organisations do not learn – individuals learn!
7. Already previously hinted at in Coleman (1997) and Tapscott (1996). Especially in the present knowledge-based society the lifestyle should be 'lifelong learning'.
8. See for example Senge (1990), Kim (1993), Tobin (1997) and Andreu and Sieber (2001).

Knowledge management and communities of practice

Communities of practice are the new frontier. They may seem unfamiliar now, but in five or ten years they may be as common to discussions about organizations as business units and teams today – if managers learn how to make them a central part of their companies' success. (Etienne Wenger and Bill Snyder)

In this chapter we begin with a brief overview of the notion of the knowledge workplace. Next, we summarise the role of knowledge management with respect to collaboration within the organisation and across its boundaries. This introduces the notion of a community of practice and its importance for knowledge management. In the second part of the study we describe the notion of collaboration and its related knowledge management technologies in detail.

The knowledge workplace

We briefly comment here on the evolving phenomenon of new experiences of physical and virtual workplaces for individuals and teams in organisations.

As argued in previous sections, knowledge work is becoming the primary work style in enterprises, and knowledge workers are becoming the key element in the workforce. Fewer jobs are well-structured or well-defined. Instead, knowledge work is defined at the point of need – as and when opportunities, issues and problems arise. Traditional hierarchical control structures can neither respond with sufficient agility to customer demands and competitive pressures nor satisfy the motivational needs of knowledge workers. The workplace must provide an environment in which the knowledge worker can most effectively perform his or her job. This environment may offer the following:

- supporting processes for analysis and decision making by individuals, teams and communities;
- providing a means to collaborate with the appropriate people to accomplish the knowledge worker's task; and
- giving access to expertise, information and knowledge assets that are relevant to the opportunity at hand.

The workplace is no longer just a physical location; it has become a blend of physical and virtual spaces in which work is undertaken.[1] People interact and collaborate with each other in physical and virtual places. Physical workplaces are about social interaction, which is an essential feature of creative and innovative efforts. The knowledge workplace therefore shifts the role of 'place' as a control feature to 'place' as a socialisation and knowledge sharing medium.

In the second part of this book we will additionally discuss how this knowledge workplace is supported by knowledge management technologies as well as the idea of whether knowledge management can become mostly virtual.

Next we consider briefly the key knowledge management concept of collaboration.

Knowledge management and collaboration

> Xerox's problem isn't with sharing knowledge – it's knowing who might want it or where to look for it. (Mary Bernhard)

Collaboration is the ability of groups of people to work together and exchange information and knowledge. Collaboration is a key part of the work activities of knowledge workers. The discipline of computer-supported collaborative work (CSCW) is concerned with computing technology serving as support for groups of people as they work together. CSCW is specifically involved with *human collaboration* and supportive software that enhances cooperation, augments interpersonal communication, and supports distributed teams. We will describe this technology – which is a key knowledge management technology in the form of 'groupware' – in detail in the second part of this book.

Unlike traditional computing technology, which has a strictly technical focus, the focus of CSCW and groupware is on social and business situations as well as organisational collaboration. The thinking is about the interrelationship of people, work and technology, as well as how to utilise technology such as groupware to stimulate innovations. Businesses, which are primarily knowledge-based, are keenly aware that leveraging the knowledge of employees and trading partners is the key to survival and success. They recognise the rough equation:

knowledge management success = technology + culture + economics + politics

in which, the further one looks to the right of the equation, the more difficult successful knowledge management becomes.

We propose in Figure 6.1 a graphical illustration of the co-evolution of knowledge management culture and technology as well as where and when knowledge management and communities of practice are positioned.

The figure illustrates how corporate culture has evolved into networked culture and to the e-mail culture which today is ubiquitous in

Figure 6.1   **Evolution of business cultures and knowledge management technologies**

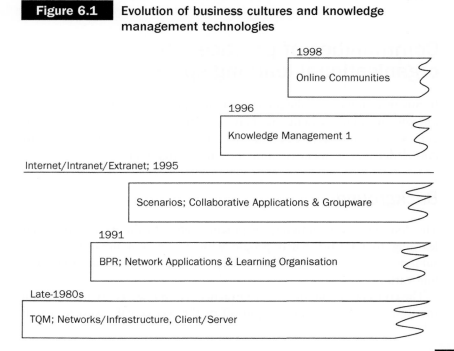

corporations. In the early post-2000 years we are experiencing a huge increase in the adoption of collaboration technologies that can rightly be seen to be key to the generation of knowledge as actionable information. Referring to Figure 6.1, we notice that the common thread through all stages is 'collaboration', the ability to work together and exchange information and knowledge. It is about groups of business individuals and how they collaborate. We also notice a fundamental change in culture: the emergence of open communications between individuals and groups, bypassing many organisational structures and boundaries. A knowledge worker or a team of knowledge workers can communicate directly with subject matter experts irrespective of their organisational ranking and position, driven mostly by the immediate project need for knowledge and information. MIT Professor Thomas Allen's studies during the 1970s showed that hierarchical distance is as much of an inhibitor of knowledge sharing as physical distance (Stewart, 2001).

As companies start to organise, access, manage and apply knowledge, knowledge tends to gather around two organising principles: relationships and people. Organisations are now realising the importance of these relationships and the people involved, and are starting to build communities. Most organisations now are a network of small communities.

Therefore, we next describe the notion of communities of practice.

Communities of practice – the organisational learning space

In this section we describe the important aspect that is closely related to knowledge management, namely communities of practice (often abbreviated as CoPs). Communities of practice and their relation to knowledge management is an important research focus.[2]

Background

The concept of a community of practice refers to the process of social learning that occurs when people with a common interest in some subject or problem collaborate to share ideas, find solutions and build innovations.

The concept of communities of practice was pioneered by the Institute for Research on Learning, a spin-off of the Xerox Palo Alto Research

Center. The basic mission of the Institute was to study how people learn. The term was first used in 1991 by Jean Lave and Etienne Wenger who used it in relation to situated learning. Their fundamental finding was that learning is a social activity, i.e. learning happens in groups. However, not every group is a learning place. Groups that learn, communities of practice, have special characteristics. They emerge of their own accord, drawn together by a force that is both social and professional. They collaborate directly, use one another as sounding boards, and teach each other.

In 1998, Wenger extended the concept and applied it to a commercial setting. More recently, communities of practice have become associated with knowledge management as people have begun to see them as ways of cultivating or nurturing new knowledge or sharing existing tacit knowledge within an organisation.

A working definition and characteristics of communities of practice

We can view a community of practice in terms of learning. This approach views learning as an act of membership in a 'community of practice'. The theory seeks to understand both the structure of communities and how learning occurs in them.

We use and support the definition of a community of practice proposed by Stewart (2001): 'A CoP is a group of professionals, informally bound to one another through exposure to a common class of problems, common pursuit of solutions, and thereby themselves embodying a store of knowledge'.

Stewart (1997) quotes Etienne Wenger in identifying characteristics that distinguish communities of practice from other groups:

- They have history – they develop over time. One can define them in terms of the learning they do over time.

- Communities of practice have an enterprise, but not an agenda – they form from a notion of 'something we are doing'.

- The enterprise involves learning – over time it develops customs and a culture.

- Communities of practice are responsible only to themselves. No one owns them. Members join and stay because they have something to learn and something to contribute.

- Communities of practice are voluntary and about fellowship rather than work.

- Communities of practice perform two main jobs of human capital formation: knowledge transfer and innovation.

Communities of practice differ from work teams in a significant way. Teams are formed by management and report to a boss. They have defined membership, deadlines and specific deliverables. In contrast, communities of practice can be voluntary, usually have longer lifespans than teams (but only last as long as they have value to their members), and have no specific deliverables imposed. They are responsible largely to themselves.

Basic communities of practice concepts

The idea of communities of practice is based on the following assumptions:

- Learning is fundamentally a social phenomenon. People organise their learning around the social communities to which they belong. Therefore, schools are simply powerful learning environments for students whose social communities coincide with that school.

- Knowledge is integrated in the life of communities that share values, norms, languages and ways of doing things. Real knowledge is integrated in the doing, social relations and expertise of these communities.

- The processes of learning and membership in a community of practice are inseparable. Because learning is intertwined with community membership, it is what lets us belong to and adjust our status in the group. As we change our learning, our identity and our relationship to the group also change.

- Knowledge is inseparable from practice. It is not possible to know without doing. By doing, we learn.

- Empowerment – or the ability to contribute to a community – creates the potential for learning. Circumstances in which we engage in real action that has consequences for both us and our community create the most powerful learning environments.

Communities of practice are simply expansions of one-on-one knowledge-sharing. Most people belong to a number of such communities, not all of them work-related. Some have names, such as the church choir or the neighbourhood council, and some may have no more of an identity than 'a group of management specialists who usually get together for lunch once a week' (Burk, 2000).

According to Lesser and Storck (2001) communities of practice help organisations to 'overcome the inherent problems of a slow-moving traditional hierarchy in a fast-moving virtual economy'. They are effective mechanisms whereby unstructured problems can be dealt with. They can be used to share knowledge outside of the traditional structured boundaries of the organisation. Furthermore, they are seen as mechanisms for the development and maintenance of long-term organisational memory, they can be used to enrich individual members' learning, and can inspire members to apply what they have learned (Lesser and Storck, 2001). For Brown and Gray (1995) the value in communities of practice lies in the fact that they can be used to build core competencies, which can energise and mobilise employees, and they can shape and enact strategy. According to Burk (2000), new staff and staff in new roles can become productive more quickly through communities of practice. Members of communities can also raise each other's competencies through sharing. Burk (2000) further regards a community of practice as a mechanism for communicating. From Allee's (2000) distinction between the value of a community of practice for the organisation, the community and the individual, it is clear that by participating in communities of practice, individuals obtain the necessary expertise to do their work effectively, and in doing so increase the organisation's intellectual capital. This is what gives an organisation the necessary competitive edge in an increasingly competitive environment.

According to Burk, communities of practice are a crucial aspect of knowledge management for the US Department of Transport:

> At work, Communities of Practice can exist solely within an organisational unit; they can cross divisional and geographical boundaries; and they can even span several different companies or organisations. They can be made up of a handful of participants or many dozen. But they all tend to have a core group of participants whose dedication to the topic provides the energy needed to hold the group together. These core participants naturally provide the groups' intellectual and social leadership. (Burk, 2000)

The positioning of communities of practice in and across organisations is illustrated in Figure 6.2.

| Figure 6.2 | Positioning of communities of practice |

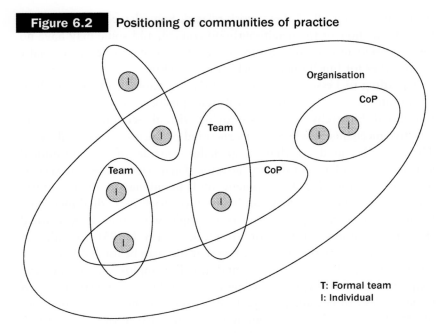

T: Formal team
I: Individual

Communities became the preferred method for groups of people that are distributed across time zones and working remotely – even across country boundaries – to communicate, collaborate and share knowledge. These communities are typically connected through an online facility such as an intranet or extranet. The communities often act as the integration points for all knowledge services provided to members. Typical communities include a leader to facilitate the community and a group of subject matter experts to contribute and evaluate knowledge assets within the community.

The services and functions provided in a typical online community include the following:[3]

- community portals;
- e-mail management;
- focus groups;
- intellectual property, best practices, work examples and template repository; and
- online events and ongoing training.

Members of communities are usually volunteers, and different rewards and other means are utilised to encourage knowledge sharing in the communities. This is a highly effective way to let members move past the old paradigm that knowledge represents power and job security.

Through communities, learners interpret, reflect and form meaning. Communities are the joining of practice with analysis and reflection to share tacit understanding and to create shared knowledge from the experiences among participants in a learning opportunity. Communities provide the opportunity for the interaction; participation provides the learner with the meaning of the experience. In essence, learning becomes a process of reflecting, interpreting and negotiating meaning among the participants of a community.

While these ad-hoc communities are valuable knowledge-sharing mechanisms, they also have real limitations. Knowledge passed in e-mail threads is lost when the thread ends. New staff or staff facing new problems are unaware of the ad-hoc communities and are unable to tap into their expertise. Lessons learned from experience are lost with retirement. Staff turnover and restructuring break down the informal networks to the point where even long-time staff members do not know who to call. Innovative business organisations are therefore formalising these communities to create new mechanisms for creating, capturing and sharing the knowledge that is critical to their success. With these communities of practice in place, this network emerges as the chartered source to build and deliver knowledge. By providing structure, support and tools, leading organisations have enabled communities of practice to function far better than their informal predecessors.

Summary

Knowledge work is becoming the primary work style in enterprises and knowledge workers are the key element in the workforce. The workplace must provide an environment in which knowledge workers can exchange information and knowledge in order to most effectively perform their jobs. In the creation of an environment conducive to learning, working and innovation communities of practice are highly valued in organisations. People are seeing them as ways of cultivating or nurturing new knowledge or sharing existing knowledge in organisations.

In the next chapter we address the issue of knowledge management best practices and other practical issues.

Notes

1. This is also supported by views of industry observers such as the Gartner Group.
2. Interested readers may consult a number of sources on communities of practice and closely related sources, such as Brown and Duguid (1991, 2000), Katzenbach and Smith (1994), Burk (2000), Gongla and Rizzuto (2001), Lesser and Storck (2001), Kimble, Hildreth and Wright (2001), Wenger (2001) and Malhotra (2002).
3. The applicable knowledge management technologies are described in detail in the second part of this book.

7

Knowledge management best practices

> Every day that a better idea goes unused is a lost opportunity. We have to share more, and we have to share faster. I tell employees that sharing and using best practices is the single most important thing they can do. (Ken Derr, Chairman and CEO, Chevron Corporation)

O'Dell, Grayson and Essaides (1998) argue that the actual learning process takes place via two main 'soft' mechanisms: networks or communities of practice (as described in Chapter 6) and best practices. In this section we consider the often quoted concept of 'best practices' that is encountered when operating in the knowledge management field.

Best or worse practices today?

> What is sensible today may be madness tomorrow. (Karl-Erik Sveiby)

In the consulting community, the term 'best practices' is often used (and sometimes misused) to select from a number of alternatives such as approaches, methods, procedures, standards and technologies in cases where the complexity or the constraints of the business challenge or business situation justify a selection based on previous experience or from a related similar situation. This term is used to justify or promote the reason for taking a specific stance or viewpoint about the business challenge. The use of best practices presumes that one can transplant the referred case directly onto this particular case. There exist reasons why this assumption can be proved wrong. First, there are subtle differences between organisations that may invalidate the assumption. Second, we are in a rapidly changing environment. Various authors have debated the applicability of best practices and point out that this tactic is potentially dangerous and should be approached with caution; we are in accordance with this view.

Knowledge management in practice – success or failure

Drawing upon lessons learned from the biggest recent failures of knowledge management and the debacle of the 'new economy' enterprises, Malhotra (2004) explains why knowledge management systems fail and how the risk of such failures may be minimised. His key thesis is that knowledge management systems are designed for the 'knowledge factory' engineering paradigm, and by unravelling, can constrain the development of such systems for business environments characterised by high uncertainty and radical discontinuous change. Design of knowledge management systems should therefore ensure that adaptation and innovation of business performance outcomes occur in alignment with the changing dynamics of the business environment. He states:

> Envisioning business models not only in terms of knowledge harvesting processes for seeking optimization and efficiencies, but in combination with ongoing knowledge creation processes would ensure that organizations not only succeed in doing the thing right in the short term but also in doing the right thing in the long term. (Malhotra, 2004)

Managing knowledge and transferring best practices is conceptually simple, but difficult to execute. The steps in the knowledge transfer process are illustrated in Figure 7.1 and aligned with the activities of our knowledge management process model (see Figure 3.6). According to O'Dell et al. (1998), every knowledge management and transfer initiative should have the design approaches to address all of the steps indicated in the knowledge transfer cycle.

Best practices take information or data and put it in the context of real people and real experiences within the company. We learn by doing and by watching what others do. The transfer of best practices helps others in the firm to learn better, faster and more effectively.

Figure 7.1   Knowledge transfer cycle

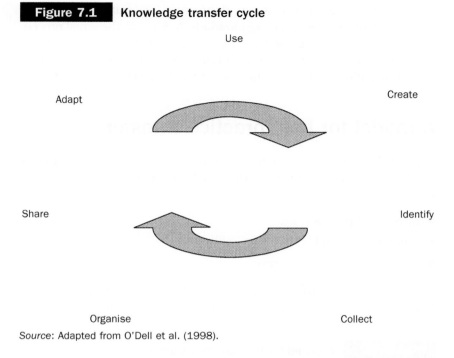

Use

Adapt

Create

Share

Identify

Organise

Collect

Source: Adapted from O'Dell et al. (1998).

We therefore define best practices as those practices that have produced outstanding results in another situation and that could be adapted for our situation.

A term that includes the word 'best' is inevitably the subject of debate, but the term 'best practice' is widely recognised in the business world. O'Dell et al. (1998) observe that Chevron recognises four levels of best practices in its corporate databases and best practice teams, namely:

- good idea;
- good practice;
- local best practice;
- industry best practice.

Contributors to these databases are responsible for deciding whether the practice is worth sharing with others and into which category of 'best' such a practice should fit. O'Dell et al. also consider the barriers to internal transfer of knowledge:

> We believe most people have a natural desire to learn, to share what they know, and to make things better ... This natural desire is

thwarted by a variety of logistical, structural, and cultural hurdles and deterrents present in our organizations. As a result, the actual process of identifying and transferring practices is trickier and more time-consuming than most people imagine. It must involve a conscious dismantling of these organizational barriers. (O'Dell et al., 1998)

A model for best practice transfer

Illustrated in Figure 7.2 is the model for best practice transfer. The model has three major components, which will be briefly discussed below, namely:

- three value propositions;
- four enablers; and
- the four-step change process.

The model is applicable to knowledge and practices about customers, products, processes, failures and successes. It applies to explicit

Figure 7.2 A model for best practice transfer

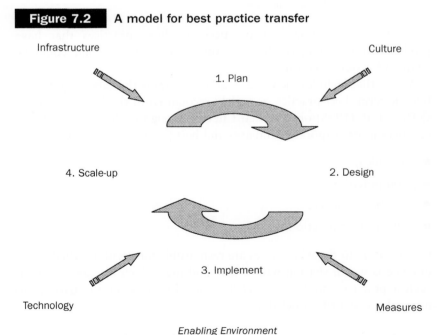

Infrastructure

Culture

1. Plan

4. Scale-up

2. Design

3. Implement

Technology

Measures

Enabling Environment

Source: Adapted from O'Dell et al. (1998).

knowledge as well as tacit knowledge such as intuition, judgment, know-why, know-when and know-how.

O'Dell et al. (1998) find that the reasons to engage in best practice transfer fall into three categories or the three value propositions, namely:[1]

- customer intimacy;
- product-to-market excellence;
- operational excellence.

Below, we now consider the four enablers and the four-step change process.

The four enablers

O'Dell et al. strongly maintain that the key reason why knowledge management efforts fail is because the enablers of the knowledge management process remain poorly understood and managed. These four enablers, as shown in Figure 7.2, are:

- *Culture*: Successful knowledge management starts with a culture supportive of knowledge management or the leadership to create such a culture. This includes skills in teaming that include cross-functional teams, and a common improvement approach such as the Baldrige Quality Award criteria; for example promoting knowledge sharing in a performance appraisal system.
- *Technology*: The huge adoption of the internet and intranet technologies turned out to be an enormous catalyst for knowledge sharing and distance learning. The key point here is that the advantages as well as the limitations of the technology should be recognised and should be appropriately employed.
- *Infrastructure*: Leadership, a healthy culture and basic IT are prerequisites but not sufficient. Successful knowledge management must be embedded into the organisation by creating new support systems, new teams and collaboration.
- *Measures*: This is the aspect of knowledge management that is least understood and developed. However, it is important to measure projects and business processes that are being improved by using knowledge management tools. The measures include having champions and facilitators, and a process for designing and managing change.

The four-phase change process

In general, the change process as shown in Figure 7.2 should follow the following four phases:

- *Plan*: This involves a self-assessment and a clear definition of the organisation's value propositions.
- *Design*: In the design phase, the roles and functions of people and technologies and their relationships to organisational structure and performance measures are designed.
- *Implement*: The implementation phase usually is done via a proof-of-concept, which tests new ideas and teaches what is feasible and what is not. During this phase 'success stories' should be gathered to widely promote enthusiasm for knowledge management.
- *Scale-up*: After a successful pilot, the project is scaled up to an enterprise-wide process to capture the full benefits of effective transfer.

Summary

The reasons for employing a knowledge management strategy relate to the current rapidly changing business environment. When appropriate, best practices still play a role in the response required to the change challenge. We pointed out, however, that best practices should be employed with caution because of the rapidly changing business environment.

This concludes the chapters that describe the 'what' and 'why' characteristics of knowledge management. These provide the foundation for describing the 'how' and 'with what' of knowledge management, to be explored in the second part of this book.

In the last chapter of the first part of the book we draw together a number of conclusions regarding the 'what' and 'why' of knowledge management.

Note

1. These are described in detail in their book (*If only We Knew What We Know: The Transfer of Internal Knowledge and Best Practice*, 1998), but we consider them to be beyond the context of this book.

8

Part 1: summary and conclusions

After all is said and done, much more will be said than done. (Anonymous)

In the emerging economy a firm's only advantage is its ability to leverage and utilize its knowledge. (Larry Prusak)

Knowledge Management is more of a strategy supported by technology that can show a quantifiable and sometimes substantial return on investment. (Greg MacSweeney)

Introduction

We conclude the first part of the book by summarising the main points of the 'what' and 'why' characteristics of the notions of knowledge and knowledge management, followed by our main conclusions about these characteristics. This serves as a foundation for the second part of the book which describes the 'how' and 'with-what' of knowledge management.

Part 1: a summary

Part 1 of this book was concerned with the 'what' and 'why' characteristics of the terms 'knowledge' and 'knowledge management'. We focused specifically on modern organisations that do business in the challenging business environment of the twenty-first century.

We argued that the current business environment has the characteristic of radical discontinuous change. This results in a highly competitive climate. The major competitive advantage an organisation has is its knowledge expertise – it is the primary differentiator in this competitive business environment.

The idea of 'knowledge management' is a contemporary response to the challenges of the economy in the new millennium. Even though humankind has perennially relied on knowledge for solutions, the recent emergence of, and emphasis on knowledge management as a critical topic, is rooted in technological developments. More specifically, it is related to the ease of access and affordability created by new technologies, primarily the set of internet-based technologies. Knowledge management is one of the key factors driving demand for IT in the new millennium.

From a business strategy perspective, knowledge management is about obsolescing what you know before others do, and profiting by creating the challenges and opportunities others have not yet considered.

Various academic and practitioner approaches are still to emerge to clarify definitions and taxonomies for positioning knowledge management. At present there is some confusion among outsiders to the field as to what this knowledge management phenomenon entails and how to comprehend various claims and issues related to it. We have proposed a set of models that jointly form a knowledge management framework for more clearly comprehending the many interrelated notions of this field of study.

We argued that the list of models we have discussed forms a framework against which we can more readily comprehend the notions and issues surrounding both knowledge and knowledge management. These models introduce much clarity and insight into the 'what' and 'why' characteristics of knowledge and knowledge management and their related issues and aspects.

We have also argued for the need and appropriateness of knowledge management technologies. We realise that these technologies are necessary but insufficient for knowledge management. We will expand on this in the second part of this book.

We also emphasised:

- the important role of learning by individuals (in their work context) as well as the importance of organisational learning;
- the close linking of knowledge, learning, working and innovation, and how those concepts relate to organisational communities of practice;
- the importance of collaboration among knowledge workers, which should employ best practices cautiously where applicable.

In the following subsections we address the phenomenon of many viewpoints of knowledge and knowledge management as well as the prediction we can make about the future of knowledge management.

Knowledge and knowledge management viewpoints

There exist many viewpoints and perspectives on the notion of knowledge. This in itself is a major contributor to the confusion about the term 'knowledge management'. Authors are often exposed to the many viewpoints of different people who have vested interests in viewing the concept of knowledge from their respective expertise domains. These viewpoints can be summarised as follows:

- *for human resource management*: 'knowledge can only be in the minds of people';
- *for document management and librarians*: 'knowledge is in documents';
- *for information system management*: 'knowledge management is information management with the word *information* changed to *knowledge*';
- *for knowledge engineering*: 'knowledge is something which can be captured in computer applications'.

Confusion is also fuelled by the many perspectives about the fundamental notions of knowledge and of knowledge management itself. These perspectives include the following:

- *Philosophical*: ideas of philosophers such as Polanyi; in contrast with
- *Pragmatists*: authors who view knowledge and knowledge management from their practical aspects and who are promoting the application of knowledge management as a response to the challenges of modern business. These authors include Nonaka and Takeuchi, Stewart, Prusak and Davenport, Sveiby, and Malhotra – to name but a few of the authors we have referred to in this book.
- *Managerial*: The vast majority of perspectives emphasise that the main focus should be about the people and managerial aspects of knowledge and knowledge management. We regarded the purely managerial aspects of knowledge management as beyond the scope of this book (although we were obliged to hint at these aspects where applicable).

- The different perspectives that we selected to describe in order to reduce the confusion were:
  - the conceptual perspective;
  - the process perspective;
  - the technology perspective (this will be covered in further depth in the second part of this book);
  - the implementation perspective.

In the first part of the book we attempted to confine these viewpoints to the more realistic and pragmatic views that are applicable in responding to the many challenges that face the modern organisation. One such view is our main premise that knowledge management technology is a prerequisite for successful knowledge management, although this in itself is insufficient.

Our study of knowledge management has initially led us to a bewildering number of viewpoints, perspectives, approaches, practices and some theories. Academics and practitioners are aiming to reconcile and comprehend this new extension to some old ideas mixed with the reality of the new millennium and its rapid change characteristic. We argue that our 'framework of models' clarifies many of the issues that present themselves in cases where such a framework is absent.

The funnel effect: knowledge management is 'just business'

Judging from similar trends in the last few decades of various business approaches and strategies, it seems that knowledge management will eventually follow a similar route to a number of these approaches. In observing these trends we noticed that a number of business approaches are not being directly applied but indirectly considered to be 'just the way business should be done'. These techniques, approaches and strategies have come to be regarded as 'normal practice' and have been embedded into the way business is perceived to be conducted.

We refer to this phenomenon as the 'funnel effect'. The funnel effect describes the convergence of different phenomena that become normal practice after other phenomena that are not robust enough to stand the test of time have been filtered out. We illustrate in Figure 8.1 the expected case where knowledge management too will become

Figure 8.1 Knowledge management becomes 'just business'

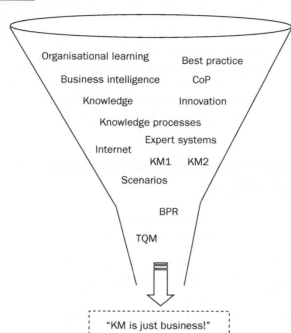

commonplace in the management of businesses, and the view will emerge that 'knowledge management is just business'.

The future of knowledge management

Knowledge management seems likely to follow one of two paths. The better one is the direction taken by the quality movement and expert system technologies. Quality management has become embedded in organisations, an integral element of organisational effectiveness. Expert systems nowadays are also very much embedded in a variety of technological solutions. As Prusak (2001) states, 'KM may similarly be so thoroughly adopted – so much a natural part of how people organize work – that it eventually becomes invisible'.

The less appealing path would be to follow the business process reengineering route; 'becoming a byword for a crude, downsizing effort that rather does harm than improve the business' (Prusak, 2001). Knowledge management could follow the same path.

Will knowledge management endure?

We may rightly ask whether knowledge management will endure. In this regard there are prominent authors who support our view that knowledge management is here to stay. For example, Ponzi and Koenig (2002) use an analytical framework for examining management fads, and conclude that, at the very least, knowledge management is more than just a trend in management practice. Koenig (2005) re-examines and reconfirms this work, stating: 'KM is simply not a fad'.

Knowledge management-related trends and implications

Our prime thesis is summarised in the following list of key knowledge management related trends and implications:

- The post-2000 era is characterised by rapid and discontinuous change in many aspects of the modern business environment – internal and external to the organisation.
- Modern business is forced to think beyond benchmarking and best practices to survive.
- Promoting knowledge sharing – unlike typical information power bases – will spawn innovation within the organisation.
- The pressure is constantly mounting on the organisation, urging it to discontinue marginal products and services before the competition does.
- Knowledge and its 'management' result in business innovation; this is the prime differentiator for competitive advantage in our fiercely competitive and challenging new economy.
- Stakeholder-focused rather than shareholder-focused strategies and execution will benefit the modern organisation in its quest for survival – a challenging task in itself.
- Collaboration forms a key ingredient in managing knowledge processes. Transforming a business will require collaboration.
- It has become of key importance to recognise the value of and to manage communities of practice – turning organisations into communities of communities to foster organisational knowledge, learning, working and innovation.

- Learning, working and innovation are closely linked; indeed, as Tapscott (1996) says, 'Increasingly, work and learning are becoming the same thing'. By implication it becomes obvious that the individual needs to adapt to the notion of lifelong learning.

- Taking individual responsibility for the learning focus will spiral into the organisation, which will in turn evolve into a learning organisation – a key prerequisite for knowledge management and survival of the organisation. Tapscott says:

> Because the new economy is a knowledge economy and learning is part of day-to-day activity and life, both companies and individuals have found they need to take responsibility for learning simply to be effective.
>
> And as you enter the digital economy, you become not only a knowledge worker but also a knowledge consumer. This places a considerable responsibility on each of us to invent our curriculum. We need to plan our lifelong learning and how, through self-paced learning, on-the-job learning, and formal education and training, we can stay robust in a changing economy. (Tapscott, 1996)

- There are at least two generations of knowledge management. The first focused more on the technical aspects and on knowledge integration. The second is focusing on knowledge production and integration but is more about human social behaviour, driven by individual and shared processes (Firestone and McElroy, 2003).

- Innovation is becoming an imperative for enterprise agility and adaptability.

- Awareness of the importance of intellectual capital is increasing.

- Knowledge management will be required by most e-business initiatives.

- Knowledge management requires a host of technologies that depend on the characteristics of the enterprise's knowledge management programmes. Debra Logan (2001) says: 'KM-in-a-box is unlikely in the near term'.

- Finally, the knowledge workplace will affect every business – its personnel policies, management approaches and style, and workplace technologies.

Main conclusions

We researched, explained, and motivated in this book why the subject of knowledge management is of such high importance for the organisation in the new millennium and ultimately for its survival. The complexity of society and business, along with its acceleration in change, and the continuing redefinition of basic principles such as the nature of work, the modernisation of the economy and its globalisation, the ever-changing demographics and related challenges in supply and demand, the onslaught of new entrants into established markets, and the leveraging effect in the explosion of new technology, information and knowledge assets, leads us to conclude that knowledge management is essential for the modern era in which we live and work.

We conclude with the following statements:

- Knowledge management is highly important for the survival of modern knowledge-oriented organisations of the twenty-first century.

- Knowledge management can only be exercised, implemented or successful if a symbiosis/balance is assured between the social, economic and technical aspects of knowledge management.

- Knowledge management technology is evolving at a great pace and there is no indication that this will diminish in the short to medium term (Koenig, 2004, 2005).

- Developing and enhancing knowledge management technologies is the only way to keep pace with the huge growth and change in knowledge assets that is most likely bound to accelerate its evolution during the twenty-first century.

Thus, responsibility for 'management' of knowledge and knowledge assets in the enterprise ultimately lies with every individual in the new knowledge-based economy. Knowledge management technologies that enable and support these roles play a key role in a holistic view of the 'management' of knowledge and of the knowledge assets of the enterprise.

Part 2
The technical perspective of knowledge management

As we grow more familiar with the intelligent environment and learn to converse with it from the time we leave the cradle, we will begin to use computers with a grace and naturalness that is hard for us to imagine today.

And they will help all of us – not just a few 'super-technocrats' – to think more deeply about ourselves and the world. (Alvin Toffler)

... people are ... shocked today by the suggestion that machines can think, but their dislike of the situation will not alter it in the least. (Arthur C. Clarke)

The real danger is not that computers will begin to think like men, but that men, will begin to think like computers. (S. J. Harris)

In the second part of this book, the 'how' and 'with-what' characteristics of knowledge management are covered. Although knowledge management is primarily concerned with non-technical issues, this part concentrates on the technical aspects of knowledge management. A new technology framework for knowledge management is proposed to position and relate the different knowledge management technologies, enablers and applications. In closure, we position the two key applications of knowledge management, namely knowledge portals and knowledge discovery (including text mining).

9

Introduction

Where is the life we have lost in living?
Where is the wisdom we have lost in knowledge?
Where is the knowledge we have lost in information? (T. S. Eliot)

Nothing is more rewarding than to watch someone who says it can't be done get interrupted by someone actually doing it. (Anonymous)

The first section of this chapter introduces our main premise: technology plays a key role in knowledge management, acting as an enabler of knowledge management. We then consider briefly what knowledge management technology should and cannot do. In closure, we position e-business relative to knowledge management because of the tight link between these two concepts.

Knowledge management technology as enabler of knowledge management

Technology has given us new ways to keep in touch with each other and share information. We have to take advantage of that technology to get better, faster. (Bill Baker, Texas Instruments)

Dutta and De Meyer report an interview with J. Jarlbaek, the Managing Partner of the Business Consulting Practice at Arthur Andersen Denmark. According to Jarlbaek, the company uses a knowledge equation:

$K = (P + I)^S$. This simple equation is the basis of our efforts to manage knowledge effectively and be competitive in the information age.

> We see knowledge (K) as being captured by people's (P) ability to exchange information (I) by utilizing technology (+), exponentially enhanced by the power of sharing (S). The power of this simple equation is tremendous. It is clear and it has universal appeal. When you explain it to someone, everything makes sense, everything falls in place! (Dutta and De Meyer, 2001).

We have attempted in this book to restrict the many viewpoints about the notions of knowledge and knowledge management to the more realistic and pragmatic views that may be of use in responding to the many challenges that modern organisations face. One such view is our main premise that knowledge management technology is an enabler of knowledge management, although by itself, this is insufficient. We take notice of a number of authors who maintain that knowledge management is not 'a technology thing' or 'a computer thing'. For example, Brian Newman has stated:

> Knowledge management is the collection of processes that govern the creation, dissemination, and utilization of knowledge. In one form or another, knowledge management has been around for a very long time. Practitioners have included philosophers, priests, teachers, politicians, scribes, librarians, etc.
>
> So if knowledge management is such an ageless and broad topic what role does it serve in today's Information Age? These processes exist whether we acknowledge them or not and they have a profound effect on the decisions we make and the actions we take, both of which are enabled by knowledge of some type. If this is the case, and we agree that many of our decisions and actions have profound and long lasting effects, it makes sense to recognize and understand the processes that affect our actions and decisions and, where possible, take steps to improve the quality of these processes and in turn improve the quality of those actions and decisions for which we are responsible?
>
> Knowledge management is not a 'technology thing' or a 'computer thing'. If we accept the premise that knowledge management is concerned with the entire process of discovery and creation of knowledge, dissemination of knowledge, and the utilization of knowledge then we are strongly driven to accept that knowledge management is much more than a 'technology thing' and that elements of it exist in each of our jobs. (Newman, 1991)

Today, in the beginning of the new millennium, we realise that modern business has in its possession far too much technology for business support to choose from. Usually business is not lacking the desire or need to exploit these technologies; neither does it lack the financial capability to acquire these technologies. What is frequently lacking, however, is access to enough skills to exploit the capabilities of this vast variety of available technology. Already there are a variety of technologies for support in the field of knowledge management. Exploiting these technologies is, however, a complex mixture of proper management of tacit/human knowledge; of differentiating the management of explicit information versus knowledge artefacts and sources; and of having to manage the knowledge management support technologies.

The value of information technology (IT) is being seriously debated – specifically its contribution to the 'productivity' of the organisation. Obviously, the application of IT has to be considered and varies widely within an organisation and between organisations. However, we argue that the organisation becomes a knowledge company when it employs IT beyond its mere number-crunching and word-processing capabilities – but rather at a 'deeper level' where information is employed and exploited for its intrinsic value and semantics as well as for its usability for reaching conclusions and taking actions. As Stewart (1997, 2001) notes, this can be achieved in different ways, namely:

- 'mining valuable detail';
- 'running simulations';
- 'making a business out of knowledge itself'.

In 1993, two MIT economists, Erik Brynjolfsson and Lorin Hitt, investigated the return on investment in 'computer capital' versus other capital equipment. They found an eight-to-one difference in favour of the former. Professor Frank Lichtenberg of Columbia University found that spending on research and development (R&D) versus spending on new plant and equipment – or physical capital – returned eight times more. For example, a new machine that assists in improving old work delivers incremental improvement. In contrast, R&D leads the organisation to innovation, which introduces new products and services that are usually more valuable than the replaced products and services (Stewart, 1997, 2001).

It is therefore important to note that knowledge management problems cannot typically be solved by the deployment of a technology solution alone. As we pointed out in the introductory part of this book, the greatest difficulty in managing knowledge is 'changing people's behaviour', and the biggest impediment to knowledge transfer is the 'culture' within the organisation.[1] As Logan explains:

> ... the state of the art is such that many of the social aspects of work important in knowledge management cannot currently be addressed by technology ... Second, the coupling between behaviour and technology is two-way: the introduction of technology may influence the way individuals work. (Logan, 2001)

In the second part of this book we argue that compelling technology is and will remain a critical success factor for knowledge management. Keeping in mind what was introduced previously, we can state that knowledge management technology:

- stimulates and supports sharing, collaboration and innovation;
- nurtures collaboration and cultural change;
- can be effectively employed to assist in the learning process, which is so critical for knowledge management;
- augments the knowledge of individual knowledge workers by providing access to the experiences, insights and ideas of other knowledge workers.

Many products and technologies with varying capabilities can be used to support knowledge management. Knowledge management programmes are likely to use a combination of products and probably do not rely on all the capabilities of each product.

Technology's most valuable role in knowledge management lies in extending the reach and enhancing the speed of knowledge transfer. Knowledge management technologies enable the extraction of individual workers' knowledge and structure it for use by other members of the whole organisation. Knowledge management technologies serve as a major enabler of knowledge management throughout the lifecycle of the knowledge management process described in the first part of this book.

In the next two sections we make brief remarks about the potentialities of technology for supporting knowledge management as well as about what knowledge management technologies cannot do.

What knowledge management technologies should do

The knowledge content required for business decisions extends beyond enterprise organisational boundaries to the network of customers, supply chain partners, and also to the internet with its virtual/ad-hoc business relationships and communities of practice. In an extended enterprise, knowledge sharing, creation and application include the people, communities, intellectual capital and processes of this business network. As enterprises begin to operate in this extended environment, the overload of information and urgency will drive the need for a knowledge management discipline and for a technical environment that assists the knowledge user in segregating relevant, applicable knowledge from the information overload. Knowledge management tools should evolve to increasingly recognise user behaviours and act on their behalf as intelligent agents to distinguish relevant, valuable knowledge and deliver it automatically or on request. 'Technology will play an increasing role as cultural barriers fall; knowledge mapping, user profiling, business rules and so on become the prominent critical success factors.'[2]

In those cases where the organisation already focuses on knowledge, technology can expand the capabilities of the access to knowledge and ease the problem of getting the right knowledge to the right person at the right time. The mere presence of knowledge management technologies may even have a positive effect on the knowledge culture of the organisation (Davenport and Prusak, 1998).

What knowledge management technologies cannot do

The ability to learn new things – or learn to learn – is paramount today. Rather, the ability to unlearn what was learnt is necessary most of the time, which is not a very smooth process unless well led. (Luiz Antonio Joia)

We thought we understood the equation, $K = (P + I)^S$, but as we go forward we continually discover new issues, interpretations and problems inside the equation. We are finding that knowledge management is not simply a task of building technological systems

> or collecting information. Questions are raised about our entire organization and about how people relate to each other. Our journey has only begun! (S. Dutta and A. De Meyer)

There exist limitations in any knowledge management programme. As noted previously, effective knowledge management only results after extensive behavioural, cultural and organisational change. Technology on its own is not enough to bring about these changes. Technology alone will not make an expert share his/her knowledge with others or create a learning organisation. Technology is common in the domain of knowledge distribution, but 'rarely enhances the process of knowledge use' (Davenport and Prusak, 1998). Technology can distribute knowledge content to the user, but cannot ensure what he or she will do with it.

One area where knowledge management technologies are still weak is the support for the process of knowledge creation. Knowledge creation remains largely an act of individuals or groups, with technology still playing a minor role. Certain technologies do support group knowledge creation, such as a group decision support system (GDSS), which supports a small group of people usually residing in the same location. A GDSS aims to create some form of group knowledge out of the group's expertise, employing techniques such as technology-assisted group brainstorming. Future development most probably may improve the knowledge creation abilities of knowledge management technologies.

Artificial intelligence and expert systems-based knowledge management technologies are often said to deliver 'the right information to the right person at the right time'. However, as we have argued in the first part of the book, new business models marked by radical and discontinuous change make the task of predicting the right information, the right person, or the right time challenging. This is because the notion of 'right' keeps shifting.[3] Artificial intelligence and expert systems are often based upon the assumption that these systems store human intelligence and experience. Technologies such as databases and groupware applications store static data and information, but cannot store the rich schemas that people possess for making dynamic sense of data and information (Malhotra, 2001b).

Malhotra (2001b) notes that the static representation of data in databases, inferential logic of computer programs, and computer memories lack inherent dynamic sense-making capabilities that are increasingly relevant for emerging business environments. In contrast, given the dynamic subjective nature of human construction of meaning and the diversity of personal constructions, different meanings could be constructed from the same assemblage of data at the same time by different individuals.

> Likewise, different meanings could be construed at different times or by consideration of different contexts by the same person … Moreover, the data archived in technological 'knowledge repositories' is rational, static and without context, and such systems cannot account for renewal of existing knowledge and creation of new knowledge. (Malhotra, 2001b)

We are in accordance with Marwick, who states:

> Sometimes in computer science 'knowledge management' is interpreted to mean the acquisition and use of knowledge by computers, but that is not the meaning used here. In any case, automatic extraction of deep knowledge (i.e. in a form that captures the majority of the meaning) from documents is an elusive goal. (Marwick, 2001)

Positioning knowledge management and e-business

Major drivers of modern business include the realisation that business can be conducted on a global scale (so-called globalisation), that the organisation can only survive if it adds value to its stakeholders, that there should be a low barrier to access its products and services, and that the customer is most important for its survival. In today's challenging environment it has become obvious that the modern solution involves a two-fold imperative: firstly, organisations should offer enhanced and low-cost electronic access to the conduct of business activities; and secondly, organisations should evolve superior management of knowledge assets. This leads to development of new knowledge-focused business models supported by a network computing-based strategy and infrastructure. Various trends support this solution, such as:

- the worldwide deregulation of telecommunications;
- the rise of consumer power;

- new enterprise business models;
- fast-changing technology innovation;
- evolving technology standards;
- the digitisation of 'everything'.

The term 'e-business' was first used and promoted by IBM in the middle to late 1990s to describe the concept of conducting business using new electronic network-based business models for electronic commerce (e-commerce), managing corporate content, and performing enhanced collaborative computing. (Thus, e-business = e-commerce + content management + collaborative computing.) IBM defined e-business as 'any activity that connects critical business systems directly to their critical constituencies (customers, employees, vendors and suppliers) via intranets, extranets and over the world-wide web'.[4]

The concept of e-business suggests that organisations should transform themselves into electronic businesses (e-businesses) by establishing new cross-organisational network-based strategies, processes, business and IT architectures, and infrastructures. New systems should be built and executed accordingly. They should integrate with and enhance the existing environment. The result should be a focus on leveraging the new business models in terms of enhanced services and products available to these 'critical constituencies'. The core of this ability to leverage the new way of operation and doing business resides in the value of the organisation's knowledge assets. The new business model depends heavily on reliable, consistent, correct and complete information and knowledge in the organisation as well as a secure infrastructure to protect these valuable assets.

However, to become an e-business is not an easy task and may take a long time to achieve – especially for large organisations with well-established old economy culture, processes and strategies. This strategy should be pursued with caution by employing a practical approach of starting small and growing quickly. This can be illustrated by an expanding implementation spiral as shown in Figure 9.1.

The positioning of knowledge management within this e-business implementation spiral is largely in the upper left quadrant. Knowledge management from this perspective is thus a continuously revisited focus area with high emphasis on the leveraging of knowledge.

The knowledge workers are the key players in leveraging the knowledge assets. Managing the knowledge workers and the knowledge

Figure 9.1 The e-business implementation spiral

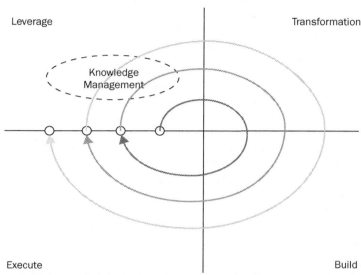

Source: Adapted from various IBM documentation on e-business.

they access becomes vital for organisations in the e-business economy. As articulated by Tapscott:

> The new economy demands that companies change their business model, and the new technology enables it … However, in the new economy much of the effort of the new enterprise is knowledge work based on teams, changing human networks, new types of jobs, serendipitous communications, ad hoc collaboration, and brainstorming for innovation. (Tapscott, 1996)

Therefore, in order to be successful with e-business, organisations are forced to regard knowledge management as a key strategy. This also implies that e-business mandates organisations to effectively employ knowledge management technologies.

In Table 9.1 we relate a list of the demands that result from an e-business initiative to the responses possible with knowledge management.

E-business has strong implications for the interaction between different processes and the integration of these processes. This interaction relies on

Table 9.1   Knowledge management responses to e-business demands

E-business	Knowledge management
Extends the enterprise and leverages its intellectual capital to customers and business partners, allowing these external parties to interact more directly with internal enterprise systems.	Supports making tacit knowledge explicit and IT systems more responsible for interactions. The result is less dependence on intermediaries that compensate for inadequacies in formal procedures and systems.
Demands increased customer and partner intimacy over new channels.	Sharing knowledge is possibly poorly developed in most enterprises.
Expands the competitive arena and also requires greater inventiveness and improved competitive intelligence.	Greater inventiveness and improved competitive intelligence are both KM focus areas.
Demands that knowledge be consolidated faster.	Drives organisational learning, innovation and responsiveness.
Requires agility and adaptation to the changing environment.	KM and collaboration act as a platform for ongoing innovation.

Source: Adapted from Logan (2001).

the electronic means to enable connections between processes to take place in fundamentally new ways. This happens at such speeds that it opens up the possibility to reconfigure each core operating process radically in order to create new sub-processes to enable new modes of integration across the operating processes. The importance of e-business for processes is described by Fahey, Srivastava, Sharon and Smith (2001). They illustrate these implications with interesting case studies such as that of Dell Computer Corporation's unique e-business model.

Figure 9.2 highlights the positioning of knowledge management relative to e-business in the e-business model. The figure includes a number of elements of importance for knowledge management (Adams et al., 2003), which we describe briefly below:

- *Customer relationship management (CRM)*: Customer relationship management is the essential business process that encompasses an organisation's end-to-end engagement with its customers over the lifetime of its relationship with them. CRM sub-processes include prospecting, marketing, sales, customer service and support. These sub-processes cover all the ways in which customers and the business

Figure 9.2 E-business model

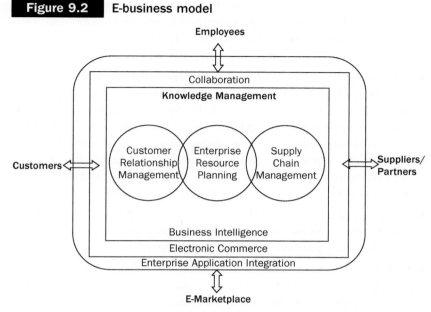

Source: Model adapted from various sources in IBM; see also Adams et al. (2003).

can interact (person to person, branch, call centre, kiosk, voice-response unit, ATM and the internet).

- *Enterprise resource planning (ERP)*: Enterprise resource planning provides the major back-office applications for many enterprises. Benefits of ERP include process automation and integration, and the availability of data to support business analysis.

- *Supply-chain management*: Supply-chain management refers to a set of solutions that allows an enterprise to tie together the internal and external people and processes associated with its flow of goods.

- *Electronic commerce*: Electronic commerce solutions allow enterprises to offer products and services to existing and new customers across new channels based on internet technologies. They also provide the foundation for managing electronic transactions and allow customers to browse for and purchase goods and services with convenience and confidence, knowing that their transactions are secure and their privacy is protected.

- *Business intelligence*: Business intelligence is the discipline of developing solutions that are conclusive, fact-based and actionable. These solutions help enterprises combine and analyse disparate data sources and derive valuable information from this data, providing key insights and data points that can be used to inform business decisions. These solutions typically include techniques such as data warehousing, data mining and trend analysis.

- *Knowledge management*: Knowledge management is the identification and analysis of available and required knowledge assets and related processes. It also includes the subsequent planning and control of actions to develop both the assets and the processes to fulfil organisational objectives. Knowledge assets are comprised of the knowledge regarding markets, products, technologies and organisations that a business owns or needs to own, and that enable its business processes to generate profits and provide value.

- *E-marketplaces*: E-marketplaces are trading exchanges that facilitate and promote buying and selling, and enable business communities among trading partners within certain industries.

- *Collaboration*: Conducting business requires collaborative interaction among employees, vendors, suppliers and business partners. A number of collaborative applications and solutions enable local work groups, or even geographically dispersed teams, to work together using real-time information sharing and distribution across the internet. In addition to e-mail, these solutions include instant messaging, group calendaring and scheduling, shared document libraries, and discussion databases.[5]

- *Enterprise application integration*: 'Integration and interoperability are critical for realizing the true potential of e-business solutions. Most "brick-and-mortar" enterprises have significant investments in legacy systems and ERP solutions. Thus, to be effective, it is important to integrate these e-business solutions with the ERP systems, legacy applications, and databases that might exist within the organization' (Adams, Koushik, Vasudeva and Galambos, 2003).

- *Implementing e-business solutions*: E-business applications are different from the traditional client/server applications developed in the 1990s. Table 9.2 illustrates the differences between these two types of applications.

The structure and nature of e-business solutions pose certain challenges to organisations that implement these solutions, including the following:[6]

- *A higher degree of integration*: E-business solutions typically implement radically new business processes and solutions that need to integrate and work with other systems in the enterprise, including legacy systems and databases, or even with external systems.

Table 9.2	Differences between client/server and e-business applications

	Traditional client/server applications	E-business applications
Reach	Within a department or enterprise	Across departments, enterprises, and geographic and national boundaries
Architectures	Deployed using a two or three-tier architecture	Deployed using a thin client architecture with one to N back-end tiers
Programming model	Event-driven, with the application state managed at each client desktop	Thin browser-based clients, with the application state managed in the server layer
Network	LAN or WAN-based	Based on LANs, WANs, private virtual networks, and internet connections
Standards	Typical proprietary technologies	Open technologies
Number of users	Predictable user loads, from tens to hundreds	Unpredictable user loads, with massive deviations in the number of users

Source: Adams et al. (2003).

- *The need for speed*: These solutions typically have a very short window for implementation.
- *Quality*: These solutions are designed to reach users beyond the enterprise, so it is extremely important to ensure the overall quality of the solution.
- *The shortage of skills*: These complex solutions require considerable skills to develop and implement.
- *Changing technology*: The internet and its technologies are evolving rapidly, causing many interesting problems for enterprises trying to implement e-business solutions.

Adams et al. maintain that:

> Many hardware and software vendors in today's marketplace claim to have strategies and approaches that will help guide companies in their transition from an industrial economy to the digital economy. However, a closer look at many of these

approaches shows that they are no more than a narrowly focused set of products thrown together to form a roadmap leading to the implementation of certain technologies. A truly powerful and viable strategy should be comprehensive and driven by all the facets of the business, supported effectively by technology. (Adams et al., 2003)

Summary

In essence then, knowledge management technologies fulfil a supportive but highly important role in augmenting human capabilities in some important aspects of knowledge management. It is important to remember that the true value of a knowledge management system comes from ensuring that knowledge activities are supported and key business needs are met and that technology enables these endeavours. However, technology alone is not the answer. The sophisticated functionality offered by technologies today is only part of the promise of knowledge management. Knowledge management remains a combination of business processes, organisational culture and technology – with technology having a major impact on the practice of knowledge management.

From the many sources and arguments stated so far (e.g. see O'Dell, Grayson and Essaides, 1998), we can derive three rules of thumb regarding knowledge and knowledge management technologies, namely:

- The more 'valuable' the knowledge, the less sophisticated the technology that supports it.
- Tacit knowledge is best shared through people; explicit knowledge can be shared by knowledge management technologies.
- The more tacit the knowledge, the less high-tech the required solution.[7]

In the next chapter we develop and propose our knowledge management technology framework.

Notes

1. Various sources support our view in this regard, for example Davenport and Prusak (1998), Logan (2001) and Malhotra (2001a).
2. Comment made by a presenter in a Gartner Group presentation on knowledge management in 2003 (at a South African IT symposium).

3. This argument is further complicated as various views of this 'definition' maintain that it is overly simplistic as we have pointed out previously. See also Thomas, Kellogg and Erickson (2001).
4. Published widely by IBM in various brochures and internal as well as external documentation.
5. See the description of collaboration in Chapter 13.
6. Covered in detail in Adams et al. (2003).
7. For example, consider discussion groups and help desks; the human knowledge in the help desk predominantly determines its success.

The knowledge management technology framework

I don't fear computers. I fear the absence of computers. (Isaac Asimov)

Introduction

In this chapter we propose a knowledge management technology framework (KMTF). We argue that this framework aids comprehension of the notion of knowledge management. The KMTF consolidates and expands many of the ideas and descriptions presented in the first part of this book. It also includes a number of categories of knowledge management enablers consisting of knowledge management technologies, infrastructure and applications.

In the rest of this book we rely on this particular set of KMTF categories for guiding and structuring the chapters, thus describing the various knowledge management enablers, as well as their relevant and mutual positioning to each other and to the overall notion of knowledge management.

Developing the knowledge management technology framework

As described in the first part of this book, knowledge management, by definition, is the management of the three different knowledge processes that we have identified, namely:

- knowledge creation and sensing;
- knowledge organising and capturing;
- knowledge sharing and dissemination.

We have previously proposed a conceptual process model for knowledge management (Figure 3.5). The model is repeated as Figure 10.1. In this part of the book we utilise the knowledge management process model as a component of our proposed knowledge management technology framework. The framework will be the general model we use to describe the position and value of the different relevant knowledge management enablers, technologies and applications.

Because knowledge management technologies and products handle (explicit) knowledge instead of data they mostly either work with existing collections of text or promote collaborative work between knowledge workers. The latter enables the sharing of the unwritten knowledge in the minds of knowledge workers. We start the framework development by considering the kind of information that knowledge workers handle and whether they know what to look for when additional knowledge is required. This approach leads us to initially categorise different

Figure 10.1   **Knowledge management process model**

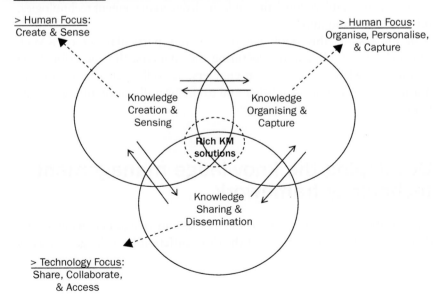

knowledge management technologies into three main categories, which will be defined in due course. This initial schema is depicted in Figure 10.2.

- Knowledge storage technologies (e.g. repositories) are used to make knowledge that one has available to others. One might say that these technologies are used in cases where 'you know what knowledge you have'.

- Knowledge sharing and transfer technologies are used to acquire knowledge that others already possess. One might cryptically say that these technologies are used in cases where 'you know what knowledge you do not have'.

- Knowledge discovery technologies are deployed to ratchet up, so to speak, knowledge storage technologies; to explore knowledge repositories and knowledge bases in such a way that new knowledge, implicit in the stored information, becomes known. One might express the matter by saying that these technologies are deployed when 'you do not know what knowledge you have'.

- The fourth category, knowledge generation, refers to the case where the knowledge worker does not know what knowledge he/she has. It implies that effort is directed at exploring, researching, and/or creating new knowledge.

Figure 10.2 **Knowledge management broad categories**

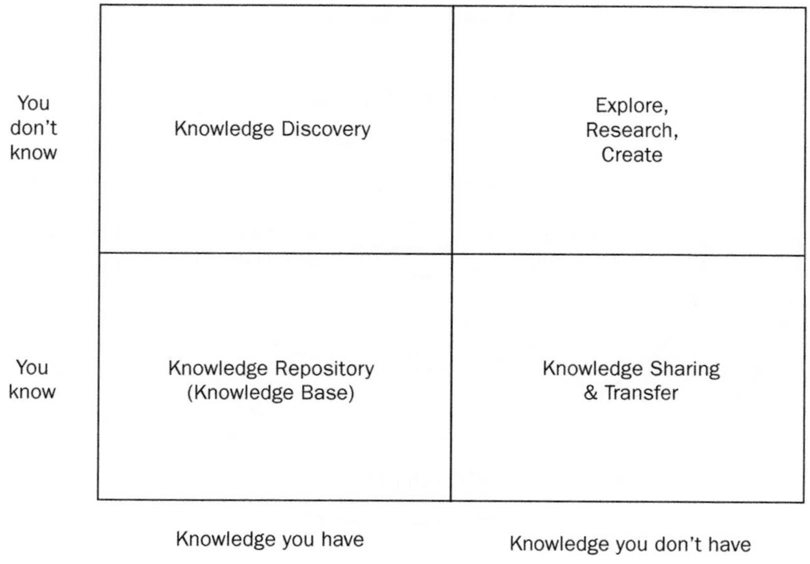

You don't know	Knowledge Discovery	Explore, Research, Create
You know	Knowledge Repository (Knowledge Base)	Knowledge Sharing & Transfer
	Knowledge you have	Knowledge you don't have

As we argued in the first part of this book, we can state that knowledge forms the core of the modern business. Therefore, our next step to develop the knowledge management technology framework is to position the knowledge processes as a layer around the knowledge core. This layer includes the organisation's leadership, strategy, culture, practices and communities of practice, as each of these has a bearing on the way in which the organisation's knowledge processes are realised. Enclosing these, we propose, are two further layers: the third layer contains the different knowledge activities, and the fourth, the knowledge management enablers, applications and technologies. These layers collectively form the conceptual model of the knowledge management technology framework and are illustrated in Figure 10.3.

We next combine the knowledge management process model and its related knowledge activities in Figure 10.1 with the knowledge management technology conceptual framework in Figure 10.3 to obtain Figure 10.4, which displays the eight different knowledge activities.

In Figure 10.5 we list the most prominent knowledge management enablers, applications and technologies[1] in order to be able to categorise them as part of the framework.

Figure 10.3 Knowledge management technology conceptual framework

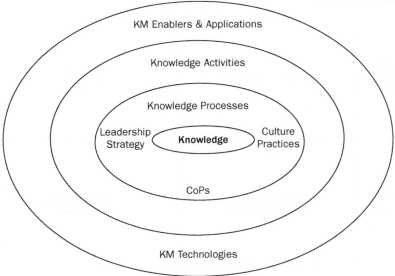

Figure 10.4 Knowledge management technology framework – processes and activities

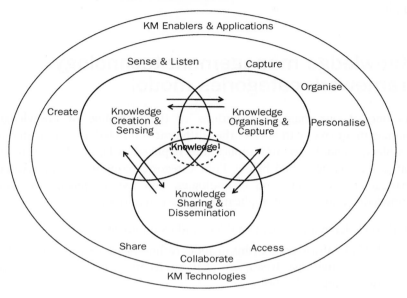

Figure 10.5 Knowledge management technology framework – enablers and applications

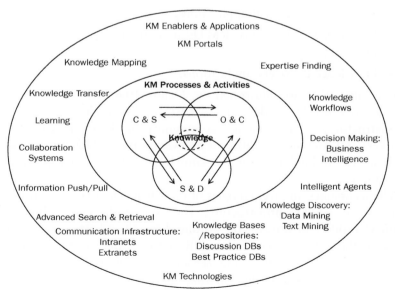

In the next two sections we first group these enablers and technologies into categories and then list the key identified knowledge management applications.

Knowledge management technology framework categories model

As one of our main contributions to the discipline of knowledge management we categorise the different knowledge management enablers, technologies and applications depicted in Figure 10.5 into six categories, as described below. Four categories contain the knowledge management enablers and technologies, and two categories the key knowledge management applications. The categories are:

- Knowledge management enablers and technologies:
  - KMTF infrastructure (this includes technologies for communication and knowledge bases, as well as technologies for knowledge organising and capture);
  - knowledge creation and sensing technologies;
  - knowledge sharing and transfer technologies;
  - advanced search and retrieval technologies.
- Knowledge management applications:
  - knowledge portals (as KMTF user interface and integration platform);
  - knowledge discovery applications.

These categories are illustrated in Figure 10.6, which shows our six-category KMTF model. At the base of this model is the KMTF infrastructure, which enables communication between knowledge workers and contains the different knowledge bases. This category also includes the technologies for the knowledge activities of capture and organising.

The techniques and technologies of knowledge discovery applications explore the KMTF infrastructure. This is also the case, albeit in a somewhat different way, for the advanced search and retrieval category. Each of these two categories logically supports the category above it. Thus, knowledge creation and sensing is supported by knowledge discovery, while knowledge sharing and transfer is supported by

Figure 10.6 Knowledge management technology framework – six categories model

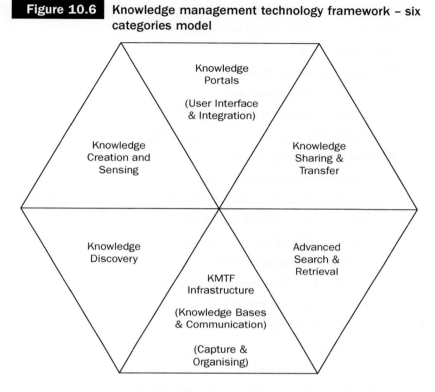

advanced search and retrieval. The top category in the model is the visual interfacing and integration category, consisting of the knowledge management knowledge portals.

Knowledge management technology framework enablers and technologies

Summarised here is the overall content of the four enablers and technology categories of the KMTF. The descriptions of each of these categories are presented hereafter in the applicable chapters.

- KMTF infrastructure:
  - knowledge management communication infrastructure
    - intranets
    - extranets

- internet-based technology
- XML as data exchange technology
- knowledge bases
  - knowledge representation
    - semantic considerations
    - XML as semantic technology
    - taxonomy and ontology (categorising and segmenting)
  - types of knowledge bases
    - discussion knowledge bases
    - intellectual capital and intellectual property knowledge bases
    - best practices knowledge bases
    - lessons-learned knowledge bases
    - research knowledge bases
    - corporate 'yellow pages' knowledge bases
- knowledge harvesting process
- Knowledge creation and sensing:
  - sense making
  - contextualising/synthesis
  - knowledge gathering (news feeds, pull, search, data entry)
- Knowledge sharing and transfer:
  - collaboration systems
    - push and pull technology
    - groupware and e-mail
    - synchronous messaging/live collaboration
  - e-learning and web-based instruction
  - e-meetings
  - technologies for the knowledge transfer cycle
    - tacit to tacit
    - tacit to explicit
    - explicit to tacit
    - explicit to explicit
- Advanced search and retrieval:

- information overload
- intelligent search, natural language processing, querying and questioning
- search engines
- searching, indexing and retrieval
  - automatic indexing
  - automatic thesaurus building
  - content recognition
  - summarisation
- information and knowledge filtering
- linking, e.g. hypertext and hyperwords (liquid information)

Knowledge management technology framework applications

We can identify a number of knowledge management applications. We selected the following list as the key knowledge management application categories to be studied. Of these four application categories, we cover the first two in depth but only summarise the categories of 'expertise mapping and finding' and 'analysis and decision making'. Although the last category fulfils a key support role for knowledge management, we regard it as a pure information technology application.

- Knowledge management portals (KMTF user interface and integration):
  - knowledge portals
  - knowledge visualisation
  - enterprise systems integration
    - expert systems
    - document management systems and content management
    - BPM and workflow systems
    - ERP, customer relationship model and supply chain model
- Knowledge discovery and mapping:
  - knowledge mapping

- – classification/navigation
- – data mining
- – text mining
- – document mining
- – intelligent agents and internet 'crawlers'
- Expertise mapping and finding:
  - – knowledge workflow mapping
  - – expertise mapping and competency linking
  - – expertise network
  - – visualisation
  - – affinity identification (locating communities of practice)
- Analysis and decision making:
  - – business intelligence (and business intelligence knowledge management)
  - – data warehousing
  - – Online Analytical Processing (OLAP), Relational Online Analytical Processing (ROLAP), Web Online Analytical Processing (WOLAP)
  - – group decisions

Summary

Based on the ideas and descriptions presented in the first part of this book a knowledge management technology framework (KMTF) was proposed. The KMTF consists of six categories of knowledge management enablers and two categories of knowledge management applications. These categories will guide and structure the rest of the chapters.

Note

1. This is a fairly complete but not exhaustive list.

11

Knowledge management technology framework infrastructure

There is the world of ideas and the world of practice. (Mathew Arnold)

Introduction

The knowledge management technology framework (KMTF) infrastructure that we describe in this chapter consists of the knowledge management communication infrastructure and the different types of knowledge bases that serve as the primary (explicit) knowledge repository. We also include in the description of this infrastructure, the process required to 'harvest' the knowledge from the organisation's knowledge processes and repositories.

Broadly speaking, one might say that the KMTF infrastructure constitutes enablers of the 'capture and organise' knowledge activities that were depicted in Figure 10.4.

Knowledge management communication infrastructure

Most successful organisations realise the need and importance of an explicit knowledge management communication infrastructure to assist the transfer of knowledge. The transfer would never happen without a process and an infrastructure of people and technology to facilitate the process.

The concept of a knowledge management communication infrastructure includes the transfer-specific mechanisms put in place to ensure the flow of knowledge and best practice through the organisation.[1]

These mechanisms include technology, work processes and networks of people (communities), as well as the necessary organisational structures.

Judging from the description of the business challenges we have described so far, we suggest that technologies that should be included as enablers for knowledge management should at least include the following:

- fast, cheap and wide bandwidth communications;
- internet-type technologies and intranets;
- interactive multimedia;
- human-centred interfaces;
- intelligent agents;
- collaboration tools.

These infrastructural technologies should be integrated together in a seamless fashion.

Knowledge management requires communication between the knowledge workers within the various communities that extends across the enterprise and even across organisational boundaries. This degree of 'reach'[2] has become readily available in the form of internet-based technologies. These include communication infrastructures such as intranets, extranets, and the internet itself. Internet-based technologies have proved to be relatively cheap and offer wide bandwidth communication. The speed and reliability of intranets are usually adequate, while extranets and the internet itself are constantly being upgraded to be fast and reliable enough to address mission-critical requirements.

The communications for knowledge management should provide either document-to-person or person-to-person linkages. Document-to-person is important for 'codification strategies'. In these cases explicit knowledge is far more important than tacit knowledge as the products or services are mostly standardised; for example, in searching and filtering applications (as described later).

Person-to-person is more a personalisation strategy. In these cases tacit knowledge is far more important than explicit knowledge. The product or service is tailor-made to the needs of the client, for example, in collaboration and portal personalisation applications (as described later).

This infrastructure is also a key prerequisite for the deployment of knowledge management portals as we describe later. The main purpose of the KMTF communication infrastructure is thus to provide access for knowledge workers to other knowledge workers and to organisational knowledge.

Knowledge bases/repositories

Organisations employ databases, repositories of various types, autonomous agents and search methodologies to enable knowledge workers to access the knowledge they require. Various definitions for knowledge repositories have been proposed. For example, according to Tobin (1997), 'A knowledge repository organizes, and makes available to all employees basic information on the company's organization, products, services, customers, and business processes'. Liebowitz and Beckman (1998), meanwhile describe the knowledge repository as 'an on-line, computer-based storehouse of expertise, knowledge, experience, and documentation about a particular domain of expertise. In creating a knowledge repository, knowledge is collected, summarized, and integrated across sources.'

In the subsections below, various themes relating to knowledge bases are discussed. These range from knowledge base concepts, to representational issues, to semantic, taxonomic and ontological considerations.

Knowledge base concepts

A knowledge base is a special kind of database for knowledge management. Typical knowledge bases consist of explicit knowledge of the organisation, embodied in such things as documentation about, and examples of best practices; links to experts (including expert mapping and knowledge mapping); articles; white papers; user manuals; etc. The main function served by these knowledge bases is the encapsulation of data and information from sources such as newspapers, journals, analyst reports, other databases, field reports, the internet and presentations. A knowledge base should have a carefully designed classification structure, content format and search engine (O'Dell, Grayson and Essaides, 1998).

Technology for knowledge management typically utilises a repository of unstructured, explicit knowledge in document format that is stored as full text and/or as abstracted artefacts. Knowledge management technology also enables access for knowledge workers to many internal and external knowledge bases. Many of these repositories have been available and accessible for a long time in the form of computerised databases of published material. Examples include Dialog, Lexis/Nexis and Medline.

The best example of a broad knowledge repository is the internet. The internet resolves issues such as worldwide knowledge access and independence of where the knowledge resides. However, this also creates the problem that a searcher has to sift through a huge number of 'hits' and has to judge the value or relevance of a particular item. Internet technologies are relatively immature and therefore one can assume that future improvements in more sophisticated search engines will probably enhance the internet as a knowledge source.

The major types of knowledge structures that can be represented in knowledge bases include the following:

- multimedia objects – images (pictures and video), sounds and signals;

- text – flat or hypertext;

- data – relational or flat files;

- document structures such as forms and templates, reports, graphs and charts;

- cases for case-based reasoning (CBR);

- rules for rule-based systems (RBS);

- processes – decomposable hierarchies, resources, performance characteristics;

- models for model-based reasoning (MBR), frameworks and simulations;

- learning material – tutorials, computer-based training, e-learning and web-based instruction course material;

- object hierarchies including taxonomies and ontology.

The typical knowledge base also contains numerous cross-links to represent relationships between different knowledge objects.

What should also be regarded as 'unmanaged' organisational knowledge that can be valuable sources for corporate knowledge bases, can be termed 'personal knowledge bases'. Personal knowledge bases include stores such as e-mail storage, calendars, personal notebooks, telephone lists, contact lists and distribution lists, as well as personal computer directories and CD libraries. Organisations are obliged to motivate knowledge workers to coordinate and share these personal knowledge bases.

Figure 11.1 illustrates the complexity of the different knowledge stores that comprise the corporate knowledge base. This figure neatly positions different knowledge management repositories and concepts in relation to individual, organisational and community content.

Figure 11.1 Complexity of different knowledge base sources

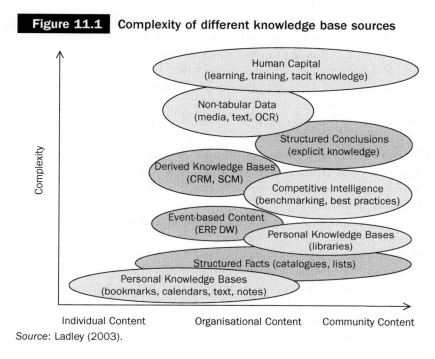

Source: Ladley (2003).

Knowledge representation

Knowledge representation is a central problem in arranging knowledge. Over a number of decades much research has been done to devise schemas to represent knowledge. The artificial intelligence community, and specifically researchers into expert systems, have considered knowledge representation in depth. These efforts have typically concentrated on managing narrow domains of knowledge such as the configurations of computer systems or the diagnosis of a particular type of disease.

The reality of expert systems and artificial intelligence in business has been much less spectacular than originally anticipated, though certainly not without value. Improvements in technology for the foreseeable future will probably be evolutionary, rather than revolutionary, with people largely augmenting knowledge-based technologies.

The problem consists of how to store and manipulate knowledge in an information system in a formal way so that it may be used by mechanisms and knowledge workers to accomplish a given task. Examples of applications that rely on knowledge are expert systems, machine translation systems, computer-aided maintenance systems and information retrieval systems (including database front-ends).

One school of thought maintains that it would be best to represent knowledge in the same way that it is represented in the human mind. Alternatively, it is thought to represent knowledge in the form of human language. Unfortunately, we do not know how knowledge is represented in the human mind, or how to manipulate human languages in the same way as the human mind does.

In general, the language used for knowledge representation determines the kind of reasoning that can take place with respect to the knowledge. The representation precedes reasoning. A knowledge representation language with limited expressivity cannot be directly used for automatic reasoning methods that require more complex expressiveness (Daconta, Obrst and Smith, 2003).

For this reason, various artificial languages and notations have been proposed for representing knowledge. They are typically based on logic and mathematics, and have easily parsed grammars to ease machine processing. To avoid excessive complexity, first-order predicate calculus is commonly used as a mathematical basis for these systems. However, even simple systems based on this simple logic can be used to represent data where useful knowledge-based processing that relies on this data is well beyond the processing capability of current computer systems.[3,4]

The recent fashion in knowledge representation languages is to use Extensible Mark-up Language (XML) as the low-level syntax. This tends to make the output of these knowledge representation languages easy for machines to parse, at the expense of human readability.

General knowledge representation schemas

Knowledge in artificial intelligence and expert systems, which sometimes play an important role in knowledge management, can be represented as three general schemas, namely cases, rules and models.

- *Case-based reasoning (CBR)* represents knowledge from experience, such as events and specific case problems and solutions. CBR involves extraction of knowledge from a series of narratives or cases regarding the problem domain. CBR technology has been commercially successful in resolving customer service problems. Unlike expert systems, which require that rules are well structured with no overlaps, case structures can reflect the unorganised thinking that takes place in the human mind (Davenport and Prusak, 1998). Applications or tasks for CBR include planning, scheduling, design, legal reasoning, story understanding and robot navigation; however, the technology has not achieved broad business application in any of these areas.

- *Rule-based systems (RBS)* use knowledge compiled into related groups of statements and conditions, called rules, which represent heuristics that human experts often use to solve complex problems.

- *Model-based reasoning (MBR)* creates an overall framework through object technology for representing and organising domain knowledge in terms of object attributes, behaviours and relationships, as well as simulating domain processes.

A fourth schema, constraint-satisfaction reasoning, can be represented as a combination of RBS and MBR.

Techniques of knowledge representation

A number of techniques are used to represent knowledge. The three most common techniques have originated from artificial intelligence research on knowledge representation. They are semantic networks, frames and scripts, which we describe briefly here.

Semantic networks are used to represent knowledge as nodes and arcs. Each node represents a concept and the arcs are used to define relations between the concepts.

In early research, the *knowledge frame* or *just frame* has been used. A frame consists of slots, which contain values; for instance, the frame for house might contain slots for 'colour', 'number of floors', etc. Frames can behave something like object-oriented programming languages, with inheritance of features described by the 'is-a' link.[5] Other links include the 'has-part' link. Frame structures are well suited for the representation of schematic knowledge and stereotypical cognitive patterns. The elements of such schematic patterns are weighted unequally, attributing higher weights to the more typical elements of a schema. A pattern is activated by certain expectations – if a person sees a big bird, they will classify it as a sea eagle rather than a golden eagle, if their 'sea-scheme' is currently activated.[6] Frames representations are more object-centred than semantic networks; all the facts and properties of a concept are located in one place – there is no need for costly search processes in the database. Frames do however suffer from the frame problem of knowledge linking.

A *script* is a type of frame that describes what happens temporally ('time-sequenced'); the usual example given is that of describing going to a restaurant. The steps include waiting to be seated, receiving a menu, ordering, etc.

Apart from the syntactic challenges of representing knowledge, the main challenge is to represent the meaning (semantics) of knowledge. This we cover and comment on next.

Semantic considerations, the semantic web and XML

In the knowledge management process we deal mostly with natural language objects in the form of unstructured text and different document types that may contain mixed data and text including multimedia. One of the main challenges for knowledge management technologies, therefore, is the issue of uncovering the semantics of the content. This is complicated further by the number of features of natural language that pose severe challenges. As an example:

> Language ambiguity – most words have different meanings or semantics. An extreme example is the following. *Time* magazine of 27 March 1989 reported on the publication of the new *Oxford English Dictionary* and noted that the term 'set' contains the longest description in the dictionary. It defines 154 main meanings and more than 60,000 words! (Botha, 1991)

Semantic considerations are key issues for managing knowledge. In this section we address three themes related to knowledge management's semantic challenge, namely:

- the semantic considerations of knowledge management;
- the semantic web;
- XML as the base technology for knowledge management.

Semantic considerations of knowledge management

Much research has been done over the last few decades regarding the representation and processing of the semantics of data and information. The most notable recent progress focuses on the semantics of the huge volume of information residing on the internet. The originator of the idea of the World Wide Web, Tim Berners-Lee, has a two-part vision for the future of the Web. The first part is to make it a more collaborative medium. The second part is to make it understandable, and therefore processable, by machines. This vision clearly involves more than retrieving HTML pages from web servers as we are presently accustomed to doing. Instead, to be able to process information in the manner envisaged by Berners-Lee will require additional metadata.

For this to happen we need a paradigm shift in the way that we think about data and information (Daconta et al., 2003). The traditional approach is to see data as secondary to processing the data. Modern approaches involve object-oriented facilities that make data important internal to the applications. 'With the Web, Extensible Markup Language (XML), and the emerging semantic web, the shift of power is moving from applications to data' according to Daconta et al. (2003). Essentially, the data is made 'smarter', meaning that more information about the content is kept with information elements. The notion of 'smarter data' is illustrated in Figure 11.2 as a data continuum consisting of four stages.

Each progressive stage is being embodied with more semantic information for machines to make inferences about. These four stages of increased semantics are as follows:

- *Text and databases (pre-XML)*: This is the initial stage where most data is proprietary to an application. The meaning is determined by the application and not by the data.

Figure 11.2 The 'smart' data continuum

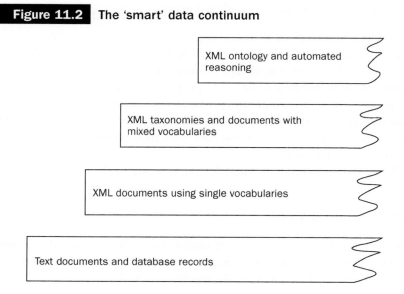

XML ontology and automated reasoning

XML taxonomies and documents with mixed vocabularies

XML documents using single vocabularies

Text documents and database records

- *XML documents for a single domain*: This is the stage where data achieves application independence within a specific domain. The data possesses enough meaning to be transferred between applications in a single domain or industry. 'An example of this would be the XML standards in the healthcare or insurance industry' (Daconta et al., 2003).

- *Taxonomies and documents with mixed vocabularies*: In this stage, data can be composed from multiple domains and accurately classified in a hierarchical taxonomy. The classification can be used for discovery of data. Simple relationships between categories in the taxonomy can be used to relate and thus combine data. Therefore, data is now 'smart' enough 'to be easily discovered and sensibly combined with other data' (Daconta et al., 2003).

- *Ontologies and rules*: In this stage, new data can be inferred from existing data by following logical rules. In essence, the data is now smart enough to be described with concrete relationships and sophisticated formalisms where logical calculations can be made on this algebra of 'semantic logic'. This allows the combination and recombination of data at a more atomic level and very fine-grained analysis of data. Therefore, with ontologies and rules as part of the data, the data no longer exists as a blob but as information with meaning. An example of this data sophistication is the automatic translation of a document in one domain to the equivalent (or as close as possible) document in another domain.

Following this sequence of increasingly 'smarter data' to another level, one can conclude that this idea is a close fit for a number of challenges and issues faced in knowledge management for which knowledge management technologies play an important role. Developments such as these have the potential to provide key benefits to knowledge management. We should however caution that developments are in the early stages and, as is usually the case with such phenomena, should be regarded as exploratory.

We next comment on the need for the semantic web.

The semantic web[7]

The semantic web is a project that intends to create a universal medium for information exchange by giving meaning, in a manner understandable by machines, to the content of documents on the Web. Currently under the direction of its creator, Tim Berners-Lee of the World Wide Web Consortium, the semantic web extends the ability of the World Wide Web through the use of standards, mark-up languages and related processing tools.

Relationship to the World Wide Web

Currently, the World Wide Web is based primarily on documents written in HTML, a language that is useful for describing, with an emphasis on visual presentation, a body of structured text interspersed with links to other documents and with multimedia objects such as images and interactive forms. HTML has limited ability to classify the blocks of text on a page or define the meaning (semantics) of the text, apart from the roles these blocks play in a typical document's organisation and in the desired visual layout. For example, the HTML tags can only specify the positioning of the item known to the user as the 'author' without having the semantic ability to interpret this item as referring to the author of this document or page.

The semantic web addresses this shortcoming, using the descriptive technologies RDF and OWL, and the data-centric, extensible mark-up language XML (see below). These technologies are combined in order to provide descriptions that supplement or replace the content of web documents. Thus, content may manifest as descriptive data stored in web-accessible databases, or as mark-up within documents (particularly in XHTML interspersed with XML, or, more often, purely in XML, with layout/rendering cues stored separately). The machine-readable descriptions allow content managers to add meaning to the content, thereby facilitating automated information gathering and research by computers.

One of the main issues to be addressed by the semantic web is that current technologies are poor at content aggregation. Putting together information from disparate sources is a recurring problem in areas such as financial account aggregation, portal aggregation and content mining.[8]

XML as basic data interchange (and representation) language

Extensible mark-up language (XML) is emerging as a fundamental enabling technology for content management and application integration. XML is a set of rules for defining data structures. Unlike

HTML, which specifies the form of how things are presented, XML specifies the function of what things are. XML makes it possible for key elements in a document to be categorised according to meaning. It enables a search engine to scan a document for XML tags that identify individual pieces of text and image, instead of selecting and presenting a document based on a meta-tag found in the document header.

XML offers the possibility of a standards-based approach to integrating many aspects of knowledge management technologies. XML brings together structured and unstructured information handling. As knowledge management works to aggregate all this information and data, XML works to categorise it. It enables advanced searching capabilities through a document's attributes, thereby increasing the speed and accuracy of searching. Ultimately, it is hoped that it enables new knowledge management technology to offer new levels of dynamic content generation, integration, interoperability and functionality through a browser interface (Silver, 2000).

The semantic web and web services

Web services are software services identified by a uniform resource identifier (URI). URIs are used as unique identifiers for concepts in the semantic web. The web services URIs are described, discovered and accessed using web protocols. The important point here is that web services often consume and produce XML-based documents and therefore further the adoption of XML and 'smart data' (Daconta et al., 2003). Web services are likely to evolve into semantic web-enabled web services. Web services also interact with other web services. As Daconta et al. (2003) describe, 'Advanced Web service applications involving comparison, composition, or orchestration of Web services will require Semantic Web technologies for such interactions to be automated'.

Figure 11.3 portrays the various convergences that need to combine to provide semantic web services (Daconta et al., 2003).

Daconta et al. (2003) argue that web services complete a platform-neutral processing model for XML. The step after that is to make both the data and the processing model smarter (i.e. more meaningful). They agree with a number of observers in the industry that there are likely to be five logical outflows of research related to the semantic web and semantic web services. We discuss these in the next topic on taxonomy and ontology.

Figure 11.3 Semantic web services

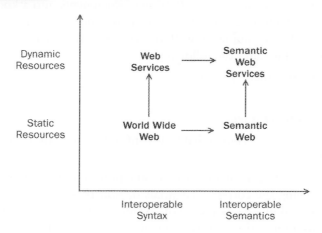

Taxonomy and ontology

As described in the previous section, web services play an important role as an enabler for the ideas of the semantic web and ultimately for knowledge management technologies. The active research in this area focuses on furthering the idea of 'smart data' to be evolved along a 'smart data continuum' according to Daconta et al. (2003). In the near term, we may expect to find important results of this research in five main areas, namely:

- *Logical assertions*: An assertion is the smallest expression of useful information. One way to make an assertion is to model the key parts of a sentence by connecting a subject to an object with a verb. The resource description framework (RDF) is designed to capture these associations between subjects and objects. As Tim Berners-Lee (cited in Daconta et al., 2003) states:

  The philosophy was: What matters is in the connections. It isn't the letters, it's the way they're strung together into words. It isn't the words, it's the way they're strung together into phrases. It isn't the phrases, it's the way they're strung together into a document.

  Assertions are not free-form commentary but rather add logical statements to a resource or about a resource.

- *Rules*: With XML, RDF and inference rules, it is hoped that the Web can be transformed from a collection of documents into a knowledge base. An inference rule allows one to derive conclusions from a set of premises. For example, a well-known logic rule is called 'modus ponens' and it states the following:

  If P is true, then Q is true.

  P is true.

  Therefore, Q is *true*.

  The semantic web is intended to use information in an ontology with logic rules to infer new information.

- *Trust*: Instead of having trust determination as a binary operation of either having the correct credentials or not, trust can be determined better by adding semantics. For example, one may want to allow access to information if a trusted entity is a stand-in for a third party. Usage of a digital signature is crucial for the 'web of trust' in digital security. By allowing anyone to make logical statements about resources, smart applications will only make inferences on statements that can be trusted. Thus, the ability to verify the sources of statements is a key part of the semantic web and therefore also of knowledge management.

- *Classification*: We classify things to establish groupings by which generalisations can be made. Classification is done to better classify resources on corporate intranets and knowledge bases. Classification is strongly related to taxonomy concepts and specific taxonomy models such as XML topic maps (XTM). However, taxonomies are typically not standardised and lack the rigorous logic that machines use to make inferences. This is the central difference between taxonomies and ontologies (which are discussed next). Figure 11.4 shows an example of a taxonomy that classifies the fox terrier Lady as a dog, which is a mammal and thus an animal.

- *Formal class models (ontologies)*: A formal representation of classes and relationships between classes to enable inference requires rigorous formalisms even beyond conventions used in current object-oriented programming languages such as Java and C++. Ontologies are used to represent such formal class hierarchies, constrained properties and relations between classes. The W3C is developing a web ontology language (OWL)[9].

Figure 11.4 Example of a taxonomy

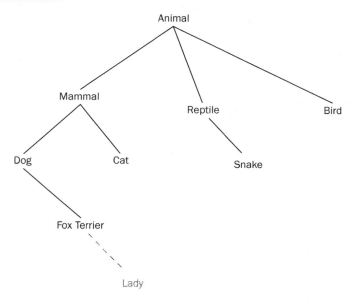

Ontology

In computer science, an ontology is the result of an attempt to formulate an exhaustive and rigorous conceptual schema within a given domain, a typically hierarchical data structure containing all the relevant entities and their relationships and rules (theorems, regulations) within that domain.[10] This area of research is a relatively new development for knowledge management. There is much excitement and hype about the supposed value-add and potential for enabling knowledge management of this technology.

An ontology defines the common words and concepts (meanings) used to describe and represent an area of knowledge, and thereby standardises the meanings. Ontologies are used by people, databases and applications that need to share domain information. (A domain is just a specific subject area or area of knowledge, such as medicine, computer configuration, etc.) Ontologies include computer-usable definitions of basic concepts in the domain and the relationships among them. Because they encode knowledge in a domain, they make that knowledge reusable.

An ontology includes the following:

- classes (general things) in the many domains of interest;

- instances (particular things);
- relationships among those things;
- properties (and property values) of those things;
- functions of and processes involving those things;
- constraints on and rules involving those things.

Ontology is often used in artificial intelligence and knowledge representation. Computer programs can use ontology for a variety of purposes, including inductive reasoning, classification, a variety of problem-solving techniques, as well as for facilitating communication and sharing of information between different systems.

An ontology, which is not tied to a particular problem domain but attempts to describe general entities, is known as a foundation ontology or upper ontology. Thus, foundation ontology is a core glossary in whose terms everything else must be described.[11] Typically, more specialised schema must be created to make the data useful for real-world decisions.

Ontologies exist at three general levels: top level, middle level and lower domain level. At the top level, the ontological information represents concerns primary semantic distinctions that apply to every ontology under the sun. These concern primary distinctions between tangible and intangible objects (objects that can be touched or held and those that cannot, or the distinction between abstract and concrete objects) as well as the semantics of parthood (i.e., what constitutes a part and what is the nature of those relations between parts and wholes). In many cases, there are multiple notions of parthood, some transitive, some not, some with other properties that need to be specified in an ontology and then inherited downward into the medium and lower domain levels of ontology representation.

Figure 11.5 depicts the three general levels of ontology. At the top is the upper ontology. This represents the common generic information that spans all ontologies. In the middle is the middle ontology. This level represents knowledge that spans domains and may not be as general as the knowledge of the upper level. Finally, the lower levels represent ontologies at the domain or sub-domain level. This is typically knowledge about more or less specific subject areas. In the figure, we point out the probable electronic commerce areas of interest, though one should note that in general, electronic commerce will be interested in all the ontology levels and areas, simply because commerce involves nearly everything.

Figure 11.5 Ontology levels

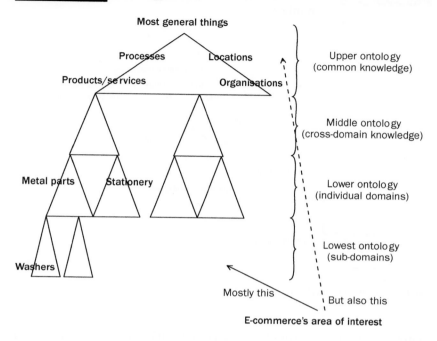

Most general things

Processes   Locations

Products/services   Organisations

Upper ontology
(common knowledge)

Middle ontology
(cross-domain knowledge)

Metal parts   Stationery

Lower ontology
(individual domains)

Lowest ontology
(sub-domains)

Washers

Mostly this   But also this

E-commerce's area of interest

In the next section we combine many of the concepts mentioned so far into an 'ontology spectrum' that shows the positioning of these concepts, ranging from weak to strong semantics.

The ontology spectrum

In this section we combine the many concepts that deal with semantics into an 'ontology spectrum'. The following concepts all attempt to address issues in representing, classifying and avoiding ambiguous meaning, namely, taxonomies, thesauri, conceptual models and logical theories. The ontology spectrum is meant to depict these concepts in a general classification or ontology space, and displays the relationships among concepts such as 'classification system', 'taxonomy', 'thesaurus', 'ontology', 'conceptual model' and 'logical theory'.

Figure 11.6 illustrates the ontology spectrum and also positions the well-known languages and technologies of the database models: the relational model, the entity-relationship language, as well as the object-oriented model: unified modelling language (UML). This model of the

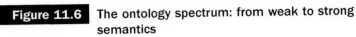

Figure 11.6 The ontology spectrum: from weak to strong semantics

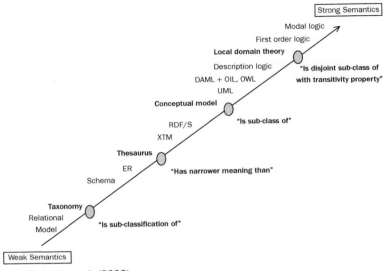

Source: Daconta et al. (2003).

ontology spectrum is from Daconta et al. (2003) and was developed for comparing the semantic richness of classification and knowledge-based models.

What is normally known as an ontology can thus range from the simple notion of a taxonomy (knowledge with minimal hierarchic or parent/child structure), to a thesaurus (words and relations such as synonyms), to a conceptual model (with more complex knowledge), to a local domain theory (with very rich, complex, consistent, meaningful knowledge).

We close this section with two summary diagrams – Figure 11.7 and Figure 11.8.

Figure 11.7 positions a range of concepts of knowledge representation and semantics by relating the types of metadata and semantic annotations. As we move up this spectrum more semantics can be utilised for actionable information and business analytics. The technologies that support these levels of semantics are therefore strong candidates for enabling meaningful knowledge management.

Figure 11.8 shows the relationship of a number of the concepts discussed so far along with current developments in technology components and standards. The figure can be seen to show the possible

Figure 11.7 Metadata and semantic annotations

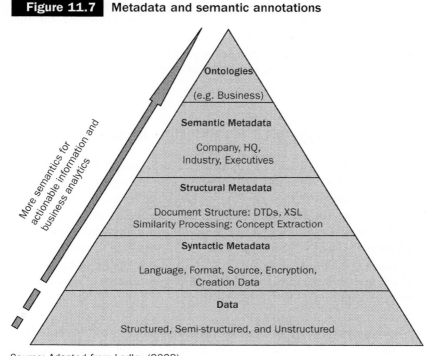

Ontologies
(e.g. Business)

Semantic Metadata

Company, HQ,
Industry, Executives

Structural Metadata

Document Structure: DTDs, XSL
Similarity Processing: Concept Extraction

Syntactic Metadata

Language, Format, Source, Encryption,
Creation Data

Data

Structured, Semi-structured, and Unstructured

More semantics for actionable information and business analytics

Source: Adapted from Ladley (2003).

Figure 11.8 Positioning the XML stack architecture

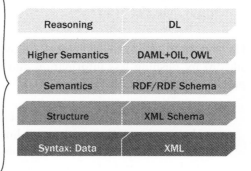

'Intelligent' Domain Applications

- Description Logic: Reasoning Methods

- OWL, DAML+OIL: Ontologies

- RDF Schema: Ontologies

- RDF: Instances

- XML Schema: Encodings of Data Elements & Descriptions

- XML Base Documents

Reasoning	DL
Higher Semantics	DAML+OIL, OWL
Semantics	RDF/RDF Schema
Structure	XML Schema
Syntax: Data	XML

Source: Adapted from Maybury (2003).

architecture for actually building and deploying these concepts for knowledge management. It relates the different technologies for the syntax of the data, the structure of the data, the semantic interpretation thereof, as well as the higher-order semantics and reasoning aspects. These layers of technologies can be combined into 'intelligent' domain applications.

Overview of types of knowledge bases

In this section we discuss a number of the knowledge bases that organisations typically employ, as well as two examples of how large organisations organise their corporate knowledge bases.

We start with the observation about the approaches of 'push' versus 'pull' dissemination of information. Stewart (1997) has cited a case study of Hewlett-Packard's experience with 'push' versus 'pull' information. One has to distinguish between information that is pushed at knowledge workers and information that they pull for themselves. Typically, as Stewart articulates:

> ...information is pushed at the knowledge worker. Standard reports – weekly sales numbers, monthly budget figures – land on their desks on a regular schedule; less formal documents like e-mail and memos pour in; other, undocumented stuff is told us at meetings, on the phone, by the coffeepot. Each of these – structured data, media, and people's knowledge – has a 'pull' counterpart: Instead of being sent a report, you can have access, the ability to get it if you need it; documents can be placed in repositories like the databases discussed ... instead of in in-boxes; corporate knowledge maps and Yellow Pages can help you pull in experts when you need them. (Stewart, 1997)

Hewlett-Packard has helped clear employees' desktops (both wood and silicon) by pushing less information and putting more where it can be pulled:

> Policies, phone directories, product descriptions (20,000 of them), and many internal reports go on-line. Rather than have publishers fulfil dozens or hundreds of individual subscriptions to magazines, newsletters, and data sources, H-P negotiates company-wide licenses and puts electronic versions into databases. (Stewart, 1997)

Types of knowledge bases

The types of knowledge bases we cover in this section are:

- corporate 'yellow pages' knowledge base;
- intellectual capital and property knowledge base;
- discussion knowledge base;
- best practices and lessons-learned knowledge base.

Corporate 'yellow pages' knowledge base

Knowledge is growing so fast that any attempt to codify all of it becomes impractical. However, the identities of the knowledge workers within the organisation change slowly. The challenge, therefore, is to locate those experts who posses the required knowledge for particular requirements. Questions asked by knowledge workers include, for example, 'Who knows whether the contract with ABC Corp. covers repair services or not?' and 'Who knows the contact details of the person who approached us about new business six months ago?' These questions may take hours to resolve. Organisations are therefore constructing and populating corporate 'yellow pages' to assist in this regard. This type of knowledge base should be a simple system that connects inquirers to experts. This will obviously save time, reduce errors and guesswork and prevent the reinvention of countless wheels. Stewart (1997) also warns that this type of knowledge base should not be a giant index because specific information changes too quickly, rather, it should be maps that show where the knowledge of the enterprise is located and who is the 'knower' (i.e. in whose head resides the knowledge). Stewart (2001) investigates why only a few companies employ these knowledge bases and again concludes that the rule remains: knowledge projects must solve a business need. This indicates that if companies employ these knowledge bases but do not adequately address a specific business need, the users will therefore not perceive the result as worthwhile.

Therefore, a good yellow pages knowledge base can be a valuable knowledge project provided it adequately addresses a business need.

Intellectual capital and intellectual property knowledge base

As discussed in the first part of this book, there are two kinds of intellectual capital:

- First, the semi-permanent body of knowledge that grows up around a task, a person, or an organisation.
- Second, tools that augment the body of knowledge by bringing relevant data or expertise to people who need them when they need them.

Value-added knowledge work is rarely routine, because each sale and each project is unique – it is impossible to predict what specific knowledge it will need.

The intellectual capital/intellectual property knowledge base therefore serves a number of purposes that are important for knowledge management. For example, it is an index of the organisation's intellectual property – items such as patents, copyrights, design rights, etc. This knowledge base will also contain information and analysis of the opportunities and challenges in the marketplace, such as the major customer files and competitor intelligence. The intellectual capital/intellectual property knowledge base is therefore primarily the repository of information and explicit knowledge about suppliers, customers, competitors, market trends and intellectual property with respect to the particular industry, etc.

Discussion knowledge base

Online discussion document bases are important repositories of more informal and unstructured information that accumulates while knowledge workers discuss certain pertinent topics among each other and with subject matter experts. For example, the issues of concern in a particular project are posted for comments, opinions and experiences. Participants then add their opinions, comments and solutions to this topic. These discussions are typically linked in a thread that combines the particular topic discussions. The threads are visually organised and displayed to emphasise relationships and the sequence of the discussions – a typical taxonomy of the discussions.

Although these databases have weak structure they are important as knowledge bases as many opinions of different expertise are accumulated. The management of this content is however more of an art than a science and needs further research.

Best practices and lessons-learned knowledge base

Teams can become more knowledgeable than the sum of their members. Interaction, conversations, dialogue and interrelationships stimulate the thought processes and creation of ideas. Team learning can result from meetings on 'lessons learned' or by solving complex problems as a team – overcoming individual assumptions and limitations as well as stimulating new thought processes and ideas.

As Nonaka (1991) points out in his knowledge-learning cycle, knowledge is created through interaction between tacit knowledge and explicit knowledge. The challenge is to expose the hidden knowledge and to share it with a team and the organisation.

Knowledge is often intended to be explicit. Many organisations hold final project review meetings to learn from a project (including the positives and the negatives) to capture and distil the project's justification, existence, history and results, as well as 'lessons learned'. This is meant to assist in capturing and reusing the intellectual capital for future projects and engagements.

However, organisations often lose this opportunity because of time pressures, by underestimating the value of such actions, or just because the team is dismantled and redistributed, making it difficult to recoup the project's potential intellectual capital.

A best practice is therefore to capture experience in the lessons-learned knowledge base as a matter of practice and as part of all knowledge projects and procedures. In effect, the important issue here is to bank lessons learned – thereby creating checklists of what went right and what went wrong. This enables the ongoing development of guidelines for others undertaking similar projects. These guidelines can then be used to leverage what was learned so that knowledge workers can do the job better and faster the next time around.

Typical knowledge bases used by a large organisation

We include here two references to case studies of how large organisations typically utilise knowledge bases: the cases of Booz Allen and Arthur Andersen of Denmark. All similar projects are ambitious attempts to organise scattered information and explicit knowledge, to convert it into organisational knowledge, and to make it easier to obtain colleagues' expertise and knowledge.

Booz Allen's Knowledge On-line

Stewart (1997) describes how Booz Allen developed their knowledge base called Knowledge On-line (KOL). KOL has been up and running since early 1995 and is supposed to save the consultants from spending long and costly hours repeating each other's work. It was also designed to make it easy to tap the company's experts and ideas regardless of geography or speciality. For example, a knowledge worker may type a name and click on an icon 'Experts/Resumé/History' to find a resumé of a particular colleague; or they may type 'customer service' and the system will deliver a list of consultant names who know the particular customer service. Another icon is labelled 'Knowledge.' Behind it are a number of databases with thousands of documents, classified into topics such as marketing, reengineering and change management. These documents can be accessed online and/or downloaded. KOL also has bulletin boards, discussion forums and training courses.

Business Consulting Practice at Arthur Andersen Denmark

Dutta and De Meyer (2001) describe the Business Consulting Practice at Arthur Andersen Denmark (AADk), which used to be known for its progressive utilisation of knowledge management technologies. AADk as a group were large users of Lotus Notes and based a number of their internal systems as well as systems for their customers on Lotus Notes. In parallel to Lotus Notes implementation they also aimed to give everyone within AADk a personal computer, a uniform set of tools and links to a common technology platform. They further focused on space management in their offices and, early on, developed a unique vision of the new office concept that included:

- *Open offices*: no boundaries – teams sit and work together in open spaces;
- *Total mobility*: no one has a pre-assigned desk or a fixed phone;
- *Clean desks*: desks have no drawers or storage areas; all work has to be filed away in the appropriate place at the end of the day;
- *Easy access*: professional staff should have all required support facilities within 10 metres of their desks;
- *Electronic networking*: all desks have a networked PC/docking station;
- *Single card access*: one card should be used by all employees to access all functions such as security, restaurants, parking garage and library.

The new office concept forced AADk to rethink the organisation of archives and knowledge stores:

- the archiving process was redefined around the client;
- it offered flexible physical storage by client and was controlled by a Lotus Notes application;
- electronic client folders were all done on Lotus Notes;
- significant volumes of material, such as local and Arthur Andersen-wide manuals, were moved online and updated centrally.

The result was enhanced teamwork and excellent knowledge sharing. Jarlbaek was reported to have said:

> Technological shifts such as the Internet and the global market space will require radical new ways of organizing knowledge and competing ... We believe that our people are our most valuable knowledge assets. Technology is now enabling us to create different kinds of knowledge assets – in real time and in virtual space! (Jarlbaek, cited in Dutta and De Meyer, 2001)

AADk's local knowledge bases include:

- employee policy manual;
- computer manual;
- ISO manuals (in line with ISO 9001);
- private addresses;
- telephone directories – lists and short codes of the telephone system;
- client list.

There were more than 50 different local knowledge-based applications in AADk in 2001. The following short list of these knowledge bases illustrates the type of knowledge bases that can be employed in such an organisation:

- *AA On-line*: This is a Lotus Notes application for internal communication worldwide, based on categories divided according to function and topic. Various forms of communication include the following:
  - publication of announcements (one to many);
  - conferences (closed, limited forum of users);
  - resources information (few to many);
  - discussions and Ask Arthur (many to many).

- *Global Best Practices*: This is the result of centralised collection of basic data for auditing, methodological and procedural standards, and the systematic consolidation and analysis thereof for reporting global best practices and useful benchmark data.

Knowledge harvesting process

It is important to establish a culture of building the organisational knowledge collection, and of recycling experiences for the benefit of other members of communities and the whole organisation (e.g. see O'Dell, Grayson and Essaides, 1998). Organisations that embark on a knowledge management strategy typically provide a variety of knowledge management services and organised networks to assist in the transfer process. Knowledge managers and knowledge integrators add value by scanning the flow of information, and 'package' the knowledge in more applicable formats and representations. They also involve networks of people who come together to share and learn from one another face-to-face and electronically utilising technology such as groupware.

However, it is not a straightforward task. Motivation to contribute to the organisational knowledge is a key part of this process. Knowledge workers need to be rewarded for valuable contributions. This implies the existence of some judging and selection process with criteria for measuring the value of the content (positive or negative). Negative experiences from which to learn may be more valuable than the successful experiences. The contributions and their importance need to be recognised by peers and leadership.

This emphasises the importance of the reflection process inherent in organisational learning.[12] There are important lessons to learn and the harvesting process ensures that team members take the time to reflect on what they have learned and then share it with others.

Harvesting previous experience and best practices gained in engagements and with real business situations is beneficial to reduce time, effort and expenses for similar future situations. This is well articulated in the title of the book *If Only We Knew What We Know* (O'Dell, Grayson and Essaides, 1998).

Organisations that actively employ knowledge management as a strategy, typically assign specific knowledge transfer responsibilities to some staff members (as job descriptions or just as additional roles). These 'change agents' are trained to assist other employees in:

- finding, capturing, codifying and transmitting knowledge and best practices to the corporate knowledge bases;
- solving and improving processes by helping these employees to use the knowledge bases and other knowledge sources;
- acting as internal consultants to facilitate implementation.

Summary

Most successful organisations realise the need and importance of an explicit knowledge management communication infrastructure to assist the transfer of knowledge. Infrastructural technologies such as intranets, interactive multimedia, human-centred interfaces, intelligent agents and collaboration tools should be integrated together in a seamless fashion.

Organisations also employ various types of knowledge bases (or knowledge repositories) to enable knowledge workers to access the knowledge they require. Various knowledge representation schemas and techniques are used to represent knowledge in the knowledge bases.

It is important for organisations to establish a culture of building the organisational knowledge collection and of recycling experiences for the benefit of the staff and the whole organisation. Harvesting previous experiences and best practices gained in engagements and with real business situations is beneficial to reduce time, effort and expenses in similar future situations.

In the next chapter we consider the aspects of knowledge creation and sensing.

Notes

1. See also O'Dell, Grayson and Essaides (1998), Chapter 11, 'Creating the knowledge infrastructure'.
2. The term 'reach' indicates the extent of connectivity between participants.
3. The case of the Prolog artificial intelligence language is also a well-known example.

4. Examples of notations include DATR for representing lexical knowledge and RDF (resource description framework) for representing relationships between objects. Examples of artificial languages intended for knowledge representation include CycL, Loom, OWL (the web ontology language) and knowledge management.

5. However, there has been no small amount of inconsistency in the usage of the 'is-a' link. In Brachman (1983) found 29 different semantics in projects whose knowledge representation schemes involved an 'is-a' link.

6. Source: *www.BambooWeb.com*.

7. Sourced from *www.BambooWeb.com* and Daconta, Obrst and Smith (2003).

8. The latter two issues are addressed in the chapters that cover the knowledge management portals and knowledge discovery.

9. The web ontology language being developed by the W3C will have a UML presentation profile.

10. The computer science usage of the term 'ontology' is derived from the much older usage of the term in philosophy, where it means the study of being or existence as well as the basic categories thereof (see sources such as: *www.BambooWeb.com*).

11. For example, 'the 2,000 English words required by Longman's Dictionary to define the 4,000 most common English idioms' – *www.BambooWeb.com*.

12. As discussed in the first part of this book.

Knowledge creation and sensing

Introduction

In this chapter we consider the different aspects of knowledge creation and sensing in the knowledge management technology framework (KMTF) model and the related knowledge management technologies. As noted previously, this category of the KMTF is the least supported by knowledge management technology because most of its focus is on tacit knowledge and the human faculties of creating new knowledge and sensing the business needs for forming new knowledge. In the next two sections of this chapter, we discuss knowledge creation and the key knowledge management technologies for this knowledge process, namely technologies associated with e-learning.

Because we still do not fully understand human intelligence and – for the lack of a better term, 'accumulation of knowledge', knowledge creation and sensing can typically be linked to the 'tacit-to-tacit' and 'explicit-to-tacit' knowledge conversion patterns of Nonaka and Tacheuchi (1995). We describe these two patterns of knowledge conversion in the last two sections of this chapter.

Knowledge creation

Individuals learn and grow their knowledge in a stimulating environment for knowledge creation. Individuals operate within teams and communities within the organisational structure and exploit organisational links to the external environment. This is especially true for knowledge workers.

Organisations create knowledge by creating infrastructure and processes that enable individuals and teams to share and improve new knowledge created by individuals. Learning can only be tested if insights are translated into actions that result in improved performance or in new/improved skills.

Hongo and Stone (cited in Coleman, 1997) suggest six points on knowledge creation to consider:

- Knowledge creation leads to continuous innovation, which leads to competitive advantage.
- Knowledge creation takes place at three levels: the individual, the team or community, and the organisation (as discussed in the first part of this book).
- Groupware creates opportunities for the sharing and spiralling of knowledge into the organisation.[1]
- Learning involves knowledge, which leads to action. In order to act on new insights an individual must internalise it, contextualise it, and add own their values and beliefs to it.
- It is the interaction of tacit knowledge with explicit business problems that creates new knowledge.
- Groupware can facilitate the reflection process only if the process of contributing to the system is well-managed and facilitated to ensure the quality of the contributions, and not just the quantity.

For competitive advantage the organisation has to know more about crucial aspects of the business than its competition. To consistently know more implies that the knowledge workers have to learn from others; but they must also continue to generate new knowledge, evolve market know-how, develop new technologies, and grow understanding of customers and their needs.

There are therefore two types of learning in organisations, namely:

- receiving wisdom and generating new (tacit) insights;
- creating new (explicit) knowledge during the run of business.

Creation of knowledge is the point at which individual learning and organisational learning come together. Most new knowledge is incremental. It is mediated more through invention than through true discovery. The former involves assembling known pieces of knowledge in new ways; the latter consists of finding ideas, approaches and technologies that are truly revolutionary. Breakthrough ideas are important to value, but cumulative small incremental gains are usually just as valuable.

The first part of this book discussed the necessity for knowledge workers to observe the way their colleagues go about their tasks, and the importance of such on-the-job training. As far as knowledge management technologies are concerned in this regard, the primary technology for knowledge creation and sensing remains e-learning technology. This is the subject of our next section.

E-learning

Many enterprises are discouraged by inadequacies in infrastructure or lack of course material and training support staff, etc. and make little use of e-learning. Nonetheless, e-learning represents a major opportunity to increase the rate and type of knowledge transfer and knowledge creation and sensing. It has long been used to support training, but e-learning can and should be different from and richer than plain computer-based training. Learning involves interaction and simulation, so e-learning must address this challenge, otherwise it risks simply becoming another unsuccessful self-service training course. E-learning supports the development of intellectual assets, workplace collaboration and innovation.

In the knowledge workplace, it can be linked to personnel and organisational competency models, compensation plans, and reward schemes for contributions to the organisational knowledge base, as well as to innovative applications of the knowledge. As the knowledge workplace becomes more complex, end users are switched rapidly and ubiquitously between applications. To make this switching easy for end users, almost all knowledge management applications offered by vendors provide just-in-time embedded e-learning capabilities. Embedded e-learning can eliminate the requirement to develop some individual competencies, thus reducing the risks of knowledge workplace competency/skill gaps and loss of experience (Logan, 2001).

Recently, the field of web-based instruction (WBI) has seen much development (e.g. see Joia, 2001). WBI systems are engines developed to use intranet or internet capabilities to enable and support distance learning in an affordable, interactive and hypertext-linked way. The only technology required by the learner is a browser. The system with the respective course content is kept either in the intranet server or in a generic internet server. These systems are typically comprised of three distinct modules, namely:

- *authoring module*: used by the content's author to create the course;
- *utilisation module*: used to process the training;

- *tracking module*: used by the course administrator to track and manage the performance of the pupils and the course as a whole.

Using a WBI system based on intranet/internet technologies and additionally exploiting videoconferencing and video-multicasting enables just-in-time education, anytime and anywhere. The utilisation of groupware to assist in communication and coordination enhances this process even further – assisting the whole knowledge management process.

Two sets of technologies for the knowledge conversion lifecycle

In the following we describe the set of knowledge management technologies in terms of two of the four steps of Nonaka and Takeuchi's organisation learning cycle, described in the first part of this book as the knowledge conversion lifecycle model. The two steps are the 'tacit-to-tacit' and 'explicit-to-tacit' phases. This is illustrated in Figure 12.1.

Figure 12.1 Concise knowledge conversion spiral model (left)

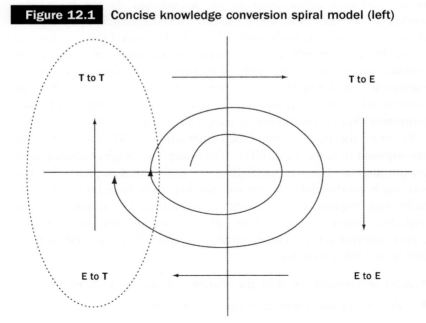

Below, the two steps on the left side of the model are described, covering the role of technologies in support of the 'tacit-to-explicit' and 'explicit-to-explicit' phases of the organisational learning spiral.

Tacit to tacit

The typical way in which tacit knowledge is built and shared is in face-to-face meetings and shared experiences, formal and informal, in which knowledge management technologies play a minimal role. However, an increasing proportion of meetings and other interpersonal interactions use groupware as online tools. These tools are used either to supplement conventional meetings, or in some cases to replace them. One has to ask to what extent these tools can facilitate formulation and transfer of tacit knowledge. We cover some of these aspects below.

As described in the previous section, *groupware* is a fairly broad category of application software that helps individuals to work together in groups or teams. Groupware can to some extent support all four of the facets of knowledge conversion. To examine the role of groupware in socialisation we focus on two important aspects: shared experiences and trust.

Shared experiences are an important basis for the formation and sharing of tacit knowledge. Groupware provides a synthetic environment, often called a virtual space, within which participants can share certain kinds of experience; for example, they can conduct meetings, listen to presentations, hold discussions and share relevant documents. Indeed, if a geographically-dispersed team never meets face to face, the importance of shared experiences in virtual spaces is proportionally enhanced. The current market leader in groupware is Lotus Notes/Domino (Marwick, 2001). It facilitates the sharing of documents and discussions and allows various applications for sharing information and conducting asynchronous discussions to be built. Groupware might be thought mainly to facilitate the combination process, i.e. sharing of explicit knowledge. However, the selection and discussion of explicit knowledge to some degree constitutes a shared experience.

A richer kind of shared experience can be provided by applications that support *real-time online meetings* – a more recent category of groupware. Online meetings can include video and text-based conferencing, as well as synchronous communication and chat, also known as 'live-collaboration'. The recent emergence of voice-over internet protocol technology – specifically the Skype technology – as a vehicle for conferencing constitutes a potential revolution in person-to-person communications. These technologies provide opportunities for relatively cheap international communication. Text-based chat is believed to be capable of supporting a group of people in knowledge sharing in a conversational mode (Marwick, 2001). Commercial products of this type include Lotus Sametime (included in Lotus Domino) and Microsoft NetMeeting. These products integrate both instant messaging and online meeting capabilities. Instant messaging is found to have properties that lie somewhere between those of the personal meeting and the telephone; it is less intrusive than interrupting a person with a question in a personal meeting; but more effective than the telephone because it can broadcast a query to a group and leave it to be answered later. In work on the Babble system (see Marwick, 2001), chat was evaluated by some users as being '…much more like conversation', which is promising for the kind of dialogue in which tacit knowledge might be formed and made explicit. However, not all online meeting systems have the properties of face-to-face meetings. For example, the videoconferencing system studied by Fish et al. (1993, cited in Marwick, 2001) was judged by its users to be more like a video telephone than a face-to-face meeting. Currently, rather than replacing face-to-face meetings, many online meetings are found to complement existing collaboration systems and the well-established phone conference. They are therefore probably more suited to the exchange of explicit rather than tacit knowledge. Online meetings extend phone conferences by allowing application screens to be viewed by the participants or by providing a shared whiteboard. An extension is for part of the meeting to take place in virtual reality with the participants represented by avatars. One research direction is to integrate online meetings with classic groupware-like applications that support document sharing and asynchronous discussion[2] (see also the discussion on electronic meeting systems in Chapter 13).

Limitations of groupware for tacit knowledge formation and sharing have been highlighted by recent work on the closely related issue of the degree of trust established among the participants (Marwick, 2001). It was found that videoconferencing (at high resolution – not internet video) was almost as good as face-to-face meetings, whereas audio conferencing was less effective and text chat least so. These results suggest that a new generation of videoconferencing might be helpful in the socialisation process, at least insofar as it facilitates the building of trust.

Another approach to tacit knowledge sharing is for a system to find persons with common interests, who are candidates to join a community. In Foner's Yenta System (Marwick, 2001), the similarity of the documents used by people allowed the system to infer that their interests were similar. Location of other people with similar interests is a function that can be added to personalisation systems, the goal of which is to route incoming information to individuals who may be interested in it. There are obvious privacy problems to overcome (see also Chapter 15 covering expertise location).

Explicit to tacit

Acquiring and possessing tacit knowledge is a necessary precursor to taking constructive action and to making business decisions. This new tacit knowledge can be internalised through better appreciation and understanding of explicit knowledge. Technology to help knowledge workers form new tacit knowledge is therefore particularly important for knowledge management. A knowledge management system should offer information retrieval and also facilitate the understanding and use of information. For example, such a system can generate metadata through document analysis and classification, supporting rapid browsing and usage of available information. One can foresee that future information infrastructures will facilitate different modes of information usage such as search, exploration, classification, categorisation and finding associations (Marwick, 2001). Users can discover relationships between documents and related concepts and learn by exploring an information space. This will assist the knowledge worker to form new tacit knowledge more easily.

When tacit knowledge is formed through learning rather than from exploring an information space a different set of technologies is applicable. Learning is increasingly done online, bypassing typical classroom formats. Online learning has the advantage of eliminating travel and of being compatible with tight modern work schedules. A wide variety of tools and applications support corporate distance learning. The trend toward self-directed learning rather than instructor-led learning has resulted in a focus on interactive web-based courseware and on downloaded courseware applications. For example, one can assume that future generations of portals will offer modules for self-directed learning (for more detail, see also Chapter 16 about knowledge management portal technology).

Summary

In this chapter the different aspects of knowledge creation and sensing in the KMTF model and related technologies were discussed. However, from the discussion it is clear that knowledge creation and sensing are the least supported by knowledge management technology, because most of its focus is on tacit knowledge and the human faculties of creating new knowledge and sensing the business needs for forming new knowledge.

In the next chapter we consider knowledge sharing and transfer.

Notes

1. See Chapter 13 for more detail on groupware.
2. An example is the IBM-Boeing TeamSpace project, which helps to manage both the artefacts of a project and the processes followed by the team. Online meetings are recorded as artefacts and can be replayed within TeamSpace, thus allowing even individuals who were not present in the original meeting to share some aspects of the experience (Marwick, 2001).

Knowledge sharing and transfer

Successful knowledge transfer involves neither computers nor documents but rather interactions between people. (T. H. Davenport)

Introduction

In this chapter we address the technologies to support the process of knowledge sharing and transfer. We begin by considering the background of the knowledge management technologies currently employed to facilitate this. We position the different technologies in terms of the two dimensions of tasks to be performed in relation to the professionals performing them. This leads us to discuss the important concept of collaboration and knowledge management. This discussion includes a brief consideration of collaboration concepts and of groupware technology. Electronic meeting systems are considered subsequently.

Because of the importance of the knowledge conversion concepts of Nonaka and Takeuchi (1995) we dedicate two sections to discussing two of their identified steps in the organisational learning cycle, namely 'tacit-to-explicit' and 'explicit-to-explicit'. These sections refer to knowledge processes that belong in Chapter 12 and we cross-reference these sections where applicable.

The early pioneers who tackled the challenges of using technology to manage knowledge built up considerable baseline experience in this area over a number of decades (e.g. see Marwick, 2001). This experience includes the following:

- Early generations of networking and computer technology offered improved access to knowledge online.

- Full-text document retrieval systems evolved into effective search technologies since the 1970s and 1980s (such as Storage And Information Retrieval System (STAIRS), Text Retrieval System (TRS), Medline).

- Collaboration solutions dated from the late 1970s/early 1980s, including first-generation text processing, office-type e-mail, and document distribution (Professional Office System (PROFS), Distributed Office Support System (DISOSS)).

- Online conferencing and discussion forums on centralised systems based on mainframe time-sharing technologies dated from the 1970s (notably based on Virtual Machine/Conversational Monitor System (VM/CMS) and Multiple Virtual Storage/Time Sharing Option (MVS/TSO)).

An important set of technologies that exist as predecessors for the eventual knowledge management technologies of today were the office systems and the eventual groupware technologies of the 1980s and 1990s. Since the early 1990s, Lotus Notes virtually defined knowledge management technology and has become the leading knowledge sharing and transfer technology available today. Many contemporary knowledge management solutions are based on Lotus Notes and its server component, Lotus Domino. It is a comprehensive integrated solution that includes many capabilities, such as a knowledge base with content search, replication for disconnected/mobile usage, well advanced security, and application development tools. With its Lotus Domino web server, content is also published and distributed on the Web. As we will discuss in due course, the native web also offers a host of tools for knowledge management (e.g. see Davenport and Prusak, 1998, Firestone, 2003, and others in this regard).

Technologies have evolved from number-crunching abilities to primarily communication abilities. These capabilities enable people to work together in a collaborative and integrated environment that is well suited for knowledge sharing and transfer activities. These technologies support knowledge management, for example, in the following ways:[1]

- they enable more than one person to work at the same time on the same document;

- they allow intelligent tracking of messages and documents within a process;

- they help employees to view and manipulate information simultaneously and efficiently.

The range of technologies that can accomplish these tasks is illustrated in Figure 13.1. The two dimensions are chosen to represent one or more tasks on one axis, as performed by a single professional or several professionals on the other axis. A single task performed by a professional requires systems for personal productivity such as office automation suites and personal information managers. Where a professional executes multiple tasks, he or she utilises integrated corporate systems such as enterprise resource planning systems or other database systems.

The two cases where several professionals are performing typical knowledge work can be differentiated into systems that are focused on information – groupware systems – versus systems that have a process focus – business process management systems and workflow systems.

In the following three sections we cover collaboration and knowledge management as a theme (including a discussion on groupware), electronic meeting systems, and technologies for the knowledge conversion lifecycle.

Figure 13.1 Systems positioning

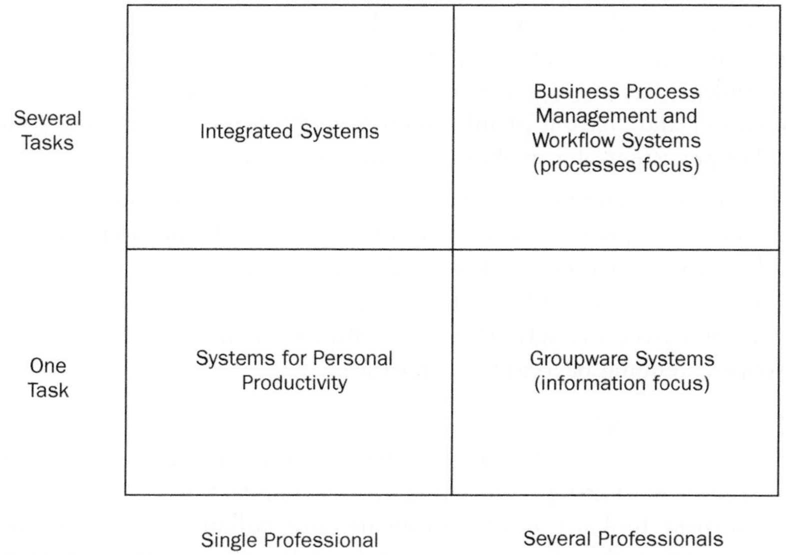

	Single Professional	Several Professionals
Several Tasks	Integrated Systems	Business Process Management and Workflow Systems (processes focus)
One Task	Systems for Personal Productivity	Groupware Systems (information focus)

Source: Joia (2001).

Collaboration and knowledge management

Knowledge management programmes must support collaboration between individuals and between communities. Doing business is a series of collaborative processes. It requires interaction among employees, vendors, suppliers and business partners. Although e-mail is one example of an indispensable communication tool used by companies around the world, a number of other collaborative applications are increasingly coming into play. These solutions enable local work groups, or even geographically-dispersed teams, to work together using real-time information sharing and distribution across the internet.

The term 'collaboration' can be used in many ways. We have found that many executives equate collaboration with e-mail. In commerce applications, it often refers to data sharing with no human dimension. In the context of knowledge management, it is important to have a full appreciation of collaboration. The idea of linking together the knowledge held by discrete parts of the enterprise for greater collaboration and learning is now becoming a strategic focus of many organisations.

Collaboration concepts

We identify two dimensions of collaboration, namely the mode and the scope:

- *The mode* is determined (a) by whether the collaboration is based primarily around conversation or the exchange of messages (which includes e-mail as well as real-time discussion); or (b) if it is based on creation and sharing of information in the form of documents and other persistent objects that are stored for reuse.

- *The scope* is determined by whether the collaboration is interpersonal, or inter-enterprise, or something inbetween. Collaboration occurs at all levels of structure. Knowledge management, groupware and intranets have typically focused on collaborative processes inside an enterprise. Increasingly, they are following e-mail in recognising a scope extending beyond the enterprise.

Various terms such as 'group support systems', 'computer supported cooperative work', and 'groupware' have been used to describe the area that studies workgroup computing and its implications. The intent of this business tool set is to coordinate and collaborate via effective communication that links people as knowledge workers to business processes and information.

Groupware is thus the technology that implements workgroup computing. Conceptually, workgroup automation is best characterised by its three 'C's, namely, communication, collaboration and coordination, as is conceptually illustrated in Figure 13.2. Table 13.1 shows the three 'C's from a technology perspective.

Figure 13.2 The three 'C's link people to process to information

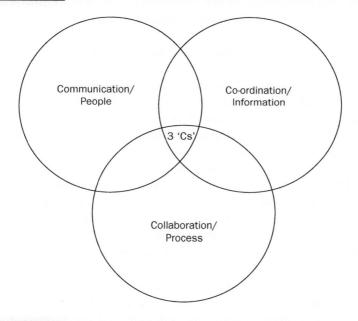

Table 13.1 Connecting people, process, and information

People connections	Electronic mail Fax Conferencing Shared folders World Wide Web
Process	Workflow Calendar/time management Development environment
Information	Database links Document management Forms Filters/search engines Security

Groupware

Important groupware technologies include applications such as e-mail, bulletin boards, newsgroups, chat, instant messaging, group calendaring and scheduling, shared document libraries, discussion databases and videoconferencing. The latter is becoming important for sharing tacit knowledge because of its 'face-to-face' or 'person-to-person' characteristics. Other technologies in this regard include distributed databases and electronic data exchange technologies such as XML.

Groupware is a combination of technologies enabling an organisation to create, share and leverage an accumulated knowledge base. Groupware technologies dramatically reduce the time and effort necessary to distribute ideas, notifications, proposals and documents throughout workgroups and communities.

E-mail has promoted information sharing. Shared calendaring and scheduling applications enable coordination of activities without the burden of personally contacting each participant multiple times to verify open dates and confirm attendance. Likewise, workflow, imaging and electronic forms (e-forms) increase the rate at which information can be entered and retrieved by individuals or groups, thus enabling better productivity and sharing of information. New multimedia technologies are emerging for real-time collaboration using PCs, cameras, teleconferencing, etc.

Currently, groupware technologies are implemented within individual organisations. As each organisation selects its own groupware technologies, frequently hardware, software and file formats are not compatible with those of other organisations. Incompatible implementations create barriers to enterprise-wide collaboration, inhibit interoperability between systems, and increase the cost of system support.

For an enterprise-wide groupware implementation to succeed, the comprised technologies must comply to a set of common protocols and infrastructure standards, allowing them to communicate with one another. Some groupware technologies, such as e-mail, have made considerable progress in the standardisation of protocols across software products. Other groupware technologies are fast maturing but have not yet standardised on protocols.

As the goal of groupware is to foster collaboration and communication, certain areas require more standards adherence than others. For example, it is more important to establish standards for communication than for

Figure 13.3 Areas of groupware

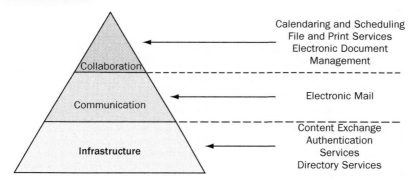

collaboration, as the impact is broader. Figure 13.3 illustrates the related groupware areas:

- *Infrastructure*. The foundation required to enable communication and collaboration across an organisation. Infrastructure includes content exchange, authentication services and directory services.
- *Communication*. The process of delivering information on intranets, extranets and the internet. E-mail is the primary backbone for communication.
- *Collaboration*. The flow of work and business information within an organisation or an ad-hoc workgroup. Automated collaborative applications include calendaring and scheduling, file and print services, and electronic document management.

Groupware technologies should overcome time and distance barriers. Figure 13.4 illustrates time and distance barriers of groupware while Figure 13.5 lists some examples of the applicable technologies.

Groupware technologies must encompass all scenarios from working at the same time at the same place to working at any time from any place. Geographical boundaries are eliminated by groupware technologies, providing communication and real-time access to information from any location. The efficiency and quality of a process are partially measured by the timeliness with which the work is performed. In order to determine whether groupware is providing value to a process, the notion of timeliness must be qualified for that process. For example, a month may be considered acceptable for passing a specific group of documents through an organisation for approval. In contrast, a month to send an e-mail to that same group of people is unacceptable.

Figure 13.4 **Time and distance barriers**

Work
Document Management
Conferencing and Meetings
Calendaring and Scheduling
Electronic Mail
Distance
Any Time
Same Place
Any Time
Any Place
Same Time
Same Place
Same Time
Any Place
Time

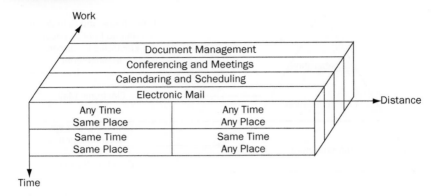

Figure 13.5 **Collaboration technologies for time and place**

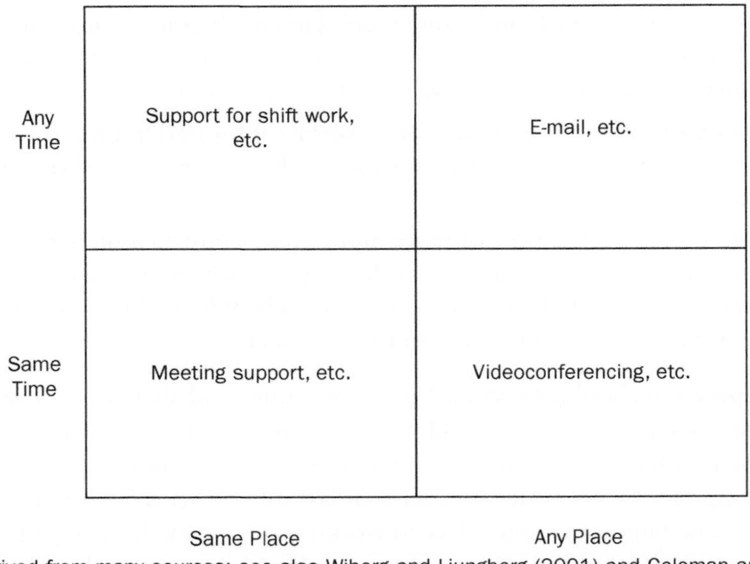

Any Time
Support for shift work, etc.
E-mail, etc.
Same Time
Meeting support, etc.
Videoconferencing, etc.
Same Place
Any Place

Derived from many sources; see also Wiberg and Ljungberg (2001) and Coleman and Khanna (1995).

Electronic meeting systems

Meetings are occasions where the minutes are kept but the hours are lost. (Anonymous)

A meeting is a gathering where people speak up, say nothing, and then all disagree. (T.A. Kayser)

An electronic meeting system (EMS) is another groupware tool for reflective learning and information sharing. Typically the average corporate 'meeting' is not well-structured and chaired. The typical knowledge worker resents meetings and regards them as a waste of time.

There are many reasons why people meet when they are working together: to share information, to make decisions, to avoid decisions, to socialise, etc. (e.g. see Nunamaker et al., 1995). Many things can go wrong with a meeting. Participants may lack focus, or may be focused on hidden agendas. Some people may be afraid to speak up, while others may dominate the discussion. Meetings are difficult and also expensive. Nunamaker et al. (1995) calculated that about 11 million formal meetings happen per day in the USA, consuming 30–80 per cent of a manager's day. However, meetings will remain essential and valuable for doing business because knowledge workers have to share and exchange knowledge in addition to their other tasks.

Using an EMS, the typical meeting and group gathering can be changed fundamentally (Nunamaker et al., 1995). An EMS is a collection of computer-based tools, each of which can structure and focus the thinking of team members in some unique way. For example, an electronic brainstorming tool encourages a group to diverge from standard patterns of thinking to generate as many ideas as possible. All users type their ideas into the system simultaneously. The system randomly passes ideas from one person to the next. The participants can argue with or expand on the ideas they see, or can be inspired to a completely different line of thought. In contrast, an idea organiser tool encourages a group to converge quickly on key issues and explore them in depth. Electronic voting tools can uncover patterns of consensus and focus group discussion on pattern of disagreement.[2]

An EMS therefore helps to break down communication and personality barriers; it helps to create a safer and more participative environment for knowledge sharing and idea generation. First-generation EMSs were purely for 'same time, same place' situations with limited functions for ways to publish the outcome of the meeting online. Putting it online enables ongoing additions and comments to the outcome. Today, most EMSs have the capability to export the knowledge created during the group session into other groupware tools or to publish it on a web server for future use. Modern EMSs offer functionality for teams to have not only 'same time, same place' but also 'anytime, anyplace' meetings and idea creation activities.

See also the discussion on the shared experiences described in the context of the tacit-to-tacit knowledge conversion in Chapter 12.

Two sets of technologies for the knowledge conversion lifecycle

In the following we describe the set of knowledge management technologies in terms of two of the four steps of Nonaka and Takeuchi's organisation learning cycle – or, more correctly, organisation learning spiral – which we have described in the first part of this book as the knowledge conversion lifecycle model. This is illustrated in Figure 13.6.

The two steps on the left side of the model have already been described in Chapter 12, where the role of groupware, online learning, etc. were noted as technologies in support of the 'tacit-to-tacit' and 'explicit-to-tacit' phases of the organisational learning spiral.

Table 13.2, reproduced from the first part of this book, summarises many of the aspects and technologies of the knowledge conversion lifecycle.

> The individual technologies [in the table] are not in themselves knowledge management solutions. Instead, when brought to market they are typically embedded in a smaller number of solutions packages, each of which is designed to be adaptable to solve a range

Figure 13.6 Concise knowledge conversion spiral model (right)

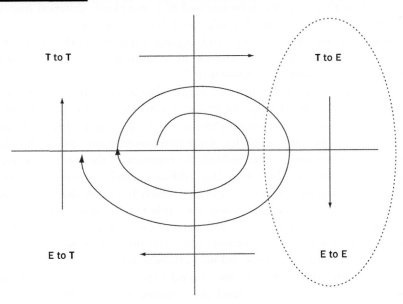

Table 13.2 Knowledge conversion lifecycle

Knowledge conversion	Tacit	Explicit
Tacit	Socialisation	Externalisation
	Sharing	Articulation; capturing
	Meetings and discussions	Write a report
	Chat rooms/synchronous collaboration	Authoring tools
	Informal e-mail	Collaborative filtering
	Conferencing tools	Capture information in course of work
	E-meetings	Answering questions
	Synchronous collaboration (chat)	Annotation
Explicit	Internalisation	Combination
	Learning	Copying; distributing
	Learn from a report	E-mail a report
	Summarisation, navigation	Current awareness – subscription
	Detect and visualise relationships	Content maps for knowledge browsing
	Personalise task and context	Organise or classify content or people
	Visualisation	Advanced text search
	Browsable video/audio presentations	Document categorisation

of business problems. Examples are portals, collaboration software, and distance learning software. Each of these can and does include several different technologies. (Marwick, 2001).

In the following two sections we describe the right-hand side of the relations of this model, emphasising the technologies that support these steps (see Marwick, 2001, in particular).

Tacit to explicit

According to Nonaka (1991) conversion of tacit to explicit knowledge (externalisation) involves forming a shared mental model, then articulating through dialogue. Collaboration systems and other groupware (for example, specialised brainstorming applications) can support this kind of interaction to some extent (Nunamaker et al., 1995).

Online discussion databases are another potential tool to capture tacit knowledge and to apply it to immediate problems. We have already noted that team members may share knowledge in groupware applications. To be most effective for externalisation, the discussion should be such as to allow the formulation and sharing of metaphors and analogies, which probably requires a fairly informal and even freewheeling style. This style is more likely to be found in chat and other real-time interactions within teams. In this regard, see also the section that covers discussion knowledge bases in Chapter 11.

Unlike typical team discussions, newsgroups and similar forums are open to all; they also share some of the same characteristics in that questions can be posed and answered, but differ in that the participants are typically strangers. Nevertheless, it is found that many people who participate in newsgroups are willing to offer advice and assistance, presumably driven by a mixture of motivations including altruism, a wish to be seen as an expert, and the thanks and positive feedback contributed by the people they have helped.

Within organisations, few of the problems experienced on internet newsgroups are found, such as flaming, personal abuse and irrelevant postings. IBM's experience in this regard is described by Foulger (cited by Marwick, 2001). For example a typical exchange in an internal company forum illustrates how open discussion group experts are used to contribute knowledge in response to a request for help. The archive of the forum becomes a repository of useful knowledge. Although the exchange is superficially one of purely explicit knowledge, the expert must first make a judgment as to the nature of the problem and then as to the most likely solution, both of which bring his or her tacit knowledge into play. Once the knowledge is made explicit, persons with similar problems can find the solution by consulting the archive. A quantitative study of the IBM system quoted by Marwick (2001) showed that the great majority of interchanges were of this question-and-answer pattern, and that even though a large fraction of questions were answered by just a few persons, an equal proportion were answered by persons who only answered one or two questions. Thus, the conferencing facility enabled knowledge to be elicited from the broad community as well as from a few experts.

Explicit to explicit

As stated by Marwick:

> There can be little doubt that the phase of knowledge transformation best supported by IT is combination, because it deals with explicit knowledge. We can distinguish the challenges of knowledge management from those of information management by bearing in mind that in knowledge management the conversion of explicit knowledge from and to tacit knowledge is always involved. This leads us to emphasize new factors as challenges that technology may be able to address. (Marwick, 2001)

Capturing knowledge

Explicit knowledge is the result of tacit knowledge being conceptualised and articulated. This needs to be captured in a persistent form such as in an e-mail, a report, a diagram, a presentation, or published as a web page. This captured knowledge can then be distributed or stored for access by the rest of the organisation. Most current documents are produced by technologies such as word processing, which automatically contribute to knowledge capture. These electronic documents are easy to share and distribute via technologies such as the Web, e-mail or document management systems. This makes explicit knowledge available to a wide group of knowledge workers. The goal of most knowledge management projects is to improve knowledge capture – deriving and controlling knowledge from experts and explicit knowledge sources.

A problem that needs to be addressed is to motivate the human contributors to the knowledge capture process. As a motivation, authors of documents can be rewarded for the quality of their contributions. The ideal is to automate this process as far as possible and reduce resistance by employing technology to reduce any barriers to generate shareable electronic documents. Barriers may include, for example, requirements for authors to fill in additional forms. Many approaches may be taken to this effect. We discuss two of these below.

The first promising approach is to automate the use of documents and measure usage patterns and behaviour. In doing so, estimates of usefulness and quality can be calculated per document and authors can be rewarded accordingly. Current technology is still evolving towards this ideal (e.g. see Copeland, 2001).

The other approach to measure quality is to measure the number of times a document is cited in published documentation or is referenced as a hyperlink on the internet. A citation or hyperlink is evidence that the author who cites or links to the document regards the target document as valuable. Analysing the links on web pages indicates the cumulative value judgments on documents. This is most valuable in ranking document value and deriving quality estimates. This technique is used very effectively in information retrieval to rank the documents in the search results list. The Google search engine uses this technique to search the internet. Marwick states:

> Citation analysis of this kind detects quality assessments made in the course of authoring documents. Quality judgments by experts are another way to capture their knowledge. There are, of course, many deployed solutions in which documents undergo a quality review through a refereeing process, often facilitated by a workflow application. (Marwick, 2001)

By far the most common way of capturing knowledge is to write a document. Other forms of media such as digital audio and video recordings are becoming easy to use, and an expert may find it easier and more convenient to speak to a recording camera or microphone than to write. It is also very easy to distribute such captured knowledge on current networks. The disadvantage of these media is that they are more difficult to search than text documents and thus less useful as material in knowledge repositories. Technologies for browsing video material are improving. These are based on summarisation techniques that can extract themes as a gallery of extracted still images – each representing a significant part of the video (e.g. see Marwick, 2001). In addition, a number of video searching systems are now available that use image searching of extracted frames.[3]

Composing a meaningful image query with these systems is usually difficult. Where possible, some systems extract text from the multimedia objects, if possible. Some videos may contain text, but in most cases the challenge is to convert speech to text.

Speech recognition

Recently, there have been major improvements in the accuracy of automated speech recognition. The aim is to have usable speaker-independent recognition with unconstrained vocabulary in the medium term. Accuracy for speech recorded under controlled conditions is already acceptable and this will lead to new ways to capture knowledge (Marwick, 2001).

Search

The most basic task for the handling of explicit knowledge is searching. Most organisations make all their electronic documents available online. The volume of these repositories grows fast and becomes very large. The challenge of online access to documents is thus transformed into the challenge of finding documents relevant for a particular task. The potential relevant information is located in a diverse number of sites such as local intranets, the internet and from commercial online publishers. The use of search technologies has increased hugely in the last decade as most knowledge workers have become more dependent on finding information to complete their tasks.[4]

Taxonomies and document classification

Domain knowledge can often be represented as a 'knowledge map' or 'taxonomy' – a hierarchical organised set of categories.[5] A typical taxonomy includes several different kinds of relations. The value of a taxonomy is twofold:

- it allows a user to navigate to documents of interest without having to search;
- a knowledge map allows documents to be put into context thus helping users to value the applicability of these documents for the specific task.

It requires significant effort and cost to assign categories manually to documents. Recently, automatic document classification has advanced to the point where accuracy of the best algorithms exceeds 85 per cent on good quality data. This is adequate for many applications for specific data types and compares very well with the best manual classification. (Results vary widely when different data types are considered.) The current generation of automatic classification includes algorithms for machine learning that train themselves from sample data (Marwick, 2001).

There are many challenges in implementing solutions that use taxonomies. The first challenge is the design of the taxonomy, which should balance comprehensibility for the users (requiring minimal training) with usefulness by describing the domain in enough detail. A number of strategies exist for building taxonomies including the use of document clustering to derive candidate subcategories (Pohs, Pinder, Dougherty and White, 2001). In the majority of cases, human input is required to ensure that the taxonomy reflects the application domain needs.

Taxonomies have become very popular as a way in which to build a domain model to assist users to navigate and search. It seems to be a trend that user groups of various sizes each have their own taxonomy. This is quite natural, as users want to see information displayed in terms of a domain model that represents their own priorities and terminology. Marwick states:

> This trend is likely to lead to a proliferation of taxonomies in knowledge management applications. It follows that there will be an increasing focus on the need to map from one taxonomy to another so as to bridge between the schemas used by different groups within an organization. (Marwick, 2001)

Portals and metadata

Portal technology provides convenient metadata about documents in a particular domain (see Chapter 16 for more detail).

Summarisation

A document summary is a kind of metadata that reflects a short view of the whole document and enables users to quickly sift out documents relevant to a particular task. Automatic generation of summaries is being actively researched (see Chapter 14 for more detail).

We cover this area of searching technologies in more detail in Chapters 14 and 15.

Summary

The knowledge management technologies to support knowledge sharing and transfer were addressed. The different knowledge management technologies were positioned in terms of the two dimensions of tasks to be performed in relation to the professionals performing them. In the discussion of collaboration and knowledge management, groupware technologies were covered. Electronic meetings were included as a groupware tool for reflective learning and information sharing. A discussion of the technologies for the conversion of 'tacit to explicit' and 'explicit to explicit' knowledge were also addressed.

In the next chapter we briefly cover the aspect of searching and information retrieval.

Notes

1. See more detail in our coverage of computer supported cooperative work and groupware later in this chapter.
2. There are many tools related to this. Nunamaker et al. (1995) provide a list of these.
3. See for example Retrievalware (www.excalibur.com).
4. See Chapter 14, which covers searching and indexing.
5. See coverage of taxonomy in the section 'Taxonomy and ontology' in Chapter 11.

14

Advanced search, indexing and retrieval

...you shall seek all day ere you find them; and, when you have found them, they are not worth the search. (William Shakespeare)

Introduction

In this chapter we make brief remarks about searching, indexing and retrieval that are relevant to knowledge management. This is an important topic for knowledge management but also a discipline in its own right, having been studied for decades (e.g. see Botha, 1991, 1992, 1995; Salton, 1989; Baeza-Yates and Ribeiro-Neto, 1999). Recently some interest is being shown in the overlap between the information retrieval discipline, library science and knowledge management.[1]

In this chapter we discuss the phenomenon of information overload followed by remarks about information retrieval in relation to knowledge management. We also cover the important aspects of information and knowledge filtering as well as linking.

Most information is currently produced online. Examples are correspondence, e-mail, travel reports, customer contacts, administrative manuals, contracts, plans, etc. The text retrieval solutions now available can enable users to avoid recreating information or making decisions without the relevant information created by unseen collaborators. The information overload discussed in the following section makes it inconceivable for most organisations to search their document bases manually. Therefore, one has to consider the electronic document in all its formats and media as the key unit for search and retrieval.

Traditional information retrieval

Research on and commercialisation of information retrieval, have produced quite sophisticated retrieval techniques for a substantial period. However, these systems continue to be limited by the semantics for retrieval. They typically process every word in a document, deleting common words (stop words), reducing words to the root form (stemming), and creating a rich-text index, which also includes the structured data related to the document. The latter includes information elements such as the title, author, abstract, creation date and other bibliographic information of the document. Sophisticated retrieval techniques have been added that measure word occurrences to make the (statistical) meaning of search terms more specific. These techniques are complemented by synonym dictionaries and thesauri that provide words with meaning. More advanced approaches utilise special concepts consisting of weighted values of search terms (e.g. see Botha, 1995; Coleman and Khanna, 1995).

Text databases are traditionally indexed on the basis of keywords and characteristics such as proximity and frequency of occurrence in the text. Typical implementations utilise inverted file indexing representation techniques. Keyword occurrence and (statistical) positioning in documents are relatively shallow aspects of knowledge. Search queries of this nature are not sophisticated enough to extract knowledge in any significant way. Further, this approach is not applicable for non-text documents. Various techniques have been proposed to address this problem. For more effective document representation than the inverted file techniques just discussed, there are three principal techniques: fuzzy search, dictionary augmentation and multi-dimensional spaces. These techniques have been employed with varying degrees of success, but will not be further discussed here.[2] The phenomenon of information overload is however a major challenge for search and information retrieval as well as for knowledge management. This is discussed in the next section.

Information overload

Modern organisations are experiencing a huge overload of information (the so-called 'information explosion'). This in itself motivates the adoption of new technology to assist in the comprehension of explicit knowledge. To make informed decisions, knowledge workers face not only the challenge of integrating the large amounts of available information, but also that of locating the pertinent information from the many sources and different locations. Information overload occurs when the quality of decisions is reduced because the decision maker spends time reviewing redundant information instead of making decisions.

Daconta, Obrst and Smith (2003) have calculated the document storage capacity on a typical PC (using a 60–80 GB drive, plain-text, and 3,500 characters per page) to be around 17–22 million pages of information. It is clear from these figures that we are only actively managing a small fraction of the total information we produce.

The World Wide Web has dramatically changed the availability of electronically accessible information. Daconta et al. (2003) contend that the Web currently contains more than 3 billion static documents, which are accessed by over 500 million users internationally. Other authors judge the number of pages on the Web as double this, at more than 6 billion pages (see www.liquidinformation.org) because the well-known Google search engine indexes more than 6 billion pages.[3] Internet search engines have barely even catalogued one-sixth of the total information available and internet traffic is doubling every 100 days according to *Interactive Week*. Wurman (referenced in www.liquidinformation.com), puts it aptly: 'everyone spoke of an information overload, but what there was in fact was a non-information overload'.

Growth in global volume of knowledge

The volume of written information/knowledge began to increase more obviously from 1447 when Johann Gutenberg invented the printing press. After about 300 years – by about 1750 – the global volume of information/knowledge had doubled. It doubled again by about 1900 and redoubled by 1950. At present, the volume of information/knowledge is estimated to be doubling every five years. Provided that this growth is sustained, some believe that by 2020 information/knowledge may even be doubling every 72 days (Dutta and De Meyer, 2001). The staggering growth of information/knowledge projected by such estimates is an important issue for knowledge management.

One should note that in addition to the familiar text-based information this volume will also consist of information and knowledge, produced and kept in media such as sound, images, animation, film and virtual reality simulation. This fast growth in the volume of available knowledge is illustrated in Figure 14.1, while Figure 14.2 illustrates estimates of the real (enormous) values that this information overload represents.[4]

Figure 14.1 Growth in global volume of knowledge

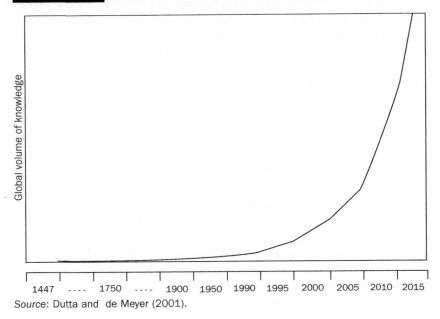

Source: Dutta and de Meyer (2001).

Figure 14.2 Examples of the values in the information overload

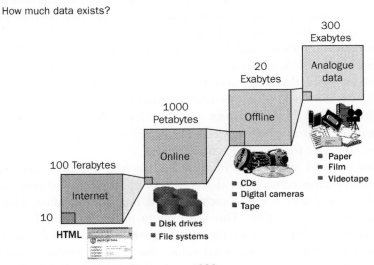

Source: IBM Almaden Research Center June, 1999.

The challenge for information retrieval

At the same time, this enormous amount of information has made it increasingly difficult to find, access, present and maintain relevant information. This is because information content is presented primarily in natural language textual format. Thus, a wide gap has emerged between the information available for tools aimed at addressing these problems and the information maintained in human-readable form.

Various approaches can be taken to assist technically in handling the information overload. Redundant information and repetition can be reduced by eliminating duplicate and similar documents. Messages can be filtered and prioritised, or compound views can ease sifting through and comprehending the retrieved information. Using visualisation techniques is an alternative and powerful approach to help the user understand the available information better.

This information explosion is challenging the ability of all companies to make constant adjustments. This may result in information chaos. It forces companies to realise the importance of controlling the information by means such as filtering, structuring, categorising and validation of the information sources. This affects the decision-making process within companies with regard to selecting the right information to perform actions, procedures, decision support, etc.

Search, indexing and retrieval

Knowledge management requires a complex suite of tools to capture the information, store it and keep access widely available. This is particularly true for search and retrieval of unstructured, document-based information/knowledge. At a minimum, the requirements will include hypertext mark-up language (HTML) publishing tools for producing web-type documents and/or preferably the ability to at least distribute knowledge in XML format and with XML extensions to incorporate taxonomies and even an ontology.

Other requirements include a relational database (for storing these documents in XML-based format), text search-and-retrieval engines, and some approach to managing meta-knowledge that describes and facilitates access to the available information/knowledge.

Another requirement for search and retrieval in knowledge management is the development of an online thesaurus or at least more semantic assistance (see Chapter 11):

Today intranets and the Internet are ubiquitous, and we are rapidly approaching the situation where all the written information needed by a person to do his or her job is available on-line. However, that is not to say that it can be used effectively with the tools currently available. (Marwick, 2001)

There is, however, little standardisation in terms of search user interfaces, different search language conventions and different ways to present the result lists. Portal technology (as described in Chapter 16) is an approach to reduce the complexity of the knowledge worker's task. The portal technology maintains its own metadata about the information available to the knowledge worker. Currently this metadata is quite simple, being a list of sources and a search index built from the content of those sources. This feature greatly improves productivity because the user does not have to visit all those sources for relevant information. Most portal systems use a single index. This requires that the documents in those sources have to be indexed via so-called 'spidering' or 'crawling'. Distributed indexes or federated indexes have failed to become popular but recent advances may change that state of affairs.[5]

In traditional information retrieval, the index of the search engine contains a list of the words that occur in the indexed documents. This is augmented by an inverted file data structure, which allows the documents in which those words occur to be efficiently retrieved at search time.[6] Researchers use a query language that contains words they think will be contained in the documents. Users face the problem that different words are used in different documents to express similar meaning. Therefore not all the documents that refer to a particular concept are retrieved. Different approaches to counter this problem when high recall is expected have been developed over a number of decades. Among these is a controlled vocabulary, which is effective when the researchers are trained users such as librarians. For the typical knowledge worker, however, the evidence is strong that searching with natural language gives better results than using a controlled vocabulary (e.g. see Botha, 1992).

The most common problem in document searching is that a query retrieves many irrelevant documents that do not address the user's needs. This is known as the problem of search precision (which is a measure of retrieval accuracy). With the tremendous growth in available information, precision becomes highly important. Recent research, however, indicates that the accuracy of natural language search engines has reached a plateau in recent years (Marwick, 2001).

The two areas that promise to improve the status quo are: 'increased knowledge of the user and of the context of his or her information need, and improved knowledge of the domain being searched' (Marwick, 2001 and Botha, 1992). We realise that the user's query contains only information about the user's needs that is known to the system. Research regarding queries submitted on the Web has found that the most common query consists of two words, with an average query length of 2.3 words (Spink, Wolfram, Jansen and Saracevic, 2001). This is obviously very little information about the user's context and needs. Advanced searching techniques are thus required to gather improved information about the context of the search. This is a challenging research area, which is aimed at building advanced search engines that can exploit such contextual knowledge along with the submitted query.

Much more advanced is the area of gathering and using more information about the domain in which the search is conducted. Limited progress has however been realised. For a number of decades the most prominent technology to tackle this challenge has been to employ a thesaurus in the search process. A thesaurus is a language assist tool for searching. In a way it is a kind of simple domain model (i.e. a more advanced taxonomy). The thesaurus is utilised by expanding the query with synonyms and other relations from the thesaurus. This approach is known to improve the recall in a text search. The expansion is effective provided the domain is well-defined with low ambiguity of words and when the validity of term relationships is less important. In broad domain searching, precision may be improved by using thesauri as well as more advanced structures such as an ontology. Results in this area have however been mixed and research is ongoing.[7]

Woods et al. (2000) have used a different approach to encode the domain knowledge. They used a semantic network that integrated syntactic, semantic and morphological relationships. Mack, Ravin and Byrd (2001) also point to prompted query refinement, relevance feedback and sophisticated ranking techniques as additional techniques in this regard.

Of high importance for knowledge management are the new developments that incorporate semantic information, XML and ontologies as we describe next.

Search and retrieval using web services and ontologies[8]

We have covered aspects of web services and semantic considerations in Chapter 11. The most promising architecture for building systems for knowledge management in the medium term is likely to be based on web services and will incorporate semantically-rich environments for search and retrieval including ontologies.

Because data is stored in an easily accessible (web services) format and is associated with ontologies and taxonomies, retrieval of information/knowledge is more powerful and easier than not having the advantages that result from employing more semantically-rich support tools. Because all information in such an environment – with web services and the semantic web – is linked with an ontology and taxonomy, searches will provide results that otherwise would be unseen.

In the specific context of web services, the semantic web offers opportunities for providing important functionality within the search and retrieval process, as described below:

- *Discovery of knowledge via taxonomies*: Because each web service can be classified in various taxonomies, taxonomic searches can be done across the web services of an organisation. A good example would be, 'I'm looking for all web services classified in the corporate taxonomy as related to "coal mining"' (Daconta et al., 2003).

- *Web service-based data searches*: Using standard SOAP interfaces, any application can query web services in the enterprise.

- *Search by association*: Because the data is mapped into an ontology, semantic searches can be made across the entire knowledge base. We have traditionally left associations out of the search equation. This is a powerful extension to previous approaches and a direct knowledge management benefit of the semantic web. A good example of such a search would be, 'I would like to perform a query on all relatives of my father, their closest friends, and their closest friends' friends'. In an electronic commerce application, associations offer additional buying opportunities to customers. For example, if a potential customer searches for a particular machine or commodity, once that product's representation is found in the ontology, its associations can be selectively displayed as related equipment, components and services.

- *Pattern-based searches*: Because all data can be semantically linked by relationships in the ontology, semantic searches can dynamically find patterns that would not have been seen by old data-mining techniques that did not directly utilise meaning. An example of such a search would be, 'Of all grocery stores listed in our corporate ontology, which stores have had revenue growth combined with an increased demand for orange juice?' (see also Chapter 17).

- *Manual and agent-based searches*: Although all of the searches can be manual, software agents can be equipped with rules to continually search the knowledge base and provide up-to-the-second results and alerts. An example of such an agent rule-based query would be, 'Alert me via SMS/e-mail whenever a new document is registered discussing a new computer virus'.

- *Rule-based orchestration queries*: Because web services can be combined to provide modular functionality, rules can be used in order to combine various searches from different web services to perform complicated tasks. An example of such a query would be, 'Find me the lead engineer of the top-performing project in the company. Based on his favourite vacation spot from his response in the human resources survey, book him two tickets to that location next week, grant him vacation time, and cancel all of his work-related appointments.'

- *Automated inference support*: Because the corporate ontology explicitly represents concepts and their relationships in a logical and machine-interpretable form, automated inference over the ontology and its knowledge bases becomes possible. Given a specific query, an ontology-based inference engine can perform deduction and other forms of automated reasoning to generate the possible implications of the query, thus returning much more meaningful results. In addition, of course, the inference engine may discover inconsistencies or even contradictions in the ontology or knowledge bases. As the corporate ontology and the knowledge base spans are elaborated over time, more complicated automated reasoning can be performed (for example, induction of new knowledge based on old knowledge, and the incorporation of probabilistic techniques). This automated inference itself can be considered a web service or set of web services, and can be utilised by software agents or human users.

Information and knowledge filtering

Because of the information overload, a number of authors have alluded to the importance of being able to determine which items to accept and retain, and which to ignore and reject (e.g. see Godbout, 1999). In knowledge management this selection can be defined as a filtering process, which the knowledge worker does or which is potentially performed automatically by a software agent. These authors perceive these activities as potentially offering the highest return on investment in knowledge management, but also as being one of the most challenging to realise. There are a number of knowledge-specific issues to resolve before this ideal can be fully automated. As decision makers, knowledge workers are not only overwhelmed with information, but they are also frequently confronted with conflicting information. They also have to judge the value of the information on which decisions should be based.

Information and knowledge linking

A major difference between a document base and a knowledge base lies in the linking of the information objects (such as documents and abstracts) to related information. This is achieved very effectively via hypertext linking. The approach of utilising hypertext ensures that the linear appearance of documents is transformed into a multidimensional appearance. Hypertext linking also enables the browser software to handle multimedia documents effectively. The problem with this approach, however, is that the hypertext links have to be assigned manually by the authors of the documents.

New research into so-called 'liquid information' utilising 'hyperwords' has a huge potential for a major enhancement to the handling and searching of documents.[9]

Summary

Organisations experience a huge overload of information. In addition to the familiar text-based information, the volume of information also consists of information produced and kept in media such as sound, images, animation, film and virtual reality simulation. Organisations are forced to realise the importance of using various information retrieval techniques and technologies and to manage the information by means of filtering, structuring, categorisation and validation.

In the next chapter we focus on the applications identified by the knowledge management technology framework.

Notes

1. See, for example, Koenig (2005) where the author has surveyed the opportunity offered by knowledge management for library science.
2. For more information on these themes, the reader is referred to references such as Salton (1989) and Baeza-Yates and Ribeiro-Neto (1999).
3. Peter Large (referenced in *www.liquidinformation.org*) quotes the following staggering figures: 'More information has been produced in the last 30 years than in the previous 5,000. About 1,000 books are published internationally every day, and the total of all printed knowledge doubles every eight years.'
4. Figures and examples sourced from Dutta and De Meyer (2001) and various IBM publications.
5. See, for example, web references covering the peer-to-peer applications such as 'Gnutella' and the collaboration application 'Groove'.
6. See detail discussed in Botha (1992, 1995) and Baeza-Yates and Ribeiro-Neto (1999).
7. See, for example, Baeza-Yates and Ribeiro-Neto (1999), who report some positive results.
8. Sourced from Daconta et al. (2003).
9. See in this regard the two websites *www.liquidinformation.org* and *www.hyperwords.net*.

Knowledge management technology framework applications

Computers can figure out all kinds of problems, except the things in this world that just don't add up. (J. Magary)

Introduction

The knowledge management technology framework (KMTF) listed two key knowledge management applications, namely, 'knowledge portals' and 'knowledge discovery' which we cover in the following two chapters. In this chapter we briefly introduce a number of other knowledge management applications we deemed important enough to be in the scope of this book.

In the next section we make remarks about intelligent agents as knowledge management technologies. In the sections thereafter we mention knowledge mapping, and discuss expertise mapping and locating. In the last section we make brief remarks about analysis and decision making in relation to knowledge management.

Intelligent agents and knowledge management

We discussed the phenomenon of information overload in Chapter 15. While the Web allows various kinds of knowledge to be created and disseminated across time and space barriers, it does not support the processes of using and updating the knowledge in a timely manner. In this regard, intelligent agents have been suggested (e.g. see Baek et al., 1999) as a promising solution for assisting and facilitating these processes. Many definitions[1] have been proposed for the concept of an intelligent agent. For example, 'anything that can be viewed as perceiving its environment through sensors and effects', and the artificial intelligence approach, 'intelligent agents continuously perform three functions: perception of dynamic conditions in the environment; action to affect conditions in the environment; and reasoning to interpret perceptions, solve problems, draw inferences, and determine actions'.

We prefer the definitions of a *software agent* and an *intelligent software agent*, as described by Firestone (2003), which is a culmination of many previous attempts and fits into our approach for knowledge management.

A software agent is a software object that acts on behalf of another software object (its client) and has the following behaviour:

- is autonomous;
- interacts with other agents;
- is proactive; meaning it influences its environment;
- is reactive; meaning it is influenced by its environment.

An intelligent software agent is a software agent that:

- has an in-memory knowledge base that includes cognition, evaluations and goals;
- is rational in the sense that it makes decisions;
- acts to attain its goal;
- learns.

Therefore, an intelligent agent that is delegated a task by a user, should determine precisely what its goal is, evaluate how the goal can be reached in an effective way, and perform the required actions that are goal-oriented and flexible. An intelligent software agent should also be capable of learning from past experiences and responding to unforeseen situations with its reasoning strategies of being adaptive, self-starting and time-sensitive (temporal). It should be reactive to its current environment and act independently to reach its goal.

Typical intelligent software agents can be employed as two major applications of intelligent software agent technology, namely, personal assistants and communication agents (Baek, Liebowitz, Prasad and Granger, 1999).

Personal assistants focus on the interaction between a user and the computer. They typically perform repetitive and burdensome tasks on behalf of the knowledge worker. For example, automatic disk backup, information filtering, automated information retrieval, mail management and meeting scheduling. What makes intelligent agents unique is two-fold: first, they use machine learning techniques to adapt to user habits and preferences; and, second, they use automated reasoning so they can decide when to help the user, what to help the user with, and how to help the user.

Communication/collaboration agents focus more on the interaction among computing agents, specifically geographically distributed agents.[2] An example would be one agent asking another agent for information instead of attempting to find the information on its own.

With regard to knowledge management, the typical tools utilised on the corporate knowledge bases and the Web have been designed for efficiency and knowledge worker productivity. Tools such as groupware are used for collaboration and knowledge sharing among teams of people inside and outside an organisation.

Agents can support knowledge workers to augment searching tools because these tools are unable to provide the user with time-sensitive knowledge. Knowledge workers, who perform knowledge-searching tasks, need to be aware of changes in the organisation's knowledge. This offers a huge opportunity for intelligent agents to assist in solving these problems. The intelligent agents perform repetitive and mundane tasks to enhance knowledge management on behalf of knowledge workers. Baek et al. (1999) have published a table of the assistance given by different intelligent agents for knowledge management tasks and processes.

Knowledge mapping

Mapping the available knowledge in the organisation for knowledge workers to locate and access forms an important part of the deployment and operation of a knowledge management programme. We have discussed this topic in part with our discussion on the types of knowledge bases, specifically the corporate yellow pages knowledge base in Chapter 11. References to knowledge mapping include: O'Dell, Grayson and Essaides (1998), who refer to 'pointer systems'; Davenport and Prusak (1998); Daconta, Obrst and Smith (2003), who describe topic maps in detail; Firestone (2003); and Maybury (2003). We regard details about this topic, however, as out of scope for our focus.

Expertise mapping and locating[3]

Suppose one's goal is not to find someone with common interests but to get advice from an expert who is willing to share his or her knowledge. Expertise location systems have the goal of suggesting the names of persons who have knowledge in a particular area. In their simplest form, such systems are search engines for individuals, but they are only as good as the evidence that they use to infer expertise. Marwick (2001) provides some possible sources of such evidence, as discussed below.

Sources of evidence for an expertise location system

Sources of evidence include:

- a profile or form filled in by a user;
- an existing company database, for example, one held by the human resources department;
- name-document associations;
- questions answered.

The problem with using an explicit profile is that persons may not be motivated to keep it up to date, as they perceive it as just another form to complete. Thus it is preferable to gather information automatically, if possible, from existing sources. For example, a person's resumé or a list of the project teams that he or she has worked on may exist in a company database. Another automatic approach is to infer expertise from the contents of documents with which a person's name is associated. For example, authorship (creation or editing) of a document presumably indicates some familiarity with the subjects it discusses, whereas an activity such as reading indicates some interest in the subject matter.

Two approaches to using document evidence for expertise location suggest themselves: either the documents can be classified according to some schema, thus classifying their authors; or when a user submits a query to the expertise location system, it searches the documents, transforms the query to a list of authors (suitably weighted), and returns the list as the result of the expertise search.

The current state of the art is to use the first three sources of evidence listed above, namely, explicit profiles, evidence mined from existing databases and evidence inferred from association of persons and documents. For example, the Lotus Discovery Server product (Pohs, Pinder, Dougherty and White, 2001) contains a facility whereby an individual's expertise is determined using these techniques, while it analyses the e-mail a person writes, to form a profile of his or her expertise. Given the properties of online discussions, discussed in Chapter 11, it is reasonable to suppose that a fourth source of evidence could be the content of the questions answered by a person in such a system, with the added advantage that such a person is already willing to be helpful.

A typical 'expert locator' should have the following characteristics:

- It allows users to search through a set of biographies for an expert on a specific knowledge domain.

- Its objective is locating people not documents.

- It contains information about human experts such as educational background, jobs held, current projects and responsibilities, skills, languages spoken, or proficiency.

- An expert locator includes a keyword-based guide to the domains of expertise in the company. For example, locating an expert on the topic of 'IT governance', should be straightforward by means of searching using that keyword-based phrase or by doing a taxonomy-based search.

Technology needed for expert locators is relatively straightforward: it requires a web browser and server software, database management system (DBMS) and search engine. The search engine should be supported by a thesaurus or ontology because expertise search may not match directly. The main difficulties encountered for companies to implement expert locators are non-technical. The systems require a considerable time commitment on the part of the expert (or some intermediary) to enter and update biographies into the database. Motivating experts to comply with this may be difficult.

Analysis and decision making

As stated before, we regard applications such as business intelligence and data warehousing as pure IT applications. These technologies play an important supportive role for knowledge management, with certain techniques shared between business intelligence and knowledge management. Codey, Kreulen, Krishna and Spangler (2002) argue that business intelligence and knowledge management may eventually be merged into a new discipline that handles data, unstructured information, and knowledge. They state:

> We call this blended technology BIKM ... The desire to extend the capabilities of business intelligence applications to include textual information has existed for quite some time. The major inhibitors have included the separation of the data on different data management systems, typically across different organizations, and the immaturity of automated text analysis techniques for deriving business value from large amounts of text. The current focus on information integration in many enterprises is rapidly diminishing the first inhibitor, and advances in machine learning, information retrieval, and statistical natural language processing are eroding the second. (Codey et al., 2002)

In their article, Codey et al. (2002) describe their contribution in this regard. For example, their 'eClassifier' is a comprehensive text analysis tool that provides a framework for integrating advanced text analytics.[4]

Summary

Before discussing the two key knowledge management applications of 'knowledge portals' and 'knowledge discovery' in Chapters 16 and 17, we briefly introduced a number of other important knowledge management applications. These include intelligent agents, knowledge mapping, expertise mapping and locating, as well as analysis and decision making.

Notes

1. See, for example, Firestone's (2003) list and discussion of intelligent agents as well as the table in Baek et al. (1999).
2. They communicate in a universal language to other agents enabling platform and implementation independence.
3. See also related description in Chapter 12 about 'tacit to tacit'.
4. See more related discussion in Chapter 17.

16

Knowledge portals

I may not know the answer to your question. But, I can find someone in five minutes who does! (Henry Ford)

Introducing the knowledge management technology framework (KMTF) user interface and integration platform

In this chapter we consider the key knowledge management application of knowledge portals. This application combines many of the previously discussed issues into a solution for knowledge management. We recognise the current publicity and popularity surrounding 'portal' technology. From the functional standpoint, portals are defined as an access point to the 'corporate' memory (the integrated interface) and represent the possibility of an integrated knowledge management 'total' solution. A knowledge portal therefore fulfils a key role in knowledge management. It is this interpretation of portals that is presented throughout this chapter.

Recently, the concept of portals – information portals, knowledge portals, as well as enterprise information portals – has become very popular. The many interpretations that result from a plethora of vendor offerings could cause confusion about this concept. It has therefore become desirable to clearly define and describe the concept and to position it for our purpose. This is the topic of the next section.

Knowledge portal concepts

A major function of knowledge management is to provide users with an interface that is comfortable and intuitive, yet powerful. Given the current pervasiveness of the internet, it is not surprising that many recent knowledge management developments have chosen the web browser to be the user interface, with access to information via a centralised access point, often known as an enterprise information portal (EIP). There are a variety of EIP implementations available, but most include the following common elements:

- personalisation, allowing users to customise their EIP workspace by means of tools such as software agents and filters;
- a unified search and retrieval system for text (and possibly multimedia objects), using intuitive techniques such as more natural language interfaces;
- collaboration, providing messaging between users, and collecting data on the relevance and usefulness of information presented, which can then be fed back to improve the EIP;
- Access to applications, in most cases eliminating the need for installing and maintaining them on individual workstations.

An information portal that is specifically utilised by knowledge workers is called a 'knowledge portal' (Mack, Ravin and Byrd, 2001). Knowledge portals are rapidly evolving into broad-based platforms for supporting a wide range of knowledge worker tasks. Mack et al. (2001) refer to these broad-based platforms as the 'knowledge workplace'. Knowledge portals serve tasks performed by knowledge workers. Knowledge workers typically gather information relevant to a task, search it, organise it, analyse it, synthesise solutions with respect to specific task goals, and then share and distribute what has been learned with other knowledge workers (Mack et al., 2001). Knowledge portals are specifically designed to assist with these tasks.

A portal is much more than a launch pad. It supports integrated access to information, applications and people, in context. One can identify at least the following functions of a full-function knowledge portal:

- *personalisation*: customising the user's interface based on their preferences;
- *access and advanced search*: delivering information in context regardless of type/media, location, platform, including multi-repository support;
- *categorisation*: cataloguing information assets and understanding relationships via metadata; employing a metadata dictionary and taxonomy;

- *collaboration*: the ability to connect users of a similar interest and assist them to work together;
- *application integration*: integrating information with processes;
- *security and directory management*: protecting assets and simplifying the user's experience with all the underlying technology;
- *development tools*: visual components, navigation and mapping;

The knowledge portal therefore provides a secure, single point of access to diverse information, business processes and expertise regardless of location or structure. This is done in the context of a user's needs and responsibilities while leveraging all forms of information, applications and expertise.

Knowledge portal technology provides convenient metadata about documents in its domain. We have already discussed two examples of such metadata: search indexes and a knowledge map or taxonomy. One of the keys to a successful knowledge portal is the establishment of a taxonomy that applies a structure, typically hierarchical, to the available information. Simple taxonomies can be seen on public portals such as Yahoo!, but a knowledge portal is usually considerably more complex, as it must handle information in diverse formats from a number of different sources. It is envisaged that increasing use of natural language processing in portals will generate new kinds of metadata (Marwick, 2001). The metadata can be automatically generated as part of the indexing service of the portal. The value of the metadata lies in encapsulating information about the document. This can then be used to build selective views of the document space; for example, listing documents in a required category.

In Figure 16.1 we illustrate the conceptual view of a typical knowledge portal. The knowledge portal offers a single point of access to a wide diversity of user devices – such as PCs and intelligent handheld devices. The users experience a secure and personalised user interface based on interface rules, profiles and roles. The presentation typically combines the content of a variety of information sources from rich content management environments in a standardised format. Personalised access is given to different applications in an integrated manner, and sophisticated collaboration is enabled with other knowledge workers.

In Table 16.1 we compare the functionality of knowledge retrieval as described in Chapter 14 with the enhanced characteristics of a knowledge portal. This clearly illustrates the richness of knowledge portals and why we argue that they play such a key role for knowledge management.

Figure 16.1 Conceptual knowledge portal

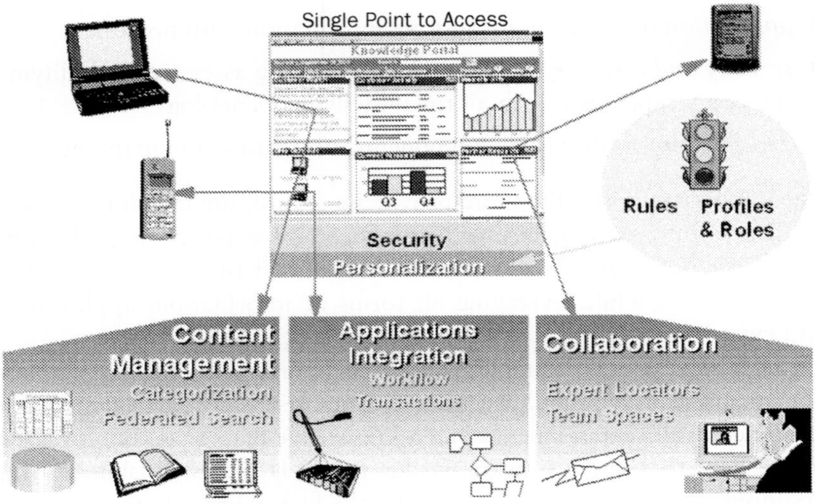

Single Point to Access

Rules Profiles & Roles

Security
Personalization

Content Management
Categorization
Federated Search

Applications Integration
Workflow
Transactions

Collaboration
Expert Locators
Team Spaces

Table 16.1 Comparison of knowledge retrieval and a knowledge portal

Knowledge retrieval	Knowledge portal
Search	Browsing, organising, suggesting, updating
User preferences	Personalisation
Interface organises to fit content	Content may be organised to fit interface
Internal content	Internal and external content
Unstructured data	Unstructured and structured data
Document-centric and impersonal	Human element, sense of community
Explicit profiling	Explicit and implicit profiling

Knowledge portal architecture

A reliable, secure, scalable and manageable knowledge portal product needs a number of architectural components. The components of a particular portal may be highly visible functions, such as personalisation, or may be totally hidden from users, such as the metadata dictionaries. Architecturally, as suggested in Figure 16.1, knowledge portals have several required services:

- a personalisation engine to personalise the look-and-feel as well as the available functionality for the particular knowledge worker;
- a search engine, including crawlers for indexing data repositories;
- collaboration functionality to let the knowledge worker collaborate with other knowledge workers – asynchronously, such as utilising e-mail, or synchronously, such as utilising instant messaging;
- application integration middleware or similar connectivity technology and networking to integrate different 'back-end' applications and combine results and presentation in a standardised format;
- a powerful relational database.

Presently, an application server may still be optional, but it is a requirement for future-generation knowledge portal technologies. A taxonomy engine is also optional today, but manually tagging documents to populate the taxonomy is a very people-intensive and error-prone exercise. Automatic taxonomy creation, document and concept classification, as well as semantic analytic taxonomy engines are still far from perfect. However, we expect automatic taxonomy engines to continue to be demanded by knowledge portal users and therefore to be included in future enterprise knowledge portal functionality when they have sufficiently matured.

In Figure 16.2 we illustrate and summarise a typical system configuration of a knowledge portal.

A number of companies are experimenting with technologies for knowledge portals and some knowledge portals are currently actively utilised by knowledge workers. The sophistication of these knowledge portals is constantly being enhanced.[1]

Summary

Knowledge portals provide most of the robust technology functions required for knowledge management. These portals serve as the common knowledge workplace for knowledge workers, and thus as the knowledge management user interface and integration platform of our knowledge management technology framework. The knowledge portal

Figure 16.2 Typical knowledge portal system configuration

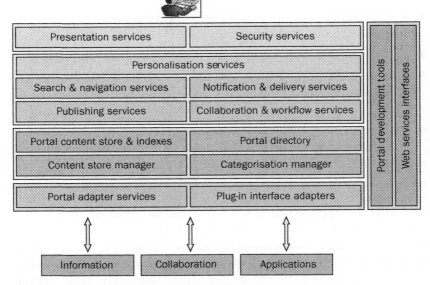

Derived from many sources such as Han (2003).

therefore combines access to the many enablers of knowledge listed in Figure 10.5, and addresses much of the knowledge management function discussed previously.

In the next chapter we cover the key knowledge management application of 'knowledge discovery'.

Note

1. See a list of candidates of commercial offerings in the survey of Firestone (2003).

17

Knowledge discovery

Ours is the age which is proud of machines that think, and suspicious of men who try to. (H. Jones)

Introduction

In this chapter we consider knowledge discovery as the other important application relevant to knowledge management alongside knowledge portals. We briefly refer to a number of technologies and techniques for performing knowledge discovery, focusing mainly on text mining.

Knowledge discovery attempts to identify and interpret patterns in information that are potentially important in performing a particular task. The patterns are defined relative to the task. Depending on the task, knowledge discovery can be partially or fully automated. Because of having to contend increasingly with information, the need for more automated knowledge discovery is becoming acute. It is becoming more feasible to contend with the huge volumes of information because of the ongoing increase in computing power at relatively affordable costs, and because of the availability of more scalable algorithms to handle huge data sets. Although the term 'discovery' means the act of finding something that already exists, this does not imply that it is necessarily a quick or easy process.

Organising information such as business rules and statistical summaries is an important interim step in the process of collecting and analysing it, so that the analysed information can be used as knowledge (tacit or explicit). With respect to generating or discovering explicit knowledge, determination of the information's context is as important as simply organising it. As previously described, having knowledge structures in the form of an ontology is an important part of knowledge discovery. Ontologies define the relationships among various bits of information in a collection. These relationships add context to the information for a particular task.

Becker (1999) utilises the diagram in Figure 17.1 to illustrate the dilemma of the knowledge worker in discovering knowledge. On the left-hand side is the ever-increasing information growth (e.g. as on the Web) and on the right-hand side the desired relevant information. Internet search engines can serve as the automated filters that return a few thousand hits to a query among the millions of available documents. The knowledge worker's role, however, is still a manual task of sifting out those relevant answers that can be confidently used for the decision-making process.

The goal of knowledge discovery technologies is to use knowledge about the user and the user's goals to move the automated filtering line in the diagram toward the right. At the same time, better data visualisation techniques are being developed that allow the user to see and work with hundreds or thousands of documents simultaneously; for example, displaying documents found as a scatter diagram or citation diagram.

Figure 17.1 Information filtering and knowledge discovery

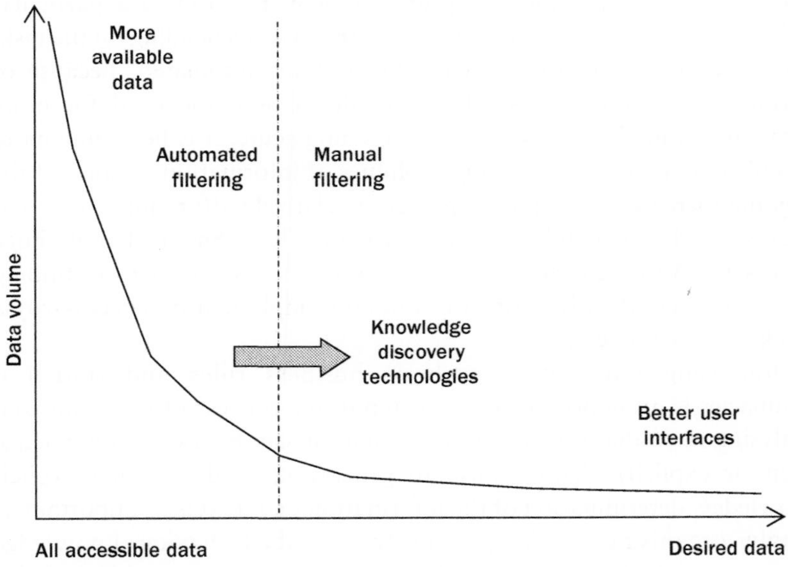

Source: Becker (1999).

Positioning knowledge discovery techniques and technologies

Individuals do not always know what they do not know, and consequently follow different strategies to obtain hitherto unknown knowledge. Sometimes, just talking to an expert is the best way to learn and thus discover knowledge. However, knowledge discovery is also achieved when the knowledge worker is supported by knowledge discovery technologies. Knowledge discovery is a way to find access to all the relevant information in a corporate environment without prior knowledge of its existence.

We can classify the different knowledge discovery techniques and technologies into three major areas in terms of explicit knowledge media:

- *Data mining in structured data*: In this area, structured information databases are analysed in the hope of discovering hidden patterns in data records that may not have been obvious in the general usage of these databases. This area of knowledge discovery is usually applied to information in data warehouses. We restrict ourselves to making some brief remarks about it in relation to knowledge management. This area is discussed in the section on data mining.

- *Text mining*: This area is important for knowledge management because of the large percentage of explicit textual knowledge in the typical organisation. We cover techniques related to this area in the section on document and text mining.

- *Data mining in multimedia*: Although most knowledge discovery is being done on structured data and text, some organisations possess large multimedia assets such as image, audio and video. It is an open question whether these assets can be made more valuable by utilising knowledge discovery techniques.

A typical knowledge discovery server should perform the following main functions:[11]

- it should automatically find, organise and map disparate content on behalf of the knowledge worker;

- it should build a network to locate subject matter experts;

- it should add value to content by maintaining its context and by incorporating the opinions and judgments of individuals.

Data mining

As stated in the introduction, we make brief remarks on this topic as we regard it as part of the business intelligence and data warehouse application set as mentioned in Chapter 15.

Over a number of years, advanced data-mining algorithms, tools and systems have been developed and are actively in production in many industries. Figure 17.2 categorises the different data-mining algorithms that are typically utilised. Pattern recognition algorithms are used to find patterns in information databases. Some of these algorithms use statistical methods and others use symbolic methods. Selecting the best algorithm for any application of data mining depends on the information format and application goals.

Statistical methods measure important characteristics (or features) of the information. These characteristics are plotted into an n-dimensional feature space (n being the number of features). These plotted values are then divided into classes and clusters. Algorithms that are classified into the statistical group include neural networks and decision trees.

Symbolic methods are utilised to find structure in the information. They look for pattern primitives using pattern description languages. Pattern primitives can be parts of speech in text, pixel patterns in an

Figure 17.2 Pattern recognition algorithms

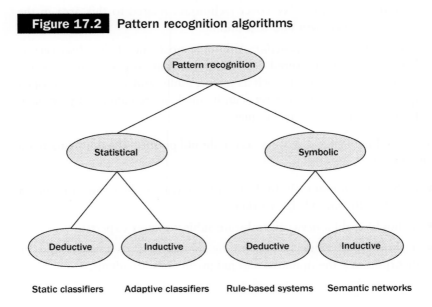

image, or a particular pattern of values in a time series. A symbolic method uses a 'grammar' to govern how patterns can be put together to form (symbolic) sentences, which are higher-order structures of pattern primitives (Becker, 1999). Recognition is done by parsing sentences, in a quest for groups of patterns that fit into the application's grammar.

Both statistical and symbolic methods may be deductive or inductive. Deduction is a process that starts with a general ontology and matches it to specific examples. Deductive methods include rule-based and case-based reasoning systems. Induction, also called concept learning, is a process that uses examples to build a general ontology that describes information patterns. Decision trees, neural networks and other machine learning techniques are all inductive (Becker, 1999).

We close this section by drawing attention to the four basic classifier approaches that are associated with the leaves of the classification tree in Figure 17.2. These include:

- static classifiers;
- adaptive classifiers;
- rule-based systems;
- semantic networks.

Text (and document) mining

A great wealth of knowledge is potentially included in large text document bases. However, from the point of view of routine computational mechanisms, natural language text represents much of this knowledge in a complex, rich and hidden way. Therefore, the typical statistical techniques used in data mining cannot be used directly for text.

On the other hand, human analysis of these volumes is becoming increasingly impractical. There is therefore considerable interest in text-mining techniques and technologies. As discussed in Chapter 14, information retrieval technologies allow the user to select documents that meet their needs. In contrast, the text-mining technologies focus on finding valuable patterns and rules in text that indicate trends and significant features about topics in the documents.

Nasukawa and Nagano (2001) have published a comparison of document-handling technologies that have been developed to reduce the work in handling huge amounts of textual data. We have adapted and included this comparison in Table 17.1.

| Table 17.1 | Comparison of document-handling technologies | | |

Function	Search documents	Organise documents	Discover knowledge
Purpose	Focus on data related to some specific topics	Overview of topics	Extract interesting information from content
Technology	Information retrieval	Clustering, classification	NLP, data mining, visualisation
Data representation	Character strings, keywords	Set of keywords (vector space model)	Semantic concepts
Natural language processing (NLP)	Keyword extraction (conversion to basic forms)	Analysis of keyword distribution	Semantic analysis, intention analysis
Output	A set of documents	Sets (clusters) of documents	Digested information (trend patterns, association rules, etc.)

In the table, different functions in the rows are compared in relation to the columns for 'searching documents', 'organise documents' and 'discovery of knowledge'. In particular we emphasise the different technologies, data/knowledge representation, as well as natural language processing (NLP). It is clear from this comparison that many of the techniques and technologies of knowledge discovery are based on the analysis of natural language text features and recognition of the semantics. In essence then, these technologies are a text version of generalised data mining. These technologies consist of NLP to extract textual concepts, statistical analysis (data mining) to find interesting patterns among these concepts, and visualisation to allow interactive analysis.

Text mining can therefore be seen as the set of techniques and technologies to achieve the following:

- find key items of information in a large collection of text, for example, by scanning a large collection of text and then indexing it by 'company name';
- rediscover authors' intentions, for example, by extracting relations between concepts;

- synthesise new insights from information implicit in a large collection, for example, by following the transfer of ideas from basic research to industrial application.

Thus, by definition, text mining is the process of analysing texts to extract information useful for a particular application.

Text, in contrast with data, has a varying degree of structure. This can range from low to high structure. For example:

- Prose does not have an explicit structure. Any structure is implicit. Text mining extracts useful information from these non-structural features.

- Documents may have some structure such as the title, abstract and author. Even utilising XML may result in text having deep or shallow structure. Text mining makes limited use of document structure.

- Metadata is highly structured and one of the applications of text mining is to generate new metadata.

The goal of text mining is to discover (or uncover) (hidden) features in the text. Features include words, phrases, names, nouns, abbreviations, acronyms, etc. A typical large text collection may contain about 100,000 features. The techniques employed for the analysis include counting, comparing of lists, discovering similarities, etc.

However, this is not a simple task, as natural language poses a number of challenging issues for automated processing. The vocabulary problem is one such challenge. For example, there is the issue of ambiguity: 'savings bank' and 'river bank' are similar in construct but have vastly different semantics. There is also synonymy to consider; for example, 'car' and 'automobile' are equal concepts. Text mining also considers other features such as hyperlinks and citations, which can convey rich relationships between documents and can be indications of the value of text documents. The analysis may also take characteristics such as sentence length and grade level of the text into consideration.

Comments on summarisation and automatic extraction

Document summaries constitute a kind of metadata that reflects a short view of the whole document and that enables users to quickly sift out documents relevant to a particular task. Automatic generation of summaries is being actively researched:[2]

> Commercially available summarizers use the sentence-selection method ... in which an indicative summary is constructed from what are judged to be the most salient sentences in a document. However, the summary may be incoherent, e.g., if the selected sentences contain anaphors. Construction of more coherent summaries, implying the use of natural language generation, currently requires that the subject domain of the documents be severely restricted, as for example, to basketball games. Summarization of long documents containing several topics is improved by topic segmentation and can be further condensed for presentation on handheld devices, whereas summarization of multiple documents, either about the same event or in an unconstrained set of domains, is another challenge being addressed by current research. (Marwick, 2001)

Marwick also comments on automatic extraction:

> Today the level of *automatic extraction* is deemed to be rather shallow because only a subset of the meaning, sometimes a very limited one, can be captured, ranging from recognition of entities such as proper names or noun phrases to automatic extraction of ontological relations of various kinds, and there is no system that can reason (in the sense of deducing something new from what it already knows) over the extracted knowledge in a way that even approaches the capabilities of a human. (Marwick, 2001)

Applications of text-mining technology

Text mining can be utilised in a host of different applications such as:

- *annotate*: annotate a document with metadata that is generated from the document;
- *search*: search for and pull related documents from the repository;
- *navigate*: navigate through a repository of text using organisation and document links to find information;
- *organise*: organise parts of text by placing them in the context of a structure.

Nowadays, the emphasis is put on problems connected to the World Wide Web and applications involving intelligent agents for text data. Knowledge discovery techniques also include different approaches to text data analysis aiming at problems such as assignment of keywords to text documents, topic identification and tracking in ordered (time) sequences of text documents, searching documents based on the content categories and not only keywords, generation and analysis of user profiles based on the usage of text databases, as well as other related problems.

The following is a list of applications of text-mining technologies that have been actively researched:[3]

- Automatic document categorisation/topic detection:
  - measuring similarity between the documents;
  - document clustering;
  - categorising to flat categories;
  - categorising to hierarchical categories (e.g. Yahoo!);
  - inventing new categories from the text;
  - custom (e.g. emotional) profile detection of documents.
- Operations on single documents:
  - document summarisation;
  - keyword assignment to documents;
  - text segmentation.
- Operations on multiple documents:
  - hierarchical subject index creation from the document set;
  - user profiling based on the text (a connection to web mining);
  - information extraction from unstructured documents;
  - topic tracking for news wires.
- Advanced topics:
  - text visualisation;
  - analysing networks of linked documents;
  - inferring communities on the Web;
  - copy detection;
  - authorship detection;
  - text-mining tools.

Text-mining technologies summary

We display the key text-mining technologies applicable to knowledge management in Figure 17.3 as a set of nine technologies that can be utilised to assemble or build the text-mining applications and solution (displayed in the diagram on top of these technologies).

To demonstrate the practical nature and extent of knowledge discovery in practice, in the next subsection we show the product features of a commercially available text-mining product providing extracted text from the product's description documentation (IBM, 1998).

Example: IBM Intelligent Miner for Text

'Text mining technology deals with all kinds of online documents: customer requests, technical reports, online newspaper articles, and many other kinds of text documents. The technology provides functions that information consumers normally do manually given sufficient time.

Figure 17.3   Key text-mining technologies

Text Mining Applications and Solution		
Feature Extraction	Categorisation	Search/ Retrieve
Web Crawling	Clustering	Language Recognition
WBI Personalisation	Summarisation	Web Search

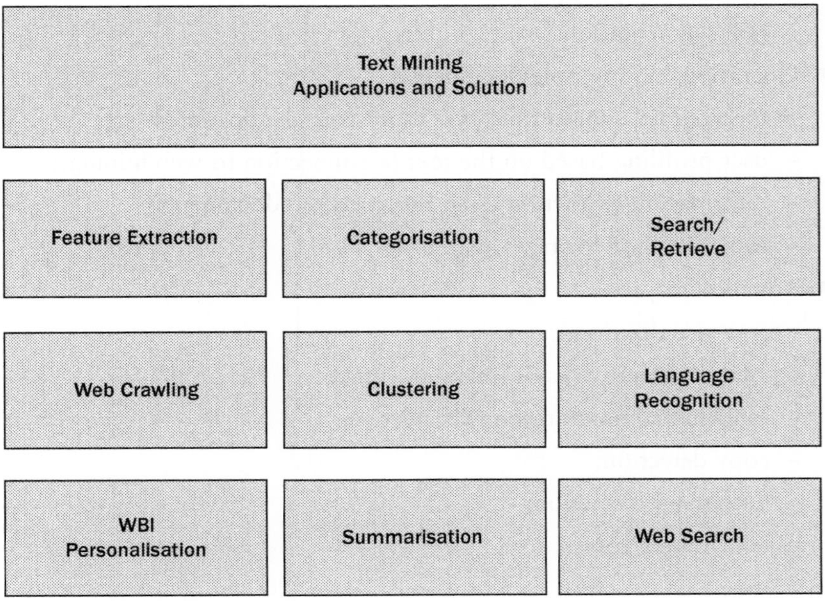

These functions include:

- *Annotate documents*: How often does one print out online information and then highlight important items, such as the names of significant companies? This can be done automatically using feature extraction.

- *Organise documents*: Today it is commonplace to have a folder scheme on a desktop. A folder scheme is a simple cataloguing mechanism for sorting items by subject. The assignment of new items to a scheme can be done automatically using topic categorisation.

- *Navigate through documents*: When following a thread of information, one may be led from one document to another looking for similar documents or predominant themes in a collection. Here hierarchical clustering can automatically give an overview.

The text mining technology is designed to be used in building applications that deal with text. Often the first step is to extract key features from text that can be used as "handles" in further processing. Examples of features are company names, dates, or technical terms mentioned.

After feature extraction, the next step may be to assign the documents to subjects from a cataloguing scheme, then to index them for searching. Or the documents can, with very little preliminary work, be grouped, or clustered to get more information about the structure of a document set, such as the distribution of subjects across a document collection, or accumulations of documents on a certain subject.'

Tools summary

'The Text Analysis Tools consist of:

- The Feature Extraction tool. This tool recognises significant vocabulary items in text, automatically, and without requiring the user to predefine a domain-dependent vocabulary.

- The Language Identification tool. This automatically discovers the language in which a document is written. A training tool lets users extend the tool to cover additional languages.

- The Topic Categorisation tool. This tool automatically assigns documents to categories, topics, or themes that have previously been defined.
- The Clustering tools. These tools divide up a set of documents into groups, or "clusters", with the members of each cluster being similar to each other by sharing common features. The clusters are not predefined; they are derived from the document collection automatically.'

Feature extraction

'An important task in text analysis is the extraction of items that provide information about document content from unstructured text. Extracting implicit data from text can be interesting for many reasons. Here are some examples:

- to highlight important information;
- to find names of competitors;
- to find and store key concepts;
- to use related topics for query refinement;
- to find the criteria that relate a collection of documents.

One can combine feature extraction with other text mining technologies. It can be used, for example, as a pre-processing step for the clustering technology to cluster documents with respect to different aspects like the names of people or organisations mentioned in a text, or key topics of the documents.'

Name extraction

'The name extraction technology uses fast and robust heuristics to locate names in text. It determines what type of entity the name refers to, for example, person, place, organisation or historical event. Even though the name extraction technology does not rely on a complete pre-existing database of names, IBM measured it to correctly recognize 90–95 per cent of the proper names present in edited text.'

Terminology extraction

'The term extraction technology discovers terms in text automatically. A set of heuristics is used to identify multi word technical terms in a document. These heuristics involve doing simple pattern matching in order to find expressions having the characteristic noun-phrase structure of technical terms.'

Abbreviation extraction

'The abbreviation recognition technology finds additional variants for terms and names in text and matches them with their full forms. "EEPROM" and "electrical erasable PROM" are, for example, recognised as a short form for "electrical erasable programmable read-only memory". A variety of common abbreviation conventions can be handled, such as conventions involving pre-fixation as in "MB" matching 'megabyte'.'

Language identification

'The language identification technology can select from a given set of languages the most likely language in which a textual document is written. This works by computing a similarity measure between the document at hand and a set of reference document collections, one for each language to be recognised. These collections, or more precisely, the statistical features extracted from them, are stored in a language identification scheme, sometimes also called a master dictionary, which is used for comparison. The language identification scheme shipped with this product supports 13 languages.'

Topic categorisation

'For text mining, categorisation means to assign categories to documents, or to organize documents with respect to a predefined organisation. These could for example be the folders on a desktop, which are usually organised by topics or themes.

The categories are chosen to match the intended use of the collection and have to be trained beforehand. By assigning documents to categories, the text mining technology can help to organise them.

While categorisation cannot replace the kind of cataloguing a librarian does, it provides a much less expensive alternative. In addition, it can be very useful in many other applications:

- Organising intranet documents. For example: Documents on an intranet might be divided into categories like 'Personal policy' or 'Computer information'. By using automatic categorisation, any document can be assigned to an organisation scheme and a link to the respective category can be generated automatically.

- Assigning documents to folders. For example: Categorising incoming e-mail items into folders.

- Sending requests. For example, by categorising problem reports, the message can be automatically forwarded to the respective expert.

- Forwarding news to subscribers depending on their area of interest.

Categorisation can of course be combined with other text mining technologies as well.'

The training phase

'Topic categorisation assigns documents to predefined categories. For this purpose the topic categorisation technology first has to be trained with a collection of sample documents for each category. These collections are used to create a category scheme.

The training uses the feature extraction technology to store only relevant information in the dictionary. The category scheme is a dictionary, which encodes in a condensed form significant vocabulary statistics for each category. These statistics are used by topic categorisation to determine the category or categories whose sample documents are closest to the documents at hand.'

Clustering

'Within a collection of objects, a cluster can be defined as a group of objects whose members are more similar to each other than to the members of any other group.

In text mining, clustering is used to segment a document collection into subsets (the clusters), with the members of each cluster being similar with respect to certain interesting features. No predefined taxonomy or classification schemes are necessary.'

Summary

Apart from knowledge portals, knowledge discovery is considered as an important application to knowledge management. A number of knowledge discovering techniques and technologies, with the main focus on text mining, were discussed. To demonstrate the practical nature and extent of knowledge discovery in practice the product features of a commercially available text-mining product were discussed.

Notes

1. See Pohs, Pinder, Dougherty and White (2001) and their description of the Lotus Knowledge Discovery System: the K-station portal and the Discovery Server.
2. See also Radev and McKeown (1998), Mani and Maybury (1999), and Boguraev, Bellamy and Swart (2001).
3. Compiled from a number of conference proceedings on text mining.

18

Summary and conclusions

There is no conclusion to managing knowledge and transferring best practices. It is a race without a finishing line. (C. O'Dell and C.J. Grayson)

The great end of knowledge is not knowledge but action. (Thomas Henry Huxley)

Summary

Not all knowledge management projects are successful. (This is obviously very true for all 'general class' projects too.) We need to investigate the reasons why such projects have failed and also why other – even similar projects – were successful. Malhotra provides such an investigation, and argues that:

> most failures could be contributed to enablers of KM that were designed for the 'knowledge factory' engineering paradigm and often become constraints in adapting and evolving such systems for business environments characterized by high uncertainty and radical discontinuous change. Design of KMS [knowledge management systems] should ensure that adaptation and innovation of business performance outcomes occurs in alignment with changing dynamics of the business environment. (Malhotra 2004)

Malhotra's article emphasises the rapid change of the business environment and the typical response made by organisations by utilising knowledge management and knowledge management technologies. Throughout this book our main thesis has been that knowledge management technology is a prerequisite for enabling knowledge management, but that such technology alone is insufficient. We have stated that knowledge management is concerned with realising the value of an organisation's intellectual assets and with determining how to manage these assets so as to more effectively make strategic and tactical decisions and solve problems. It is technology's role to support this process.

In both parts of the book we have adapted and employed different models to assist in the comprehension of the notion of knowledge management and its different perspectives. The first part covered the 'what' and 'why' aspects of knowledge and knowledge management; the second part covered the 'how' and 'with-what' characteristics. We have concentrated on the perspective of knowledge management technologies and have proposed a knowledge management technology framework. This framework enabled us to categorise knowledge management technologies and knowledge management applications into six major categories. We exploited this framework to comment on and describe the six categories and their implications as they affect knowledge management.

We stressed the value of the two key applications of knowledge management, namely 'knowledge portals' and 'knowledge discovery'. The importance of XML technologies and other semantically-rich efforts to move toward the semantic web were emphasised and we pointed to the richness of functionality and the huge potential of many developments in knowledge management technologies.

Conclusions

We can conclude that knowledge management technologies will be increasingly recognised as one of the prerequisites for successful knowledge management, specifically in medium-to-large-scale organisations.

In the fist part of he book we reached the conclusion that knowledge management itself will eventually become 'just business' and therefore 'invisible' in organisations. Organisations will incorporate the concepts and principles of knowledge management into the day-to-day running of business. In the second part we described various knowledge management technologies that we may also regard as becoming 'invisible' as they are converged and incorporated into fast-evolving areas as 'business enabling' technologies and are no longer regarded as pure knowledge management technologies. This may take quite a while though, as so-called 'common knowledge' and the human faculties that we take for granted are so complex and rich that they cannot easily be translated into software, as researchers are constantly rediscovering. Knowledge management and the effort to develop and evolve knowledge management technologies humble us as we come to realise just how elusive a full comprehension of the concepts of knowledge and its related ideas are.

On a more technological note, we also are in agreement with the industry consultants, Gartner Group, as they have observed a new type of 'suite product' (Gilbert, Caldwell and Hayward, 2002). This suite covers the enterprise needs for content management, knowledge management and collaboration, and supports the extended virtual workplace – inside and between enterprises. They refer to previous examples of aggregation of functionality into suites, which have created dominant product categories. Examples include 'office suites', which integrate what were originally independent personal-productivity tools, and 'enterprise resource planning suites', which grew from manufacturing planning and finance systems, and now cover a wide range of business application functionality. In the workplace area, groupware products combine messaging, scheduling and some basic document-sharing functions. It is likely that these smart enterprise suites will emerge as an aggregation of the functionality offered today by portals, team collaboration support and content management.

Bibliography

Adams, J., Koushik, S., Vasudeva, G. and Galambos, G. (2003) *Patterns for E-Business: A Strategy for Reuse*, Indianapolis, IN: IBM Press.

Allee, V. (2000) 'Knowledge networks and communities of practice', *OD Practitioner* 32(4), available at: *www.odnetwork.org/odponline/Vol32no4/knowledgenets.html* (accessed 7 November 2003).

Andreu, R. and Sieber, S. (2001) 'Organizational learning and knowledge management: where is the link?', in: Y. Malhotra (ed.) *Knowledge Management and Business Model Innovation*, Hershey, PA: Idea Group, pp. 60–76.

Argyris, C. (1991) 'Teaching smart people how to learn', *Harvard Business Review*, May–June, pp. 99–109.

Baek, S., Liebowitz, J., Prasad, S. Y. and Granger, M. (1999) 'Intelligent agents for knowledge management: toward intelligent web-based collaboration within virtual teams', in: J. Liebowitz (ed.) *Knowledge Management Handbook*, Boca Raton, FL: CRC Press: 11.1–11.17.

Baeza-Yates, R. and Ribbeiro-Neto, B. (1999) *Modern Information Retrieval*, Reading, MA: Addison-Wesley.

Becker, G. (1999) 'Knowledge discovery', in: J. Liebowitz (ed.) *Knowledge Management Handbook*, Boca Raton, FL: CRC Press: 13.1–13.27.

Beckman, T. (1999) 'The current state of knowledge management', in: J. Liebowitz (ed.) *Knowledge Management Handbook*, Boca Raton, FL: CRC Press: 1.1–1.22.

Birkinshaw, J. and Sheenan, T. (2002) 'Managing the knowledge life cycle', *MIT Sloan Management Review* 43(3): 75–83.

Boguraev, B., Bellamy, R. and Swart, C. (2001) 'Summarization miniaturization: delivery of news to hand-helds', proceedings of Workshop on Automatic Summarization, Annual Meeting of the North American Chapter of the Association for Computational Linguistics, Pittsburgh, PA, 3 June.

Bontis, N. (2001) 'Managing organizational knowledge by diagnosing intellectual capital: framing and advancing the state of the field', in:

Y. Malhotra (ed.) *Knowledge Management and Business Model Innovation*, Hershey, PA: IGI Publishing, pp. 267–97.

Botha, A. C. (1991) 'Inligtingsaspekte vir Inligtingherwinning', *SA Archives Journal* 33: 3–23.

Botha, A. C. (1992) 'Herwinning van teks (en ander inligting)', *SA Archives Journal* 34: 32–48.

Botha, A. C. (1995) *Moderne kantoorstelsels*, Pretoria: A.C. Botha.

Brachman, R. J. (1983) 'What IS-A is and isn't: an analysis of taxonomic links in semantic networks', *IEEE Computer* 16(10): 30–6.

Brown, J. S. and Duguid, P. (1991) 'Organizational learning and communities of practice: toward a unified view of working, learning and innovation', *Organization Science* 2(1): 40–57.

Brown, J. S. and Duguid, P. (2000) *The Social Life of Information*, Cambridge, MA: Harvard Business School.

Brown, J. S. and Gray, E. S. (1995) 'The people are the company: how to build your company around your people', *Fastcompany Magazine* 1: 78–82.

Burk, M. (2000) 'Communities of practice', *Public Roads* 63(6): 18–21.

Codey, W. F., Kreulen, J. T., Krishna, V. and Spangler, W. S. (2002) 'The integration of business intelligence and knowledge management', *IBM Systems Journal* 41(4): 679–713.

Cohen, D. (1998) 'Toward a knowledge context', *California Management Review* 40(3): 22–39.

Coleman, D. (1997) *Groupware: Collaborative Strategies for Corporate LANs and Intranets*, Upper Saddle River, NJ: Prentice Hall.

Coleman, D. and Khanna, R. (eds) (1995) *Groupware: Technology and Applications*, Englewood Cliffs, NJ: Prentice Hall.

Collison, C. and Parcell, G. (2001) *Learning to Fly*, London: Capstone.

Consortium for Service Innovation (Canada) (year unknown) 'Knowledge-centred support operational model version 5.0', available at: *www.serviceinnovation.org* (accessed 5 June 2007).

Copeland, R. (2001) 'Mind your intellectual assets', available at: *http:www.informationweek.com/824/lotus.htm* (accessed 2 August 2005).

Daconta, M. C., Obrst, L. J. and Smith, K. T. (2003) *The Semantic Web: A Guide to the Future of XML, Web Services and Knowledge Management*, New York: Wiley.

Davenport, T. H. (1998) 'Some principles of knowledge management', available at: *www.mccombs.utexas.edu/kman/kmprin.htm* (accessed May 2005).

Davenport, T. H. and Prusak, L. (1998) *Working Knowledge: How Organisations Manage What They Know*, Boston, MA: Harvard Business School Press.

Davis, S. and Botkin, J. (1995) *The Monster under the Bed: How Business is Mastering the Opportunity of Knowledge for Profit*, New York: Simon and Schuster.

Davis, S. and Meyer, C. (1998) *Blur: The Speed of Change in the Connected Economy*, Reading, MA: Addison Wesley.

Demarest, M. (1997) 'Understanding knowledge management', *Long Range Planning* 30(3): 374–84.

Depres, C. and Chauvel, D. (1999) 'Knowledge management(s)', *Journal of Knowledge Management* 3(2): 110–20.

Depres, C. and Chauvel, D. (2000) 'A thematic analysis of the thinking in knowledge management', in: C. Depres and D. Chauvel (eds) *Knowledge Horizons: The Present and the Promise of Knowledge Management*, Boston, MA: Butterworth/Heinemann, pp. 55–86.

Drucker, P. F. (1988) 'The coming of the new organisation', in: *Harvard Business Review of Knowledge Management (1998)*, Boston, MA: Harvard Business School Press, pp. 1–19.

Drucker, P. F. (1993) *Post-Capitalist Society*, Oxford: Butterworth-Heinemann.

Dutta, S. and De Meyer, A. (2001) 'Knowledge management at Arthur Andersen (Denmark): building assets in real time and in virtual space', in: Y. Malhotra (ed.) *Knowledge Management and Business Model Innovation*, Hershey, PA: Idea Group, pp. 384–401.

Fahey, L., Srivastava, R., Sharon, J. S. and Smith, D. E. (2001) 'Linking e-business and operating processes: the role of knowledge management', *IBM Systems Journal* 40(4): 889–907.

Firestone, J. M. (2003) *Enterprise Information Portals and Knowledge Management*, Boston, MA: Butterworth-Heinemann.

Firestone, J. M. and McElroy, M. W. (2003) *The Key Issues in the New Knowledge Management*, Amsterdam: Butterworth/Heinemann.

Garvin, D. A. (1993) 'Building a learning organization', in: *Harvard Business Review on Knowledge Management (1998)*, Boston, MA: Harvard Business School, pp. 47–80.

Gilbert, M., Caldwell, F. and Hayward, S. (2002) 'The smart enterprise suite is coming: do we need it?' Gartner Group article AV-16-2189 (internal document), 10 May.

Gilley, J. W. and Maycunich, A. (2000) *Beyond the Learning Organization*, Cambridge: Perseus Books.

Gingrich, N. (1995) 'Foreword' in: A. Toffer and H. Toffler, *Creating a New Civilization: The Politics of the Third Wave*, Atlanta, GA: Turner Publishing, Inc.

Godbout, A. J. (1999) 'Filtering knowledge: changing information into knowledge', *Journal of Systemic Knowledge Management*, January, available at: *www.tlainc.com/articl11.htm* (accessed 7 June 2007).

Gongla, P. and Rizzuto, C. R. (2001) 'Evolving communities of practice: IBM Global Services experience', *IBM Systems Journal* 40(4): 842–62.

Grey, D. (1998) 'Knowledge management and information management: the differences', available at: *www.smithweaversmith.com/km-im.htm* (accessed 13 August 2007).

Grulke, W. and Silber, G. (2000) *Ten Lessons from the Future: 21st Century Impact on Business, Individuals and Investors*, Parklands: @One Communications.

Han, S. (2003) 'Commercial portal products: Digital Enterprise Research Institute (DERI)', Research Report 2003-12-31, available at: *www.deri.ie/publications* (accessed 2 August 2005).

Henderson, J. C. and Venkatraman, N. (1993) 'Strategic alignment: leveraging information technology for transforming organization', *IBM Systems Journal* 32(1): 4–16.

Hildreth, P. and Kimble, C. (2002) 'The duality of knowledge', *Information Research*, 8(1), available at: *http://InformationR.net/ir/8–1/paper142.html* (accessed 10 June 2005).

Hitt, W. D. (1995) 'The learning organization: some reflections on organizational renewal', *Leadership and Organizational Development Journal* 16(8): 17–25.

IBM (1998) Program manual for: 'Intelligent Miner for Text', Version 2.2, Program Number 5765-IMT, Text Analysis Tools, Second Edition, June 1998, pp. 3–11.

Ilbury, C. and Sunter, C. (2003) *The Mind of a Fox: Scenario Planning in Action*, Cape Town: Human and Rousseau and Tafelberg.

Jackson, C. (2001) 'Process to product: creating tools for knowledge management', in: Y. Malhotra (ed.) *Knowledge Management and Business Model Innovation*, Hershey, PA: Idea Group, pp. 402–12.

Joia, L. A. (2001) 'Information technology for intelligent megabusiness', in: Y. Malhotra (ed.) *Knowledge Management and Business Model Innovation*, Hershey, PA: Idea Group, pp. 95–113.

Katzenbach, J. R. and Smith, D. K. (1994) *The Wisdom of Teams: Creating The High-Performance Organization*, Boston, MA: Harvard Business School Press.

Kim, D. H. (1993) 'The link between individual and organisational learning', *Sloan Management Review* 35(1): 37–51.

Kimble, C., Hildreth, P. and Wright, P. (2001) 'Communities of practice: going virtual', in: Y. Malhotra (ed.) *Knowledge Management and Business Model Innovation*, Hershey, PA: Idea Group, pp. 216–230.

Koenig, M. (2004) 'Knowledge Management Lessons Learned: The US Perspective', Online Information 2004 Proceedings, available at: *www.online-information.co.uk/0106/files/conferenceproceedings. brochure?1070303112904.pdf* (accessed 2 August 2005).

Koenig, M. (2005) 'KM moves beyond the organization: the opportunity for librarians', in: Proceedings of World Library and Information Congress: 71st IFLA General Conference and Council, 14–18 August, Oslo (CD-ROM).

Ladley, J. (2003) 'Beyond the Data Warehouse: Beyond Rows and Columns – Unstructured Information, Part 3', available at: *www.DMReview.com* (accessed 10 November 2005).

Lave, J. and Wenger, E. (1991) *Situated Learning: Legitimate Peripheral Participation*, Cambridge: Cambridge University Press.

Lesser, E. L. and Storck, J. (2001) 'Communities of practice and organizational performance', *IBM Systems Journal* 40(4): 831–41.

Liebenberg, J. (2003) 'The misapprehension of Polanyi in KM literature, with specific reference to Nonaka', unpublished MIT dissertation, University of Pretoria.

Liebowitz, J. (ed.) (1999) *Knowledge Management Handbook*, New York: CRC Press.

Liebowitz, J. and Beckman, T. (1998) *Knowledge Organizations: What Every Manager Should Know*, New York: St Lucie Press.

Logan, D. (2001) 'Knowledge management scenario: measuring and managing intellectual assets', paper presented at Gartner Symposium/Itxpo Africa, 30 July to 1 August 2001, Sandton, South Africa.

Luger, G. F. and Stubblefield, W. A. (1989) *Artificial Intelligence and the Design of Expert Systems*, Redwood City, CA: Benjamin/Cummings.

Luger, G. F. and Stubblefield, W. A. (1993) *Artificial Intelligence: Structures and Strategies for Complex Problem Solving* (2nd edn), Redwood City, CA: Benjamin/Cummings.

Mack, R., Ravin, Y and Byrd, R. J. (2001) 'Knowledge portals and the emerging digital knowledge workplace', *IBM Systems Journal* 40(4): 925–55.

Malhotra, Y. (1993) 'Role of information technology in managing organizational change and organizational interdependence', available at: *http://www.brint.com/papers/change/* (accessed 15 May 2005).

Malhotra, Y. (ed.) (2001a) *Knowledge Management and Business Model Innovation*, Hershey, PA: IGI Publishing.

Malhotra, Y. (2001b) 'Expert systems for knowledge management: crossing the chasm between information processing and sense making', *Expert Systems with Applications* 20(1): 7–16.

Malhotra, Y. (2002) 'Enabling knowledge exchanges for e-business communities', *Executive's Journal* 8(3): 26–31.

Malhotra, Y. (2003) 'Is knowledge the ultimate competitive advantage?' *Business Management Asia* Q3/4: 66–9.

Malhotra, Y. (2004) 'Why knowledge management systems fail? Enablers and constraints of knowledge management in human enterprises', in: M. E. D. Koenig and T. K. Srikantaiah (eds.) *Knowledge Management Lessons Learned: What Works and What Doesn't*, Medford, NJ: Information Today Inc., pp. 87–112.

Mani, I. and Maybury, M. (eds) (1999) *Advances in Automatic Text Summarization*, Cambridge, MA: MIT Press.

Marquardt, M. J. (2000) 'Five elements of learning', *Executive Excellence*, 19(9): 15–16.

Marwick, D. (2001) 'Knowledge management technologies', *IBM Systems Journal* 40(4): 814–30.

Maybury, M. T. (2003) 'Knowledge management: an introduction', paper presented at the 11th International Conference on Information and Knowledge Management (CIKM'02), 4 November 2002, Washington, DC, available at: *www.mitre.org/resources/centres/it/maybury/mark.html* (accessed 15 May 2005).

McNurlin, B. and Sprague, R. (2002) *Information Systems Management in Practice* (5th edn), New York: Prentice-Hall.

Nasukawa, T. and Nagano, T. (2001) 'Text analysis and knowledge mining system', *IBM Systems Journal* 40(4): 967–84.

Newman, B. (1991) 'An open discussion of knowledge management' (quoted in 'What is Knowledge Management', The Knowledge Management Forum, 1996), available at: *www.km_forum.org/what_is.htm* (accessed 7 June 2007).

Nonaka, I. (1991) 'The knowledge creating company', *Harvard Business Review* 69(6): 96–105.

Nonaka, I. and Takeuchi, H. (1995) *The Knowledge-Creating Company*, New York: Oxford University Press.

Nunamaker, J. F. (Jr), Briggs, R. O. and Mittleman, D. D. (1995) 'Electronic meeting systems: ten years of lessons learned', in: D. Coleman, and R. Khanna (eds.) *Groupware: Technology and Applications*, Englewood Cliffs, NJ: Prentice Hall, pp. 146–95.

O'Dell, C., Grayson, C. J., Jr. and Essaides, N. (1998) *If Only We Knew What We Know: The Transfer of Internal Knowledge and Best Practice*, New York: Free Press.

Pohs, W., Pinder, G., Dougherty, C. and White, M. (2001) 'The Lotus knowledge discovery system: tools and experiences', *IBM Systems Journal* 40(4): 956–66.

Polanyi, M. 1964. *Personal Knowledge: Towards a Post-Critical Philosophy*, Chicago, IL: University of Chicago Press.

Polanyi, M. 1967. *The Tacit Dimension*, New York: Doubleday.

Ponzi, L. and Koenig, M. (2002) 'Knowledge management: another management fad?' *Information Research* 8(1), available at: *http://InformationR.net/ir/8–1/paper145.html* (accessed 2 August 2005).

Prusak, L. (2001) 'Where did knowledge management come from?' *IBM Systems Journal* 40(4): 1002–7.

Quinn, J. B., Anderson, P and Finkelstein, S. (1996) 'Managing professional intellect: making the most of the best', *Harvard Business Review* 74(2): 71–80.

Radev, D. R. and McKeown, K. R. (1998) 'Generating natural language summaries from multiple on-line sources', *Computation Linguistics* 24: 469–500.

Rajan, R. G. and Wulf, J. (2003) 'The flattening firm: evidence from panel data on the changing nature of corporate hierarchies', available at: *http://www.nber.org/papers/w9633* (accessed 27 April 2004).

Rich, E. and Knight, K. (1991) *Artificial Intelligence*, New York: McGraw-Hill.

Salton, G. (1989) *Automatic Text Processing: The Transformation, Analysis, and Retrieval of Information by Computer*, Reading, MA: Addison-Wesley.

Schlier, F., Hunter, R., Harris, K. and Berg, T. (1998) 'Enterprise 2003: The Technology-Enabled Enterprise', Industry Trends and Directions Document R-ITD-120 (internal document), Gartner Group, 29 January.

Senge, P. 1990. *The Fifth Discipline: The Art and Practice of the Learning Organization*, New York: Doubleday.

Silver, C. (2000) 'Knowledge management and technology in context', available at: *www.inst-informatica.pt/v20/cid/biblioteca_digital/ gestao_connecimento/business_knowledge_management.pdf* (accessed 7 June 2007).

Snowden, D. (1998) 'A framework for creating a sustainable programme', in: J. Reeves (ed.) *Knowledge Management: A Real Business Guide*, London: Caspian Publishing, pp. 6–19.

Spink, A., Wolfram, D., Jansen, B. J. and Saracevic, T. (2001) 'Searching the web: the public and their queries', *Journal of the American Society of Information Science* 53(2): 226–34.

Standfield, K. (2001) 'Time capital and intangible accounting: new approaches to intellectual capital', in: Y. Malhotra (ed.) *Knowledge Management and Business Model Innovation*, Hershey, PA: Idea Group, pp. 316–24.

Stewart, T. A. (1997) *Intellectual Capital: The New Wealth of Organizations*, London: Nicholas Brealey.

Stewart, T. A. (2001) *The Wealth of Knowledge: Intellectual Capital and the Twenty-first Century Organization*, London: Nicholas Brealey.

Sunter, C. (1992) *The New Century: Quest for the High Road*, Cape Town: Human and Rousseau/Tafelberg.

Sunter, C. (1996) *The High Road: Where Are we Now?* Cape Town: Human and Rousseau/Tafelberg.

Sveiby, K.-E. (2001a) 'Intellectual capital and knowledge management', available at: *http://www.sveiby.com/articles/IntellectualCapital.html* (accessed 27 April 2004).

Sveiby, K.-E. (2001b) 'A knowledge-based theory of the firm: to guide strategy formulation', *Journal of Intellectual Capital* 2(4): 344–58.

Tapscott, D. (1996) *The Digital Economy: Promise and Peril in the Age of Networked Intelligence*, New York: McGraw-Hill.

Thomas, J. C., Kellogg, W. A. and Erickson, T. (2001) 'The knowledge management puzzle: human and social factors in knowledge management', *IBM Systems Journal* 40(4): 863–84.

Tobin, D. (1997) *The Knowledge-Enabled Organization: Moving from Training to learning to Meet Business Goals*, New York: AMACOM.

Tobin, T. (2003) 'Ten principles for knowledge management success', available at: *http://itresearch.Forbes.com/detail/RES/1063624180_419.html* (accessed 2 August 2005).

Toffler, A. (1970) *Future Shock*, New York: Random House.

Toffler, A. (1981) *The Third Wave*, London: Pan Books.

Toffler, A. (1990) *Powershift: Knowledge, Wealth, and Violence at the Edge of the 21st Century*, New York: Bantam Books.

Toffer, A. and Toffler, H. (1995) *Creating a New Civilization: The Politics of the Third Wave*, Atlanta: Turner Publishing, Inc.

Turban, E. and Frenzel, L. E. (1992) *Expert Systems and Applied Artificial Intelligence*, New York: Macmillan.

Visser, W. and Sunter, C. (2002) *Beyond Reasonable Greed: Why Sustainable Business is a Much Better Idea*, Cape Town: Human and Rousseau/Tafelberg.

Von Krogh, G., Nonaka, I. and Aben, M. (2001) 'Making the most of your company's knowledge: a strategic framework', *Long Range Planning* 34(4): 421–39.

Waite and Company (1997) *Beyond Expectations: How Leading Companies are Using Lotus Notes to Jump-Start the I-net Revolution*, Cambridge: Lotus Development Corporation.

Waterman, D. A. (1993) *A Guide to Expert Systems*, Reading, MA: Addison-Wesley.

Wenger, E. (1998) *Communities of Practice*, Cambridge: Cambridge University Press.

Wenger, E. (2001) 'Communities of practice: learning as a social system', available at: *www.co-i-l.com/knowledge-garden/cop/lss.html* (accessed 10 June 2005).

Wiberg, M. and Ljungberg, F. (2001) Exploring the vision of 'anytime, anywhere', in: Y. Malhotra (ed.) (2001) *Knowledge Management and Business Model Innovation*, Hershey, PA: Idea Group: 153–65.

Woods, W. A., Bookman, L. A., Houston, A., Kuhns, R. J., Martin, P. and Green, S. (2000) 'Linguistic knowledge can improve information retrieval', Proceedings of the Applied Natural Language Processing Conference (ANLP-2000), Seattle, May 1-3 2000, available at: *www.springerlink.com/content/6lwv3mnr9fl6jj2m/* (accessed 15 May 2005).

Index

Printed and bound by CPI Group (UK) Ltd, Croydon, CR0 4YY

08/05/2025

01864969-0002